Philosophy Without Women

27. august 2004

To Joan Scott,

in remembrance of the
days you spent in Bergen.
We are proud to have you
as our honorary doctor!

— from Vigdis.

Philosophy Without Women

The Birth of Sexism in Western Thought

VIGDIS SONGE MØLLER

Translated by Peter Cripps

continuum
LONDON • NEW YORK

Continuum
The Tower Building, 11 York Road, London SE1 7NX
370 Lexington Avenue, New York, NY 10017-65503
www.continuumbooks.com

British Library Cataloguing-in-Publication Data
A catalogue record for this book is available from the British Library.

ISBN
0-8264-5848-3 (hardback) 0-8264-5849-1 (paperback)

Typeset by Acorn Bookwork, Salisbury, Wiltshire
Printed and bound in Great Britain by MPG Books Ltd, Bodmin, Cornwall

Contents

Translator's Note

For the Norwegian original of this work, many of the passages quoted from Greek sources were translated by the author herself. This allowed her to highlight those nuances in the classical texts that were of significance to her argument but which might not always have been apparent in translations made for other purposes.

The translations of Greek texts that appear in the current edition have, except where otherwise stated, been prepared in conjunction with the author on the basis of various widely available English translations. This applies in particular to the translations of Hesiod and Parmenides. Owing to the process of collation, selection and occasional emendation that has been necessary to convey the frequently contentious meanings of the originals, it is impossible to credit any single scholar for the renditions presented here. Even so, we must acknowledge a particular debt to the following:

Kirk, G. S., J. E. Raven, and M. Schofield. *The Presocratic Philosophers*. Cambridge University Press, 1983.

Hesiod. *Theogony. Works and Days*. Translated with an introduction and notes by M. L. West. Oxford University Press, 1988.

Hesiod. *Theogony. Works and Days* (published together with Theognis. *Elegies*). Translated and with introductions by Dorothea Wender. Harmondsworth: Penguin, 1973.

Parmenides. *Parmenides. A Text with Translation, Commentary and Critical Essays*. By Leonardo Tarán. Princeton University Press, 1965.

Preface

My thanks are due to many for being able to complete this work. A three-year study grant from the Norwegian Research Council for Science and the Humanities (NAVF) (which due to childbirth and reduced work time was spread over the period 1983 to 1988) provided the economic basis for the project. From 1984 to 1985 I received extra funding for a stay in Paris together with my family. The Norwegian Research Council (NFR) supported publication of the book in Norway. The English translation has been made possible through the generous support of the Faculty of Arts at the University of Bergen and by a grant from the NFR.

The essays in this book are largely based on lectures I have given over the years. I have received inspiring and constructive criticism and much thought-provoking feedback from my audiences. My thanks to them.

Above all I must thank various good friends and colleagues for many years of academic support and inspiration. My gratitude is particularly due to Margarita Kranz, who initiated the actual process of writing when in 1984 she invited me – together with Konrad Gaiser – to hold a lecture at the University of Tübingen on what would henceforth be my focal theme: 'Ein griechischer Traum: die Überflüssigkeit der Frau' (A Greek Dream: the Superfluity of the Woman). Margarita has read and diligently commented on several of the manuscripts out of which the current essays grew. It would be difficult to thank Elina Almasy enough. During my lengthy period of research in Paris she arranged working conditions for both me and my husband that would never have been so good without her help. By taking the personal initiative to publish the first essay of this book in her journal *Social Science Information* (in 1986) she provided an immensely valuable impetus. During my study period in Paris I was fortunate to come in contact with Pierre Vidal-Naquet. I wish to thank him for his kindness, generosity and intellectual support. Special thanks are also due to Toril Moi. She read preliminary drafts of several of the essays, and she also read and commented on the final version of the book as a whole. Thanks to colleagues and students in Bergen who have taken the time to read and give valuable comments on one or more of the book's essays, especially Thomas Hägg, Gro Rørstadbotten and Kristin Sampson. I would also like to thank the Norwegian Research Council's anonymous consultant for useful criticism, and Peter Cripps, who has not only translated the book into English, but has also been a critical reader and has pointed out both philological and philosophical inaccuracies in the text.

My husband, Kjell Roger Soleim, has read all the essays in their various drafts and commented extensively on both thematic and linguistic aspects. Without his invaluable help and support I would have been unable to complete this project. Neither would it have come about if it had not been for my children, who not only prompted the undertaking, but have also been my companions along the way.

Bergen, October 1998 / April 2002
Vigdis Songe-Møller

Introduction

The essays in this book build on articles that were originally written independently of one another, although all deal with the same themes: gender, sexuality and reproduction in the myths and philosophy of ancient Greece. I began to focus on this thematic complex following the birth of my first child in 1980. At that time I was freshly qualified, with a German doctorate in philosophy from the University of Tübingen, where I had spent three years studying Greek philosophy. It was my experience of pregnancy, birth and the early period of motherhood that prompted me to look again at the Greek philosophers in a new light. For my doctoral thesis I had studied the Presocratic philosopher Parmenides, whose thought is – perhaps more than that of any other – characterized by the notion of identity. Parmenides claims that all things that exist do so in virtue of being one and self-identical. What he deduces from this is that, ideally speaking, there is no such thing as plurality, or difference, indeed, that there is no such thing as change, which implies in turn that there is no such thing as becoming or death. According to Parmenides, these phenomena – plurality, difference, birth and death – are attributable to a mistaken grasp of the world. For a pregnant woman, the Parmenidean idea of all things existing ultimately as one and self-identical is, to say the least, far from self-evident. An expectant mother is both herself and her child, and although the child does not yet have any existence independent of the mother's body, still it is not one with the mother. During pregnancy I was neither one nor self-identical, yet beyond all doubt I existed.

I am – and was – clearly aware that a pregnant woman's experience of being both one and two, which also means being neither one nor two, poses no great threat to Parmenides' philosophy of identity. Parmenides was hardly suggesting that a human being – any more than any other single entity – is completely one and self-identical. Unity and self-identity must rather be viewed as ideals. Unity and self-identity were crucial not only to Parmenides, but also to Plato and Aristotle, as preconditions of unchanging – and this meant eternal – divine existence. With its message of forthcoming plurality, change and growth – and hence also death – the pregnant body is quite literally ambiguous; as such it is a far cry from the ideals of Greek philosophy – ideals that we might even regard as the central pillar of that period of thought. The simple, but for me decisive, experience of physically bringing forth the negation of the philosophers' ideal of identity and unchangeability gave me a new perspective on the philosophy of identity. It also provided the starting point for my new research project. I wanted to inquire whether there was any connection between the Greek philosophers' ideals of unity, self-identity and eternity and their attitudes towards sexuality, reproduction and sexual difference.

This book is the provisional result of that research project, which got underway in 1984 with a lengthy period of study in Paris. While there I came in contact with the circle around Pierre Vidal-Naquet and Jean-Pierre Vernant. In his works Vernant draws attention to a fundamental attitude which in his view characterizes much of the intellectual life of ancient Greece. Implicit not only in Greek myths, literature, philosophy and scientific theories, but also in the architecture, town planning and political and social institutions of the Greek city state, there seems to be a masculine dream whereby men yearn to get by on their own, independently of women. It is this insight that inspires the title of the first chapter in the current book: 'The Greek Dream of a Womanless World'.[1]

The central philosophers in this book are Parmenides and Plato. It is in the works of these two thinkers that the ideals of unity, identity and unchangeability are developed with the greatest clarity. These ideals can however be traced back to the poet Hesiod, who serves as the starting point of my study. In Hesiod's texts, these ideals and their opposites are related to sexual difference; whereas unity, identity and unchangeability tend to be symbols of the man and the masculine, plurality and death are seen as representing the woman and femininity. Parmenides and Plato significantly augment this picture: since the unity of existence can only be grasped by means of *thought*, this too becomes associated with the man and the masculine. This view is unambiguously developed in Plato's *Symposium*, to which one of my chapters is devoted. In that dialogue, Plato depicts the philosopher as a man whose love of ideas allows him to aspire to a higher form of reality than that attained by the woman in giving birth. By means of his thought the philosopher immortalizes himself, thereby gaining independence of women and indeed heterosexuality in any form. Masculine spiritual love and creativity is contrasted here with female sexuality and the process of giving birth.

For this reading of Plato I am indebted to two very different philosophers, namely Luce Irigaray and Michel Foucault. Whereas Irigaray reads Plato in a critical, feminist perspective, we could say that Foucault glorifies the masculine aspect as it comes across in Plato and other Greek authors. Irigaray's spectacular reading of Plato's cave myth and Foucault's analysis of sexuality in antiquity form the basis for two of the book's essays.

The Platonic tradition in Greek thought – stretching back to Parmenides and Hesiod – is characterized by a strongly dualistic and *hierarchic* attitude. Reality is conceptualized in terms of dualistic pairs of contraries such as unity/plurality, unchangeability/change, immortality/mortality; the first term in each pair defines the ideal, whereas the second denotes something that is regarded as inferior.

Nevertheless, early Greek philosophy also includes another, non-Platonic tradition. The central names in this case are Anaximander, Heraclitus and Empedocles. These philosophers also thought in terms of dualities, but not hierarchically. They regard existence as a battleground, where opposed but equally important forces clash. From this point of view the woman and the feminine can be seen as something *different* from the man and the masculine, and not just as a negation, which is how they appear in the tradition deriving from Parmenides and Plato. This non-hierarchical way of thinking is exemplified not only in philosophy, but also in the Greek tragedies, where the struggle between the sexes constitutes a central theme. The comparison and contrast of these two attitudes constitutes the subject of two of the essays in this volume. First I discuss what we can call Anaximander's *inclusive* as opposed to Plato's *exclusive* philosophy. Subsequently I compare the view of sexual relationships conveyed in the tragedies with that to be found in Plato. It is a disturbing conundrum in the history of thought that the Platonic, hierarchic way of thinking is the one that came to dominate later European philosophy. In contrast, the approach that seemed to accommodate a view of man and woman as creatures of equal status was considerably less significant for subsequent philosophy – and thought in general.

The view of the relation between the sexes that we find in Hesiod, Parmenides and Plato signals the beginning of the tradition that treats the man as definitive of what it means to be human and the woman as the Other, which is nothing in itself and only has meaning in relation to the man. By focusing in this book on this tradition I wish to pursue a small but central aspect of the story analysed by Simone de Beauvoir in *The Second Sex*. One of the aims of de Beauvoir's work was to cleanse the concept of reason of its sexual aspect so as to make it accessible also to women. In this sense my own text is motivated by de Beauvoir's project. I shall briefly explain what I mean by this.

There is a tendency running through all Greek thought – be it mythology or philosophy – to attribute sexual characteristics to the various elements of existence. When this is combined – as it is for example in Plato – with a hierarchic attitude, the result is that all inferior things – such as forms of becoming, change and plurality, and aspects of the body – become associated with the female, whereas the positive elements of existence – such as unity, identity, unchangeability and reason – are regarded as male. There are many historical and perhaps even biological reasons to explain a linkage between the female and what belongs to the body, although none are logically necessary. And in simple terms, this is my point: since there is no necessity in this linkage, it is in the final analysis arbitrary and must be motivated by extraneous considerations. The body does of course have a sexual character, and this can be associated with either sex. Thought, on the other hand, is not sexual in nature and in itself neither masculine nor feminine. Neither are concepts such as unity and plurality, identity and difference, change and unchangeability, becoming, decay and eternity in themselves sexual in nature. This observation is banal, yet it does not repudiate the fact that the linkage between such concepts and sex has been of decisive importance both for the history of thought in general and for the history of sexual attitudes in particular. It is my hope that this book will throw some light on the ubiquitous significance of the linkage that the early philosophers made between sex and the fundamental concepts of philosophy. I hope moreover that the light thus thrown will have a demystifying effect.

All the essays in this volume build on articles that were previously published either in Norwegian or international journals. They were written over a ten-year period, a fact that is undoubtedly reflected in the shape of the current book. For their publication here the essays have been revised – some of them extensively, others less so – in order to form them into a single entity. In practical terms I have aimed to reduce unnecessary repetitions and to highlight the connections between the various sections, which in many ways mutually support one another.

Chapter 1 is based on the following articles: 'A Greek Dream – to render women superfluous', *Social Science Information*, 25 (1986), pp. 67–82; 'En gresk drøm: Å føde uten kvinnen', *Norsk Filosofisk Tidsskrift*, 21 (1986), pp. 117–29 (both published under the name Vigdis Soleim); 'Ein griechischer Traum: die Überflüssigkeit der Frau', *Zeitschrift für Didaktik der Philosophie*, 10 (1988), pp. 8–16; 'The Definition of Male and Female – an Unsolved Problem', *Studia Theologica*, 43:1 (1989), pp. 91–8.

Chapter 2 is a revision of 'Tenkning og seksualitet: et problematisk forhold', *Norsk Filosofisk Tidsskrift*, 28 (1993), pp. 169–206. The latter part of this manuscript provided the basis for two articles: 'Sexual Metaphors in Early Greek Philosophy', in Elin Svenneby and Inga Bostad (eds), *Nordic Women in Philosophy*, no. 2, Oslo, 1994, pp. 101–20; 'The Road of Being and the

Exclusion of the Feminine', in Erik C.W. Krabbe et al. (eds), *Empirical Logic and Public Debate: Essays in Honour of Else M. Barth*, Amsterdam and Atlanta: Rodopi, 1993, pp. 275–9.

The latter part of Chapter 3 provided the basis for the conference paper 'Parmenides – en polistenker', which was published in J. Lindhardt (ed.), *Staten: Platonselskabets konferencerapport, nr. 13*, Århus, 1997, pp. 10–22.

Chapter 4 is adapted from the conference paper 'Fra tragisk konflikt til platonsk harmoni', which is published in *Konstituering av kjønn fra antikken til moderne tid*, Norwegian Research Council, Oslo, 1995, pp. 64–74. Only small alterations have been made here, and the informal style is largely preserved.

Chapter 5 is based on an article originally published in German with the title, 'Sexualität und Philosophie in Platons *Symposion*', in *Symbolae Osloenses*, LXIII (1988), pp. 25–50.

Chapter 6 is based on a lecture that was published in *Kvinnovetenskaplig tidskrift*, 4 (1987), pp. 3–13, under the title 'Kunnskap och fallisk makt: Platon och fransk feminism' (the author's name at that time was Soleim), and in *Norsk Filosofisk Tidsskrift*, 24 (1990), pp. 95–107, under the title 'Erkjennelse og maskulin reproduksjon: Platon i et kvinnespeil'. As presented here the text has been extensively revised.

Chapter 7 is a revision of the article 'Fra pederasti til filosofi', published under the name Soleim in *Norsk Filosofisk Tidsskrift*, 20 (1985), pp. 139–62. The introductory pages of this chapter are new, and the remainder of the text has been revised in various respects.

PART I

Sexuality in Myths and Early Philosophy

CHAPTER I

The Greek Dream of a Womanless World

If only children could be got some other way, Without the female sex!
(Euripides, *Medea*)[1]

So says Jason, the male hero of Euripides' tragedy. Evidently he dreams of a world where the female sex is no longer needed, a world where men get along fine on their own. There are few places in Greek literature where the dream of women's superfluity is expressed so bluntly, yet there are good reasons to suppose that many aspects of ancient Greek culture were nourished by some such ideal of male self-sufficiency. I myself would suggest that this vision even helped shape the political institution that was the very bedrock of the Greek *polis*, namely democracy. In the following reflections I shall focus especially on the city state of Athens. Here as elsewhere among the Greek city states of the fifth- and fourth-centuries BCE, democracy was the preserve of male citizens, who were known as 'the equals' (*hoi homoioi*) in virtue of their equal political rights. Yet the term 'equals' presupposes the existence of 'the unequals', those whom the democratic city state excluded, and these were first and foremost women and slaves.

It has been suggested that the democratic Greek city state can best be defined in terms of a double exclusion: 'the exclusion of women, which made it a "men's club", and the exclusion of slaves, which made it a "citizens' club".'[2] If this is correct, we should regard the exclusion of women and slaves as rather more than mere historic fact, since it plays a part in the very foundations of the democratic tradition. Numerous aspects of early Greek thought are marked by the exclusion of women and the feminine. The claim I shall pursue is that some of the ideas that recur both in early philosophy and in the democratic ideology of the Athenian city state derive from the notion of women's superfluity. This is not to say that the first philosophers were directly responsible for the development of democracy in Athens. But I wish to show that the philosophy of the period and the principles underlying the city state are characterized by the same type of gender ideology.

Most significantly, the dream of a womanless world seems to inform one of the main currents of Greek philosophy, namely the Platonic tradition, which I shall regard as stretching from Parmenides to Plato himself. Among the early philosophers there was, however, another brand of thinkers who did not exclude women and the feminine from their conception of the world. Here I have in mind philosophers such as Anaximander, Heraclitus and Empedocles, who conceptualized the world as a struggle between opposing but equally valid principles. In such a world-view there is nothing that entails the exclusion of women and the feminine. If anything, the opposite is true. In a later chapter I shall look more closely at Anaximander as the exemplar of such an inclusive form of thought. It is no accident that Anaximander's fragments are generally not so well known today, since the branch of Greek philosophy that he represents proved relatively uninfluential for subsequent intellectual developments. In all essential respects it is the Platonic tradition that provided the foundations for what is generally called Western philosophy.

In this opening chapter my main concern is philosophical, although I shall also dwell on a couple of the most important Greek myths. Among the questions to be asked is what these myths tell us about how the Greeks – and especially the Athenians – saw themselves. In addition to this mythological analysis, I shall focus on a number of Athenian social practices, such as the institution of marriage and the general status of the woman in the family. From these angles I hope to illuminate how Greek male citizens thought of themselves, of women and of the relationship between the sexes. We shall see that despite ambiguities and apparent contradictions the relevant concepts seem invariably to have drawn sustenance from the dream of women's superfluity.[3] This opening chapter anticipates many of the questions that will be pursued and developed later in the book.[4]

A MYTH OF ATHENIAN ORIGINS: MAN AS THE SOURCE OF THE CHILD

The Athenians believed they could trace their descent back to Erichthonius, who was also called the 'earth-born' (*autochthon*), and they were proud to call themselves 'the earth-born race'. This autochthonic myth relates the circumstances of Erichthonius' birth. Athena once asked Hephaestus, the Olympian blacksmith, to make her a set of weapons. Hephaestus gladly accepted the commission, but declined any payment for his labours. He said he would do it for love. Without considering what this might entail, Athena visited Hephaestus in his smithy to watch him at work on her weapons. Hephaestus availed himself of the opportunity by attempting to ravish the goddess, but

Athena proved an unconquerable virgin. As she tore herself from Hephaestus' embrace, his seed fell on the earth, the soil of Athens, and inseminated that instead of her. And in due course the earth gave birth to a boy, Erichthonius.[5]

The first thing to note is that this tale does not distinguish clearly between sexual and vegetative reproduction. The earth is like a woman; it is fertilized by a man and brings forth a human child. The child springs from the soil like a mere seedling. He sprouts like a plant, whereas the earth gives birth like a woman. The confusion of asexual, vegetative reproduction with sexual procreation is reinforced in the remainder of the story. The virgin Athena behaves as if she had in fact received Hephaestus' seed and *she* were the child's mother. She receives the child and assumes responsibility for his upbringing. Moreover, this means that Erichthonius is acknowledged as Athena's legitimate offspring. According to tradition, it was he who founded Athens as a political entity, and who was therefore the first true Athenian.[6]

Whereas the paternity of the earth-born child presents no problem, it is hard to name the mother: neither Athena nor the earth contribute substantially to procreation. In purely physical terms the earth-born boy is a product solely of the father's seed. The myth associates fertility with virginity, thus implying a model of reproduction devoid of sexuality: reproduction without female participation. The Athenian boy has a father but no mother. What this suggests is some ideal of one-sex humanity, where all children are boys, and each child originates from the father alone.

Athenians regarded themselves as the descendants of earth-born Erichthonius, and could thus explain their origins without recourse to women. The myth tells us not only that Athenians have a common origin in the same earth, but also that they are the progeny of a single individual ancestor. It could be said that the myth implies a vision of the human as a plant that puts out runners: the man can perpetuate himself to eternity without needing to mix himself with anything that differs in nature from himself.

Thus offspring represent the faithful continuation of their source. Or to put it another way: the source survives in the offspring without alteration. And in its turn this ensures the identity and continuity of the race and of the city state. But not only that. It also guarantees the basic concept on which Athenian democracy is built; Athenians are like identical brothers and as such they have identical rights. In other words, the story provides mythological justification for the fundamental principles of the democratic city state, namely the political equality of its citizens and their interest in a stable and unitary society.

What I have called 'the fundamental principles of the democratic city state' can be captured in a single term: *the same (to auto)*. The idea behind many of

Athens' social and political institutions was the preservation of the city's
unity and identity through time. Or put another way: one of the objectives of
the Athenian city state was its self-reproduction, that is the endeavour always
to remain *the same*. The myth of Erichthonius' birth provides an image of
such reproduction of the same and thus serves to guarantee that the same will
continue unaltered through many generations (cf. Loraux, *The Children of
Athena*, p. 50f.).

In this myth the male element symbolizes that which remains the same,
identical and one, while the female is the other, the alien, that for which the
story has no use simply because the story already allows the Athenians to
explain their origins in terms of man alone. What the myth does is simply
reaffirm political realities: there are only male citizens. But it goes further.
Not only does it deny woman a political function, it deprives her of any
function whatsoever and renders her utterly superfluous. Reasonably enough,
the city state needed women in their reproductive capacity, and indeed it was
only as the mother of a citizen's legitimate children that the married Athenian woman enjoyed any kind of social status. Yet the myth of Athenian
origins denies her even 'that sphere of fertility to which the city, in practice,
confines [her]', as Nicole Loraux puts it (*The Children of Athena*, p. 122).
The ultimate consequence of this myth is that it denies the woman her right
to existence.

ASYMMETRICAL SEXES: MAN AS CITIZEN, WOMAN AS SEXUAL BEING

The dream of women's superfluity is also apparent in the Greek tragedies. In
a well-known passage from Aeschylus' tragedy, the *Eumenides*, it is justified
by a physiological theory:

> *The mother is not the true parent of the child*
> *Which is called hers. She is a nurse who tends the growth*
> *Of young seed planted by its true parent, the male.* (658ff.)[7]

This is reminiscent of the autochthony myth: the man is like a plant that
sows its seed in the soil of the woman, which provides conditions suitable for
the seed's growth. The man is the sole source of the child, who consequently
has no mother in the biological sense. In the Greek original this comes across
more forcefully. The original speaks of the child and the mother as friends,
yet the Greek word for friend (*xenos*) can also mean 'guest' or 'stranger':
mother and child are like strangers to one another. The implication is that

there is no natural bond between the two. The woman is not a natural part of the family, and her social status, or rather her connection to the city state, is consequently unclear.

Woman's status as an outsider in relation to the family and society in general is fundamental to the ideology of the Athenian city state, insofar as it is required to explain, or justify, the concept of masculine democracy. This is reflected in an interesting way in a myth which could be described as an extension of the autochthony myth.[8] During the reign of Cecrops in Athens – himself one of the earth-born – a vote was held to decide who should be adopted as the city's patron deity, the sea-god Poseidon, or Athena. Both men and women took part in the vote. While the men voted for Poseidon, the women voted for Athena, and since the women were in the majority, Athena was duly elected as the city's guardian.

The men, however, still retained sufficient power to impose effective revenge. From that time on women were denied the right to vote, children would never again bear their mothers' names as they had done formerly, and the feminine form of 'Athenian' was no longer to be used. The myth also tells us that it was at this time that the institution of marriage was established. Thus male democracy and marriage have a common mythological origin. This is no mere coincidence, since one of the prime objectives of Athenian marriage was to legitimate the heirs of male citizens – meaning those who participate in Athenian democracy. In this way marriage ensured the continuation of the masculine, democratic city state. I shall return to this in greater detail later in the chapter.

As the myth suggests, the concept of woman as an outsider, with no clear rights within the family and only ambivalent social status, is also embodied in the Greek language; men have their own form of the word 'Athenian', or 'Athenian citizen', *athēnaios*, but there are no feminine inflections of these terms. Athenian women are simply called 'women', *gynaikes*, and are characterized as belonging to Athenians, as their wives or daughters. There are, as it were, no Athenian women, only Athenians' women.[9]

There is obviously a radical asymmetry between the sexes. On the one hand, Athenians, on the other, women. Man is defined in terms of his involvement in a political community, whereas woman is defined through belonging to a sex. It would seem that only the Athenian men can be subsumed under Aristotle's definition of the human as 'a political animal'. For Aristotle, it is part of man's nature to belong to a political community, and anyone who does not do so fails to fulfil his human potential.

Although ancient Greek has no word for 'Athenian women', it is a female figure that gave the Athenians' their name: the goddess Athena. This might seem paradoxical. But we must remember that Athena is the most masculine of the goddesses, a daughter worthy of her father Zeus, and born of him alone. Without female involvement she leapt from his head, full-grown and bearing weapons which were otherwise reserved exclusively for men. The figure of Athena seems pervaded by that of Zeus, insofar as her female qualities are largely suppressed; the female is present but remains unfulfilled in this rather masculine maiden. In the *Eumenides*, Aeschylus has Athena comment on her fundamental masculinity as follows:

> No mother gave me birth. Therefore the father's claim
> And male supremacy in all things, save to give
> Myself in marriage, wins my whole heart's loyalty. (736ff.)[10]

This adds a peculiar irony to the myth of the women who elect Athena as their city's patron goddess. It might appear that, in electing a goddess as their guardian, the women had achieved at least a partial victory. But rather the contrary seems true: the fact that the city takes its name from a female goddess tends to conceal the woman's status as a stranger to family and society. The name 'Athens' might encourage the belief that women play a central role in the city state.

THE PANDORA MYTH: WOMAN AS DEATH-BRINGER

It is hardly surprising that there is no myth to explain the origin of Athenian women, no feminine parallel to the masculine autochthonic myth. There is, however, a myth about the origin of the female sex, or the 'race of women', as Hesiod calls it in his *Theogony*. In this poetic work about the origins of the gods and mankind, composed around 700 BCE, Hesiod writes that the 'death bringing sex, the race of women' (*Theogony*, 591)[11] originated with Pandora, the first woman, who was both evil and beautiful. She was the punishment inflicted on Prometheus for having set mankind against the gods. It should be noted that Pandora is not born, but formed from clay like a mere artefact. It is the craftsman of the gods, Hephaestus, the father of Erichthonius, who shapes her. Thus 'the race of women' comes into being without any form of reproduction, either sexual or vegetative.

Prior to the creation of Pandora, mankind had lived in harmony with the gods. The race was untouched by worries or sorrow and had eaten at the table of the gods. The revocation of this communality meant that mankind had to toil for the continuation of his race, and this led in turn to the loss of any intimate unity with nature. Furthermore – and this is the crucial point in the current context – mankind also forfeited unity with himself. Taken alone, the individual was no longer self-sufficient, but would henceforth be dependent on someone else of a different nature in order to reproduce. Humankind was now divided in two, into man and woman. This division was Pandora's doing, and it largely explains why women were regarded as evil. Henceforth, humankind would be constrained by sexuality. In order to reproduce, men had to plough not only their fields but also their women. This is not merely a figure of speech. In Greek the noun *arotos* refers both to the ploughing of earth and to man's impregnation of woman. For Hesiod, the work a man does on the soil and his sexual activity belong to the tiring but needful demands of life.

Sexuality entered the world with women, and with it the asymmetry between the self and the other. Women introduced plurality, dissent and disharmony to human existence. Hence woman is seen as a 'great affliction' (*Theogony* 592) and an 'evil for mankind' (*Theogony* 570). She is the origin of all human ills: the curses of old age, sickness and death. The consequences of the two-part separation of mankind, for which Pandora, and with her women in general, is responsible, are therefore far-reaching and fateful. Hesiod emphasizes the fundamental and decisive nature of this division in his choice of words; it is only after the new race has been named as 'woman' (*gynē*) that he begins to refer to the original humans (*anthrōpoi*) as 'men' (*andres*). 'And so they remain,' comments Loraux in her revealing analysis of the Pandora myth; henceforth it is the men who represent mankind, whereas women merely represent their own sex (*The Children of Athena*, p. 77).

In the light of Hesiod's tale about Pandora it is reasonable to ask what men and women actually have in common. The implicit answer is: nothing. Men and women are portrayed as different 'races'. Nonetheless, man and woman need each other for reproduction, suggesting they must have something in common after all. A basic feature of the genealogical lines we meet in the *Theogony* is that those who have sexual relationships with one another belong to the same ancestral tree and thus ultimately constitute a unity. In allowing men and women – who are so different – to reproduce by means of one another, Hesiod makes humans into creatures that are both singular and dual, self-identical and different. Although he does not explicitly examine this kind of problem, his conception of human origins, of sexual difference and of sexuality is, if not paradoxical, at least problematic. I shall pursue this Hesiodic paradox in the next chapter. In the autochthony myth the Hesiodic paradox is avoided, but at a price. Human reproduction is represented here as a vegetative process and in a sense the result is a reduction of humans to the level of plants.

What I have called the dream of women's superfluity is something we find in both the autochthony and the Pandora myths. In both places it occurs as a dream about an original unity, about a time when there was only one sex and people multiplied in ways that had no need of sexuality. This dream of unity is especially clear in the Pandora myth. Not only were people originally one with themselves, they also lived in harmonic union with nature and the gods. The implication is that the appearance of woman destroyed the unity once enjoyed on all these levels.

It is interesting to note how sexual difference is regarded as a condition for the *distance* people establish between themselves and their surroundings, or for the liberation of humankind from the gods and nature. Yet distance and liberation are portrayed as a fall rather than as marks of progress, as something evil rather than good. Since it is woman who introduces the distinctions and dissimilarities, she comes to symbolize what we can call the category of difference: man stands for original unity, whereas woman is the *other*.

Humanity's original condition allowed each man to see himself reflected in any other. The governing principle was sameness. In Hesiod, that original, unified condition assumes the aspect of a lost dream, a utopia. This emphasis is not so apparent in the autochthony myth. In the latter, women simply do not figure in the origins of humankind – or more correctly, of the Athenians. The autochthony myth suggests that the Athenians clung to the dream of sameness and refused to accept it as something past. Hesiod's Pandora myth, on the other hand, makes a concession to sad reality. Whereas the autochthony myth sees the source of humankind as singular, the Pandora myth tells us that it was – regrettably – dual.

With the Pandora myth, Hesiod laid the foundations for a long tradition in which woman was characterized as the other sex. The true, original human is the man, and as such he represents the ideal. Hesiod's theory of sexuality also provides the basis for an influential metaphysics which counterposes the original, ideal unity with a condition of discord and otherness. Oneness and otherness, singularity and plurality, the One and the Other; these dualistic pairs of principles found their expression above all in the Platonic tradition. Thanks not least to Hesiod and his Pandora myth, these paired principles embody clearly sexual connotations. Oneness stands for the masculine element of existence, whereas Otherness stands for the feminine.

PLATO AND SEXUALITY: THE ONE AS MALE PRINCIPLE, THE OTHER AS FEMALE

To indicate how Plato developed Hesiod's reflections on the relationship between man and woman, I shall briefly sketch an aspect of his philosophy that tends to be overshadowed by his better-known theory of forms, namely his dualistic theory of principles. What we know of his theory of principles has come down to us first and foremost from Aristotle's *Metaphysics*. The theory speaks of the One (*hen*) and the Other (*allo*) – of which the latter is also sometimes called the Duality (*dyas*) – as the two fundamental principles.[12] According to the theory, everything that exists can be traced back to these two principles, insofar as it results from a 'meeting', a 'mixing' or a 'confluence' of the One and the Other. Thus, everything that exists is an embodiment of these two principles. What is meant by 'principle' here is something like a fundamental property that we cannot imagine a thing not to possess. Plato believes that, for us to be able to say of a certain thing that it exists, it must exhibit both a type of unity and a type of plurality. The fact that we can say of something that it is 'one' implies that it manifests some kind of stability and identity. The principle of otherness, by contrast, accounts for differences, plurality, change and movement. For Plato there is a clear hierarchy between these two principles. The One is essentially good and positive, whereas the Other, or Duality, is essentially negative. In Platonic thinking, plurality, difference and change are what we can call forces of annihilation.

In Plato's language the One is also called the Good, and it represents the true ideal, that which we ought to strive for. He stresses the importance of limiting wherever possible the role of Otherness in existence, a point which is most clearly made in his ethical and political works. The goal of the ideal state, for example, is to achieve the highest possible degree of unity, harmony and stability. For Plato, unity and stability are the main criteria of a good state. State censorship and state-approved killing have to be characterized as 'good' within this system, provided they lead to greater stability and unity. But even if unity is indisputably good, it cannot exist in isolation. Everything that exists must of necessity have a form of plurality, and even *time* is dependent on the existence of something other than the One. The existence of nothing more than the One would imply total standstill. There would be no activity of any kind. This means that the One cannot of itself bring anything into existence. It must first be 'mixed' with its contrary, Otherness. Reproduction – in other words, coming-to-be and birth – require both the One and the Other.

This may sound rather abstract, but for Plato the meaning is quite specific. Anything that exists – whether it be a tree, a person, a chair or a state – is in Plato's opinion a combination of the two opposed principles of unity and otherness. The One and Duality/Otherness are not things in themselves, but principles of all existing things. It should be stressed that although unity is the ideal and plurality merely a necessary evil, both are nevertheless required for *reproduction*. Thus Plato does not allow himself to be entirely seduced by the Greek dream but, like Hesiod, is realistic enough to acknowledge the Other, in the sense of 'that which is not one', the non-identical, etc., even if he ascribes it a lower value.

There is good reason to believe that, for Plato, the One is a male principle, whereas Otherness is a female principle. However, the demonstration of this will require some space, and I shall therefore reserve the subject for Part II of the book, where Plato will stand in focus. At this point I shall merely show the probability of the claim by considering Plato's philosophy as a part of the Pythagorean tradition. In much the same way as Plato, the Pythagoreans conceived of existence as a combination of contrary principles, which for them were called the 'limited' and the 'unlimited'. These two principles were seen as analogous to a series of other pairs of contraries, which the Pythagoreans recorded in their so-called table of principles (cf. Aristotle's *Metaphysics* I 986a). Here male, good and light all stand on the same side of the divide as unity and limit, whereas plurality and the unlimited are grouped together with female, evil and darkness. For the Pythagoreans the principle that constitutes unity, or limit, is therefore masculine in character.

The masculine, or good, principle is an active principle that separates out and delimits individual things from the unlimited, indeterminate and formless female element. Everything that exists has come into being by means of some such process of distinction, which for its own part arises through a kind of birth. Things come into being when the masculine principle impinges on the feminine. Thus for the Pythagoreans, sexual fertilization and birth served as a model for all forms of becoming. There is no doubt that Plato's theory of principles is indebted to the Pythagorean tradition. I also believe his account of how all things come into existence has to be understood as analogous to sexual fertilization and birth. In short, Plato was not unfamiliar with the problem of sexual difference, as we shall see in greater detail in Part II.

AN INVERSION: WOMAN AS ONE, MAN AS OTHER

The topics discussed so far – the autochthony and Pandora myths, and the Platonic theory of principles – add up to a rather simple and one-dimensional picture of the relationship between the sexes, or more correctly, between the masculine and the feminine. The man originally symbolized unity and self-identity. The woman stood for the Other, the alien, that which is extraneous and brings difference, plurality, disharmony, conflict and ultimately destruction into the world. However, it is rare for a system of thought or a mythology to be as straightforward as I have presented this one to be. A closer look at Greek mythology soon discovers figures that do not easily fit the scheme of male and female presented here.

Two divinities in particular are worthy of mention here, Hermes and Hestia, such as they emerge in the works of Jean-Pierre Vernant. The starting point of Vernant's essay 'Hestia-Hermes'[13] is the statue of Zeus at Olympia. On the pedestal on which the statue stands we find Hestia and Hermes depicted as a couple together with a number of other divine couples. Although it is clear what kind of partner relationships hold between the other gods – Zeus and Hera, for example, are man and wife, Apollo and Artemis are brother and sister, Aphrodite and Eros are mother and son – there is no clear connection between Hestia and Hermes. Vernant's essay endeavours to account for this conjunction. Hestia and Hermes are said to belong together in virtue of their *functions*, which stand in a complementary relationship to one another. Both have functions in relation to the human sphere, or rather, they both provide dimensions of the physical world and the society in which people live. I shall explain what this entails, and then take a look at these gods – one male, one female – in relation to what has already been said about Greek notions of male and female.

Hestia refers not just to a goddess; it is also the usual Greek term for the round hearth, or fire-place, that stood at the centre of the Greek citizen's home. By means of Hestia, as if by means of a navel, or *omphalos*, the house and the family were rooted to the earth. In both the literature and visual arts of Greece, Hestia is frequently associated with the navel. One example is the *omphalos* at Delphi, a stone in the form of a pregnant woman's navel, which was regarded as the seat of Hestia. In characterizing Hestia as the navel of the individual family, it is important to realize that the Greek word for 'family' – *oikos* – also means 'house'. The place where the family lives is not clearly distinguished from the family itself, which consists of the family members, living as well as dead, together with the family's property. Thus a family belongs to the place where it lives for many generations, indeed, it belongs to the very earth. As the family's navel, Hestia constitutes a root fixing the house, home and family to the earth. In keeping with this symbolism, a new addition to the family was associated with the produce of the earth; the birth of a child was like the appearance of a new shoot. Here again we suspect that no clear distinction is made between vegetative and sexual reproduction, and, as we shall see, this has implications for Hestia's function.

As the focal point of the home, rooted to the earth, Hestia also symbolizes the link between generations, that is the continuity of the family through time. Moreover, she represents the family's unity and identity at any given time. When outsiders were invited into the home, they were received beside the hearth; here one was assured of hospitality and protection from the world outside. The family forms a ring, as it were, around their divine Hestia, thus creating a closed sphere of which she is the centre point.

During the cosmic procession of the Olympian gods in Plato's *Phaedrus*, Hestia is described as remaining alone in the 'gods' dwelling place', while all the other divinities troop across the heavens (*Phaedrus* 247a). Thus Hestia has a cosmological function as well. She can be said to hold the world together by remaining at the 'centre of the sphere', which is also where the Pythagorean Philolaus places her (fragment 7).[14] Plato also accords her an ontological function. In *Cratylus*, he notes an etymological connection between *hestia* and *ousia*, the Greek term for the essence of things (*Cratylus*, 401d). In other words, not only does Hestia hold the universe together and guarantee the family's continuity through the succession of generations, she also fixes individual things, securing their existence and identity.

The function of Hermes is the opposite of that of Hestia. Hermes *angelos*, the messenger of the gods, is the one who comes from afar and leaves without delay. He is always in motion and forever changing; one cannot say he *is*, since he is never at rest. He communicates between the gods and humankind and is constantly crossing the borders between the divine world and that of mortals.

Like other Greek gods, Hermes also takes on a variety of guises. Most of these are related to his function as a transgressor of borders. His name is used to signify various types of boundary stones. It is Hermes who stands at the threshold of the house and welcomes strangers. He rules over the border between the home and beyond, between inside and outside. He also stands as milestones along roads and points travellers in the direction they need to go. We find Hermes on gravestones, this time as the soul's companion on its journey to the underworld, Hermes *psychopompos*. Thus Hermes presides not only over the border between mortals and the gods, but also over the border between life and death.

In the public sphere, Hermes has a central place among the citizens. He is Hermes *agoraios*, he who dwells in the marketplace (*agora*), which is where the citizens of the city state met to exchange produce and opinions. Hermes is the mediator *per se*, the one that forges links between various elements without himself being linked to any of them. He is and is not in everything and everywhere.

Hestia is marked by a number of traditionally feminine associations. She is linked to the domestic sphere, the introverted and above all darker aspects of the dwelling place. She stands at the centre of the house, that which is closed off from the outer world, that which rests in itself. Hestia secures the continuity of the family. She represents the motionless focus of the home, a point that provides unity and identity, calm and stability.

Hermes, on the other hand, opens the home to the outside world, towards other families, indeed towards everything alien and 'other'. Hermes symbolizes the masculine publicness of the city state and the openness of the marketplace. Hermes is movement. It is through him that one thing is able to meet the other. In their polarity, Hestia and Hermes can be said to determine one another reciprocally. Together they constitute the human space in society and on earth. Hestia takes care of the secure, immobile foundation, which gives all things their orientation, whereas Hermes creates movement away from this fixed point.

Xenophon, an Athenian contemporary of Plato, describes the nature of man and woman in a way that agrees fairly closely with this analysis of Hermes and Hestia. According to Xenophon, man's soul and body are created for work out of doors, under the open sky, in motion, away from the home, whereas woman's nature suits her to remain at rest, occupying herself with indoor work.[15] This characterization of male and female roles matches what we can call the social reality of Athens. The woman, meaning in this context the married woman, was by and large confined to the home, where her main function was indubitably to bear legitimate children, and thereby to ensure the continuity of the family and the city state. The man, meaning here the Athenian citizen, pursued his activities outside the home, in the public and political sphere. He was the head of the family, without himself being restricted to the family sphere.

If we now recall what was said about the autochthony and Pandora myths, with the support they gained from the Pythagorean and Platonic theory of principles, the picture seems to have been turned on its head. There the man symbolized unity and identity, yet these are the qualities we have just fixed upon as characteristic of Hestia and the feminine. In both the myths and the theory of principles, woman and the female symbolize otherness. Yet these qualities have just been equated with the masculine Hermes, whose function it is to open the inward-looking family to the outside world. How can this be explained?

In order to grasp the contradiction – or at the least, the ambiguity – in these notions of the feminine and the masculine, we need to probe a little deeper into the Hestia and Hermes figures. Plato provides a useful starting point. In *Cratylus*, he postulates etymological connections not only between *hestia* and *ousia*, but also between *hestia* and *ōthoun*. Plato sees in Hestia not just the essence of things (*ousia*), that which holds them at rest or maintains their unity and unalterability, but also that which enables motion, change and growth, a kind of 'pushing principle' (*ōthoun*; *Cratylus* 401d). The implied ambiguity in Hestia's nature is not merely the result of Platonic wordplay, for it was also apparent in the myths. The situation becomes clearer when we adduce still further aspects of the Hestia figure.

As a goddess, Hestia is a virgin. In this respect she is comparable with
Athena and Artemis, the only goddesses capable of fully withstanding the
influence of Aphrodite, the goddess of love. There are also indications that
Hestia is identified with Mother Earth, *Gaia-Mētēr*, the basis of all fertility
in nature. Hestia therefore symbolizes not only virginity but also the earth's
fecundity. Once again she appears ambiguous. She combines fertility and
virginity, which comes to the same thing as reproduction without sexuality.
Hestia is the virginal hearth, the firmly rooted mid-point of the home and
family, securing as such the continuity of the ancestral line over generations.
We now see that the notion of continuity itself is ambiguous. On the one
hand, it denotes a fixed point that remains unchanged despite things changing around it. On the other, it suggests the very process of change. That
which is to secure the family's continuity should not only be a fixed,
unchanging point, it must also take care of reproduction, which amounts to
change.

Since it is the woman who gives birth to the child, it seems reasonable to
regard her as the physical link between one generation and the next. For the
Athenian *oikos*, however, she was an unstable link, insofar as a new woman
had to be fetched into a man's family for each new generation. The *oikos*
belonged to the man, and it was therefore the son who inherited the home –
the house and the property – from his father. Thus the secure link in the
family was the man, the master of the house, the paterfamilias. It was he who
symbolized the family's unity and continuity, that is who enabled the family
to remain *the same* through time. In this sense, there was a close symbolic
link between Hestia and the paterfamilias.

This connection between the feminine Hestia and the masculine head of
the family was reflected in an Athenian ritual, the *amphidromia*, which
Vernant has called a ritual of integration (*Myth and Thought*, p. 157). This
ritual was performed when a new-born baby was to be integrated into the
family. Several days after birth, the child was carried around the hearth of
the house. This signalled that the child was acknowledged by the father as his
legitimate offspring, and worthy of being taken into the family. Failure to
perform the ritual generally indicated the opposite, namely, rejection by the
family, and in such cases the child might not even be allowed to survive. A
child that was recognized by the father was known as 'issue of the hearth'
(*Myth and Thought*, p. 134). The expression suggests that the child is des-
cended from Hestia, or born of her. Hestia is like a navel that roots not only
the earth to its place at the 'centre of the spheres' and the home to the earth,
but also the child within the family. Here as well, Hestia serves as an asexual
fertility symbol: the child springs from Hestia much as a shoot springs from
the earth.

The family's legitimate child is the child of the father and the virgin Hestia. The masculine dream of reproduction without sexuality is thus expressed not only through mythology, but also in ritual. The man has conquered both Hestia and Hermes, insofar as he embodies both feminine and masculine aspects. By contrast, the woman seems to have been entirely disregarded. In terms of her gender at least, she was neutralized, or condemned to total passivity; on the symbolic level, her role in the reproductive process was reduced to invisibility. In claiming that the man, through his association with Hestia, has absorbed the feminine elements of the city state, a further distinction is still required. Although it is clearly the male citizen, or master of the house, who acquires Hestia's aspects of immovability and stability, Hestia's introverted and private aspects continue to define the woman.

It remains for us to tie these threads to the concept of the female such as it emerged from the autochthony and Pandora myths, and from the Pythagoras–Plato tradition: woman as the other, as the principle that corrupts masculine unity. We can establish this link by means of a brief look at the Athenian institution of marriage. When a woman married, she left her father's home and moved into the family home of her husband. Even so, she never became entirely integrated into the new family. To some degree she remained a perpetual alien (*xenē*), a kind of guest (*xenē*) on a long-term visit,[16] and like any guest, she had a right to protection. According to one Greek author, a wife was someone who merely sought refuge at her husband's hearth (*hestia*).[17] This tenuous status meant that a woman kept a bond to her original family throughout her marriage. Her dowry was to be maintained intact for as long as she was married so that it could be returned to her father in the case of divorce.

The man and his domestic Hestia, which was passed down from father to son, were inseparably linked. Each represented in its own way the home and the family. The wife, by contrast, was an intruder, certainly a necessary intruder, but still an alien element within an otherwise self-contained unit. It was only as a virgin, as an unmarried girl, that the woman could be said to belong to a Hestia, namely that of her father, which she left on marrying.

From the point of view of marriage the woman therefore constituted an element of mobility, someone who provided the family with an opening to the outside world and who linked different families together, yet these qualities we have already identified as 'masculine', and characteristic of Hermes. In accounting for this anomaly, Vernant claims that the institution of marriage involved an *inversion* of the woman's evident social situation: whereas the woman was bound to the home, confined to the family, the man was the mobile element who moved within the public sphere, outside of the family. This inversion seems to confirm the picture of the woman established earlier on the basis of the autochthony and Pandora myths. Here as well the woman (or the female) is characterized as the Other, the alien, that which comes from outside and breaks up the self-contained masculine unity. The reason for a man to take a woman into his family through marriage was to make a reality of what he yearned to do alone, which was to secure the continued existence of his line.

The concepts of the feminine and the masculine seem to have been turned on their head not once but twice. It turns out that Hestia, the ostensible home-hearth, represents essentially masculine values, while Hermes, the mediator and creator of public, masculine space, also has a feminine aspect. Does this imply that the terms 'feminine' and 'masculine' have lost their meanings?

I think not. In the daily life of the *polis* the man clearly remains the mobile element, symbolized by the masculine Hermes, whereas the woman is the stable element, symbolized by the feminine Hestia. In his imagination, however, the man seems to have seen himself as the unmoving, stable element, symbolically linked to Hestia. In her daily life, the woman, meaning once again the married woman, the wife of the citizen and the mother of citizens-to-be, was bound to the home where her task was to bear legitimate children for the family father. But it is precisely this function – the woman's reproductive capacity – which is not symbolically acknowledged. It is missing not just in the myths and rituals, but also in the thought and legislation associated with the institution of marriage.

The woman entered the family from outside, and were she to vanish again, the family's identity would not be affected. In this respect she resembles – but only resembles – the masculine Hermes. We should remember that, while for the man the world outside the home was a highly significant space – indeed, the space that gives his life meaning – for the woman it was a void, a nothingness. The married woman had no function outside the home. In the extra-domestic realm she was nothing.[18] In this way, Hermes thoroughly retains his 'masculinity'. The man seems to have conquered both the masculine and the feminine aspects of the city state.

So what is left for women? How should we characterize her status in the Athenian *polis*? Compared to the man and the culture he perpetuated, the woman is first and foremost a negation; she is the 'otherness' that disrupts the unity of masculine society. She is physically present without being acknowledged as such; she is a kind of nonentity that nevertheless has to be reckoned with. In the Periclean law of around 450 BCE, for instance, it says that an Athenian must be 'born of two citizens', implying that both mother and father must be citizens, even though there are no female citizens (cf. *The Children of Athena*, p. 119). The definition of the Athenian citizen is therefore self-contradictory. The woman both is and is not a part of society. She is both insider and outsider, yet neither of these. Graphically speaking, she stands on the border. No matter where she is, she is alien. We begin to suspect something profoundly paradoxical in the city state's ideology, in that it seems defined by the exclusion of women, although in practice such exclusion would of course be impossible. Woman's exclusion from the city state was at one and the same time an ideological necessity and a practical impossibility (cf. *The Children of Athena*, p. 75).

In attempting to determine more precisely the border on which woman stands, we discover that we are in fact dealing with two borders at diametric extremes. Firstly, woman symbolizes the city state's 'outer border', that is the border towards that which lies outside the political space of the *polis*. In this respect women constitute a fringe group, and as such they are associated with other fringe groups: slaves, foreigners, youth.[19] As this particular borderline phenomenon, the woman is the opposite of Hestia; despite her essentially feminine connotations, the latter has been appropriated by the man. The married woman has no place in the city state simply because the man represents wholeness, or totality.

There is however one aspect of Hestia unencompassed in this totality, namely the inner, the aspect of darkness, the hidden, everything that is most private and intimate, that which not even the city state's pervasive publicness and clear *logos* could render visible. The second of the two borders on which woman stands is therefore the 'inner border'. In this we detect a hint of the woman's physical inside as a space concealing something that has not yet been brought to light, which has not yet been born. Here as well the woman stands symbolically on the border between existence and non-existence.

CHAPTER 2

Thought and Sexuality: A Troubled Relationship
An analysis of Hesiod and Parmenides

INTRODUCTION

Motionless in the limits of mighty bonds it is without beginning and never-ceasing, since coming into being and perishing have been banished far away, driven out by true conviction.

(Parmenides, fragment 8.26 ff.)[1]

This is how Parmenides, one of the earliest Greek philosophers, describes Being, or existence. In these terms he sets the tone for a philosophical tradition that culminated in the works of Plato a few generations later. True reality is independent of all coming-to-be, growth, change and destruction. The ideal is eternity and immutability, in other words, a form of divine reality in which mortal phenomena such as life and death play no part. Parmenides can be characterized as Plato's spiritual father, and the extent of his influence on European philosophy right up to the present day can hardly be overestimated. Philosophers of the Platonic tradition – from Parmenides and Plato through to Kant and Hegel – have for example found it natural to think in terms of hierarchies. Immutability is superior to ('better than') change; eternity is set above time, immortality above decay and death. According to this attitude, only things that display perfect unity and self-identity can be raised to the sphere of the eternal. Unity and identity are thus regarded as ideals and hence 'better than' plurality and difference.

An investigation of this Platonic – or perhaps we should say Parmenidean – tradition will help us understand the misogyny inherent in so much Western philosophy. Within this tradition woman and the female principle are identified as the cause of phenomena that philosophers ought to avoid. The woman tends to be more closely associated with the body and sexuality than the man, with the result that woman generally symbolizes not only growth and plurality, but also the decay and death of the body.

Woman, sexuality, birth and death form a group of concepts with symbolic connotations and an almost natural kinship in our philosophical heritage. Contrasted with these are the man, thought and eternity. Corresponding to this distinction we find two ways of conceptualizing the world: either as a product of sexuality and birth, such as it appears in myths, or as something that can only be grasped by means of thought, which is how Parmenides describes it.

The philosophers' idealization of thought is linked to a concept of the world which at first glance seems far-fetched and rather absurd, but which nevertheless turns out to permeate our culture in numerous ways. One reason why this tradition can seem so incongruous is that it regards birth, growth and development – the very stuff of a rich and varied existence – as inessential aspects of life. By focusing on what I consider the principal source of this tradition, I hope to get beneath some of the clichés and improve our understanding of the influences that nourished it.

Parmenides' philosophy has come down to us in the form of a poem he composed in the first half of the fifth-century BCE. This text is considered one of the most obscure statements of Greek philosophy. It is short and terse, and calls for detailed analysis on the level of individual words and expressions in order to yield the author's meaning. The poem comes across as an intense attempt to convince the listener that the phenomena of birth and becoming, death and destruction are incompatible with genuine thought and hence also with 'Being'. Accordingly, Parmenides denies any form of origin, or *archē*, to existence as such.

However, the question of the origin of things was not raised for the first time by what we now think of as philosophy. It was also posed in the Greek myths, especially as recounted in Hesiod's *Theogony*. This exemplary verse work from around 700 BCE, could be described as a single lengthy answer to the question of origins, and it is common to regard Hesiod as a precursor of philosophy. The continuity between Hesiod and Parmenides is particularly striking.[2] Parmenides writes in epic hexameters, which is the verse form of both Homer and Hesiod, and much of his imagery and many of his expressions are also characteristic of Hesiod. In fact, we can formulate Parmenides's main philosophical objective as the direct repudiation of the way Hesiod describes the world. In his *Theogony* Hesiod presents a genealogical account of existence.[3] In other words, he describes the creation of the world and its subsequent development as a kind of ancestral history in which everything happens as a result of births. And it is precisely this approach to reality that Parmenides undertakes to refute in his own poem.

To prepare the ground for what will be a fairly detailed analysis of Parmenides' work, I shall begin by taking a close look at the *Theogony*. It will become clear that Hesiod's genealogical account of reality runs into serious theoretical difficulties, something which Parmenides takes into account in his own work. Parmenides' concern is to find an alternative to the genealogical perspective. He attempts to grasp the peculiarity of existence without reference to the question of origins. But his intense refutation of everything connected with birth and becoming also results in a rejection of the female and the postulation of an ideal of existence correspondingly remote from sexuality, a type of existence which is in many ways purely masculine; only once we get beyond sexuality can we glimpse immortality. I am aware that it is unusual to attribute such thoughts to Parmenides, who has often been called 'the father of logic'. But in emphasizing the Hesiodic tradition to which he so obviously belongs, I hope to throw this aspect of his thought into clear relief and thereby expose his philosophy in an unfamiliar shape.[4]

WHAT IS THE ORIGIN OF ALL THINGS? HESIOD REPLIES

In the *Theogony* Hesiod describes how the world came into being as a story of births. Ultimately, everything that exists can be traced back to one of two sources: a bottomless, gaping abyss, which he calls Chaos, or the firm, safe Earth (*Gaia*). At the same time, Eros, the force of love, also appears. Chaos, Earth and Eros function in the poem like principles (*archai*) in the philosophical sense; they describe that from which all else derives, although they themselves have no further foundation, and they recur throughout the poem and govern its development. Chaos, Earth and Eros are therefore crucial to the origin of the entire universe, which develops out of them.

> *Chaos was first of all, but next appeared*
> *Broad-bosomed Earth, secure seat for all*
> *[The gods who live on snowy Olympus' peak,*
> *And misty Tartarus, in a recess of broad-pathed earth,]*
> *And Love, most beautiful of all the deathless gods.*
> *He makes men weak, he overpowers the clever mind,*
> *And tames the spirit in the breasts of men and gods.*
> (Hesiod, *Theogony* 116–22)[5]

Hesiod invokes Chaos and Earth as two mutually independent sources for everything that exists, in the broadest possible sense. Not only the physical parts of nature such as Heaven and Earth, mountains and rivers, but also phenomena such as day and night, war, age and mendacity can be traced back to one of these two principles. This means there are in fact two genealogies in Hesiod's universe, with either Chaos or Earth as the 'primal mother' of each ancestral line. Eros caters for loving embraces, thereby helping the lines of both Chaos and Earth. In the poem there is no sexual mixing between the genealogies of Chaos and Earth, but we shall see that the two are nevertheless interwoven, a fact that should also warrant a rethinking of the basic principles of existence.

Whereas Earth is generally acknowledged as a feminine principle, Chaos is usually regarded as a principle of neutral gender. I myself believe that also Chaos – if not Chaos in particular – can be seen as essentially feminine, in that it functions as a kind of sexual symbol: Chaos was the original cleft or chasm. Clear parallels can be found between antique representations of the female sexual organs and Hesiod's description of Chaos, which thus serves as an image of female sexuality.[6] Chaos does not have a safe lap, as does Earth, but is rather her contrary: an enormous gap that opens above a terrifying void, without form and consistency.

Chaos is contrasted, however, not just with the safe, feminine Earth, but also with the masculine Eros. Whereas Eros is the harmonizing principle that brings opposites together, Chaos is a divisive and destructive principle. Chaos gives birth to Night, which gives rise in turn to a range of destructive and sometimes formless powers, including Deceit, Love (*philotēs*), Age, Strife, Work, Forgetfulness, Famine, Pains, Battle, Murders, Killings of Men, Quarrels, Lies, Disputes, Lawlessness, Ruin and Death (*Theogony* 212 and 224ff.). Later in the *Theogony* it is precisely these destructive forces that are associated with woman's entry into the world.

Each of the three basic principles of existence stands in a contrary relationship to the other two. Earth, which is 'a secure seat for all' and the cradle of the gods that rule over clearly defined domains, stands in contrast to bottomless Chaos, the source of formless and destructive powers. The positive features of Earth are set against the negative aspects of Chaos. Eros, the unifying, harmonizing principle, is still opposed to Chaos, as the divisive principle. But Eros and Earth can also be seen to stand in a dichotomous relationship. Whereas Earth is a feminine goddess of birth, Eros is a masculine god of love. In the course of the poem, these dichotomies become increasingly cumbersome and eventually break down completely.

The Hesiodic universe begins of necessity with autogenesis. This is true of both the generation that begins with Earth and that which begins with Chaos:

And Earth bore starry Heaven, first, to be
An equal to herself, to cover her
All over. (Theogony 126f.)
From Chaos came black Night and Erebos.
(Theogony 123f.)

Earth's first offspring, Heaven, is soon gripped by an irresistible urge to couple with the source of its own origin. But the first union between Earth and Heaven, which provides a model for later sexual relationships, is not a great success. The birth does not come to fruition; for fear of being overpowered by his own progeny, Heaven prevents the child from seeing the light of day by forcing it to remain in the bowels of Earth, thereby causing the mother immense pain and despair:

> As soon as each was born, Heaven hid
> The child in a secret hiding-place in Earth
> And would not let it come to see the light,
> And he enjoyed this wickedness. But she,
> Vast Earth, being strained and stretched inside her, groaned.
> (*Theogony* 156–60)

In other words, there is not much that is 'natural' about this first meeting between the sexes. Evidently it is not the harmonizing principle of love, Eros, who has been at work here, but rather the disruptive, divisive love-principle, Philotēs, a child of Night and a sister of Deceit and Strife.[7] Thus Chaos also manages to play a part in this first of all fertilizations. This unfortunate start to the meeting between the sexes has lamentable consequences. Earth initiates a cunning and treacherous conspiracy with her sons against their father. Initially, Earth supports her son Kronos, 'last', and 'most terrible' of Earth's children (*Theogony* 138), by castrating Heaven. This allows Kronos to assume – at least for the time being – his father's hegemony.

Hesiod's genealogical project, initially based on two 'pure', that is mutually independent, lines, already seems to be breaking down. For Kronos' evidently 'chaotic' aspect cannot be explained in terms of his origins; he is the son of Earth and Heaven, and the latter is for his own part a simple duplication of the former (cf. *Theogony* 126f.). If it were only the genealogical principle that mattered here, then it should be possible to give a full account of the descendants in terms of their origins. But Kronos' treacherous qualities can only be explained with reference to the family line of Chaos, with which, in genealogical terms, he has no connection whatsoever. The families of Earth and Chaos are thus connected with one another right from the start.[8] As we would expect, this also has consequences for Earth, whose properties were initially safety, stability and security. As the poem proceeds, she becomes so marked by 'chaotic' elements that she seems in danger of transformation into her opposite, which is Chaos. We will see that, at the point where this happens, Hesiod abandons his genealogical strategy.

Earth overthrows one patriarch but only to instate another, Kronos, whom she deceives in turn in cooperation with Kronos' son, Zeus. When Zeus succeeds to the throne, he guesses where the story is going and is determined to avoid the fate suffered by both his father and his grandfather. The strategy he uses to secure his own power for generations to come is to exploit the chaotic powers to their utmost by undermining the fundamental position of Earth. The first thing Zeus aims to do is to render harmless his immediate enemies, namely his father and his entire generation. This is evidently no easy undertaking since the gods are immortal. But Zeus comes up with an ingenious plan: he hurls his father and all the other Titans down into Tartarus, the deepest region within Earth (*Theogony* 731).

Hesiod devotes as much as 100 lines to the description of Tartarus, which is repeatedly invoked with an almost incantatory 'there' (*entha*). Following the violent conflict between Zeus and his supporters on the one hand, and the Titans on the other, it turns out that Tartarus has become an enormous, 'yawning mouth' (*Theogony* 740), and is quite incapable of providing even a hint of the safety characteristic of Earth. Anyone who is unfortunate enough to enter Tartarus, 'would not,' according to Hesiod, 'reach the bottom for a year; / Gust after savage gust would carry him / Now here, now there' (*Theogony* 741ff.). The contrast to 'Broad-bosomed Earth, secure seat for all' (*Theogony* 117f.) could hardly be greater. Tartarus is further described as 'Murky and awful, loathed by the very gods' (*Theogony* 739), a 'fearsome' place associated with Night (*Theogony* 743). In other words, although Tartarus is a part of Earth, it is still a chaotic place. Earth herself seems to have become chaotic.

Hesiod seems deeply troubled by what is in effect a fundamental problem. His universe requires a new foundation, and no sooner has Earth's chaotic nature been revealed than he produces one. Immediately after the Tartarus episode just described, he writes:

> *There are gleaming gates, and brazen threshold unshaken, fixed with*
> *continuous roots, self-grown.*
> (*Theogony* 811ff.)[9]

Here we find

> *... springs and limits*
> *Of gloomy earth and misty Tartarus,*
> *And of the barren sea and starry heaven.*
> (*Theogony* 807f.)

This description suggests we are dealing here with an absolute beginning. The place described is the source of all other things, but it does not itself need to be traced back to anything else insofar as its roots of bronze are 'self-grown'. As the 'springs and limits' of all things, this place seems to combine beginning and end in a single unity. This description has much in common with definitions of the first principle (*archē*) given by later philosophers: an *archē* is that which can exist in and of itself and which enables all other things to exist.[10] This new, non-genealogical principle seems here to take over from the three original birth principles. Let us take a closer look at this.

The new *archē* – principle or origin – is a kind of threshold, or portal, where everything comes together and is unified, and which gives the world a new, more secure foundation, although not necessarily in the physical sense. The endless roots, which themselves are not secured in nor have grown from anything, ensure that the gates are unshakeably stable. The fundamental characteristic of Earth, which has now been lost, is transferred to the gates, or concentrated in the threshold (*Theogony* 746–51).[11]

A threshold is a border between two different spaces, or rather, between two different spheres: the internal and the external. The threshold links these two spheres to one another. By means of this picture of a doorway and a threshold, Hesiod suggests a view of reality as a building, as a kind of house for the gods and mankind. The ways of Day and Night, for example, meet at the threshold (*Theogony* 748ff.), and Hesiod explains that these two are never inside the house at one and the same time:

> ... *never are both at home,*
> *But always one, outside, crosses the earth,*
> *The other waits at home until her hour*
> *For journeying arrives.*
> (*Theogony* 752ff.)

Various phenomena can thus go in and out of 'the house of Being'. If the house is taken to be that which is present, then 'outside' would correspond to what is currently absent. In other words, the threshold links what is absent to what is present. The threshold can be seen as the unifying ground of Being.

But more than just the house metaphor is significant here. Of equal importance is the image of the roots that grow of their own accord. The subject is the house of *life*, and it is evident that this involves both growth and reproduction. The new *archē* is a principle from which all things can grow, albeit without the need for sexual fertilization; the model here is vegetative reproduction. Neither is there any further mention of generations succeeding one another, since everything now seems to spring directly from this one locality. The new *archē* is the taproot of all existence.

In order to understand the scope of this newly established *archē*, we must also acknowledge its non-biological aspects. For instance, in saying about 'this place' that 'there, are the springs and limits of gloomy earth and misty Tartarus, and of the barren sea and starry heaven' (*Theogony* 736), it is hardly likely that Hesiod intends the word 'limits' in a physical or spatial sense, that is as the outer boundary of the universe. It seems more likely that he is struggling to grasp what would later – among the Pythagoreans, and in Parmenides and Plato – become a philosophical concept of boundedness, in the form of a delimiting, or form-giving, principle. Evidently the new *archē* is also a collective, unifying principle, and as such it clearly explodes both the anthropomorphic and biological modes of thought.

This place appears to combine the two fundamental contraries: Chaos, the source of Night and Day, and Earth. As the highest unifying principle and origin of all things, it is described partly in terms of biological metaphors and partly as a logical-metaphysical abstraction. This combination of genealogy with a unifying principle became decisively influential for Plato,[12] albeit conveyed to him via Parmenides' critique of all and every genealogical project.

*

What place does Hesiod accord to humankind in his universe? Again, we can approach the question from the angle of origins: how did the human race come into being? In purely genealogical terms, the question is easily answered. Humankind – mortals, as Hesiod likes to call them – are the progeny of Earth. But we shall see that the three fundamental principles – Earth, Chaos and Eros – pose difficulties also in relation to mortals. At first, the human race, initially composed only of men, lived in harmony with the gods. They shared their meals with the gods, and food was a source of pure delight and festivity, not just a means to still hunger or to hinder the body's decay.[13] Men received what they needed without exerting themselves. They communed directly not only with the gods, but also with nature. They knew neither toil nor sorrow, and were equally unfamiliar with sickness and old age.[14]

The body does not seem to have been a burden for these men; it simply does not feature in the text. Neither are we told what death might involve, although it certainly could not result from corporeal decay. The simplest suggestion is that it was imagined as a mild and everlasting sleep, which is how Hesiod's *Works and Days* describes the fate of mankind during the Golden Age: 'Death came to them as sleep' (*Works and Days*, 116). These first men were probably not acquainted with Eros, whose agency seems to presuppose some kind of difference between the parties he draws together.

The text gives no indication that either Eros or the 'chaotic' and divisive powers were active during this period. Harmony and stability seem to reign throughout.

All this changed when Pandora, the first woman, entered the world. She destroyed the utopian, masculine state of innocence, which involved the intimate fellowship of men and gods. Pandora initiated a new age in the history of humankind, an age in which men and the gods no longer lived in harmonious union. This is underlined by the fact that the story occurs at the point in time when

> *the gods and mortal men separated at Mecone.*
> (Hesiod, *Theogony* 535)

Characteristically, Pandora is not portrayed as an agent acting of her own free will, but rather as a tool in a larger intrigue, which begins with Prometheus' theft of fire.

Prometheus' aim in stealing fire from Zeus and giving it to the original mortals was to liberate them from the patriarchal care and authority of Zeus. With fire at their disposal they could make weapons and tools, which would allow them both to hunt and to cultivate the earth. Fire would allow them to prepare their own food, which would make them partially independent of the gods. But Prometheus' theft of fire achieved the opposite of what he intended. Zeus responded to the crime by transforming human existence from something easeful and carefree into a life of toil and pain (*Theogony* 594–602). With fire man acquired freedom, but Zeus added a gift that would turn him into a slave, binding him hand and foot. He gave him Pandora, a woman.

Hesiod seems to have regarded men and women as distinct races. Pandora brings with her 'the race of women' (*genos gynaikōn*) (*Theogony* 590). Hesiod can hardly find strong enough words to describe the evil that this represents:

> *'They'll pay for fire: I'll give another gift*
> *To men, an evil thing for their delight,*
> *And all will embrace this ruin in their hearts.'*
> (Hesiod, *Works and Days* 57ff.)

Thus the evil lies in the embrace, in the sexual desire that woman arouses in man. Correspondingly, Hesiod refers to Pandora as a 'lovely curse' (*kalon kakon*; *Theogony* 585).

Pandora is the sum of the gods' gifts, all of which are associated with her body, or more precisely, her sexual nature. Athena prettifies her with all the tricks of art, Aphrodite gives her 'charm ... and painful, strong desire, and body-shattering cares', while Hermes 'put in her breast / Lies and persuasive words and cunning ways'.[15] The gift of the gods is meant to tempt man's sexual desire. And Pandora succeeds in her task. This living artwork, formed from a lump of clay, is of such beauty that 'this hopeless trap' is 'irresistible to men' (*Theogony* 589).

Pandora is described as a creature without precedent. No one has seen the likes of her before; she is 'a wonder to behold' (*Theogony* 581). What seems to warrant this amazement is a certain ambiguity in her nature. She has the beauty of a goddess but is mortal nonetheless. Her similarity to the immortals arouses desire among men, while her mortal aspect makes her potentially attainable. And it is here Zeus demonstrates his cunning: men's desire to be one with the gods, their yearning for immortality, is what seals their fate as mortals.[16]

Thus it is not only sexuality that Pandora brings into people's lives, but also death:

> From her comes all the race of women,
> The deadly female race and tribe of wives
> Who live with mortal men and bring them harm.
> (Hesiod, *Theogony* 590–92)[17]

Mortals owe their mortality to woman. For this to be meaningful, the death introduced by woman must be different in nature from the death that men already know; henceforth death will be a result of the body's ageing process.[18]

Even if woman – or rather, the woman's body – is beautiful and arouses wonder and desire in man, she brings him little joy. The nature of sexual desire, and the fact that man is dependent on woman in order to reproduce, mean that humankind is subservient to demands of the body. This too is explained in the text, this time in terms of an altered attitude to food. Whereas food formerly implied a festive communion with the gods, it is now associated with the toil required to fill one's belly – and not just one's own, but also woman's, which is depicted as all but insatiable. Hesiod illustrates his point by comparing the woman with a drone and the man with a worker bee:

> And daily, all day long, until the sun
> Goes down, the workers hurry about their work
> And build white honeycombs, while [the drones] inside
> In the sheltered storeroom, fill their bellies up
> With the products of the toil of others.
> (*Theogony* 596ff.)

For both Homer and Hesiod, hunger and the need for food are defining characteristics of mortals, and it is woman above all else that represents this aspect of the physical body.[19] The implication is that the coming of woman into the world exposes something of the true nature of these mortal creatures; in contrast to the gods, 'who are forever' (*Theogony* 801), the human turns out to be 'the one that exists from day to day'.[20] The body is worn down by the toils of daily existence and requires food and sleep for its restoration, a need that can only be met in part. Day by day the body moves closer to death, which is no longer a gentle conclusion to life, but its constant accompaniment. The process of destruction begins at the moment of birth. The human has become mortal in our contemporary sense of the word.

It should not be forgotten that what makes the body mortal is its sexuality. Things are different for the gods, who remain immortal despite being both physical and sexual. The body of an immortal is differently constituted from that of the mortal. For instance, the former is not subject to temporal rhythms like the latter, but remains eternally young, full of strength, vitality and beauty. Probably the most revealing example of the absence of 'natural' temporality among the gods is the tale told in the Homeric *Hymn to Hermes*. Here we learn that Hermes leapt from his cradle soon after birth to steal Apollo's cattle. Having accomplished this trial of manhood, he whips on his nappies again and is back in his cradle well before mother gets home.

The immortal body seems inalterable, whereas the human body is characterized by its vulnerability for change. Whereas people eat to stave off bodily decay, and have intercourse to continue their race, the gods eat and make love only for pleasure. Viewed in this way, the divine body can hardly be regarded as a body at all, since the qualities we regard as characteristic of a body – mutability, decay and death – are absent. For the gods, sexuality is not a problem, as it is for mortals. This is shown by the fact that divine reproduction can occur by means of either autogenesis or sexual reproduction. It seems of little consequence, either for the parent or the offspring, which type of propagation is involved. This is a far cry from the human situation. For the latter, sexual reproduction is a fateful exercise. It is what makes them mortal.

Whereas the *arche* of the first human beings could be identified as Earth, this origin loses its significance once woman has been added to the race. Thanks to her, humankind seems to become 'chaotic' in its nature. There is a parallel between her arrival and Zeus' struggle against the Titans. The latter conflict deprived the gods of the safe ground beneath their feet by opening Earth to reveal Chaos beneath, and in a similar way, the advent of woman introduced a fundamental insecurity into human existence by opening the imminent prospect of death. Woman, and by extension sexuality, has a counterpart in Chaos and its formless, destructive powers.[21] This is reflected in the names Hesiod gives to the offspring of Chaos, such as Deceit, Age, Strife, Work, Famine, Quarrels, Lies, Ruin, Death, etc. Such are the phenomena that woman introduces into human existence.

*

Hesiod's genealogical project evidently assumes the ideal of 'pure' race, free of foreign elements. This is true not just of the races of Earth and Chaos, but also for that of men, which in its primeval state was pure and unmixed. Yet it is an ideal that cannot be maintained. The fact that Chaos, as a cosmological power, cannot be excluded from all aspects of the world's genesis poses problems for theory. Similarly, Hesiod seems to regard woman as a necessary and problematic phenomenon for our understanding of human origins.

We have seen that Hesiod attempts to compensate for the shortcomings of his genealogical hypothesis. The contradictions in his text oblige him to abandon the idea of two distinct, but mutually dependent principles. By postulating a new principle, he obtains the unity he needs to reconcile the opposites. In many ways his project is successful, at least from a historical perspective, insofar as his rudimentary principle of unity proved decisive for philosophy in the tradition of Parmenides and Plato. But the project is not pursued to its conclusion. Hesiod does not reconsider his concept of humankind in the light of his newly found principle of unity. Had he attempted to do so he would have had to rethink his view of the part played by woman – and sexuality – in human life. His omission seems to leave humankind without a foundation. In other words, Hesiod regards humankind as a mixture of two races – the female and the male – of essentially different natures, yet he makes no attempt to bring the two together on some higher level, as his unifying principle would seem to demand.

It is here we find a connection between Parmenides and Hesiod. Parmenides takes up Hesiod's novel insights and gives them a radical twist, while at the same time clearing the ground for a view of human life compatible with a principle of unity. Parmenides evidently regards genealogy to be incompatible with a principle of unity. For him, a unifying principle provides access to the eternal and he undertakes an explicit refutation of the genealogical approach as something that stands in the way of establishing a dimension of the eternal in human life. This leads him to exclude sexuality and sexual difference from all true thought and Being. In the following I shall focus first on the connection between Hesiod and Parmenides, and secondly on Parmenides' concept of existence, which to my mind unifies notions of life and immortality, albeit as a purely masculine and virile entity.

PARMENIDES' POEM: THOUGHT INSTEAD OF SEXUALITY

Parmenides' poem tells a story. A young man, the narrator of the poem, reports on a spectacular journey that ends beyond the world of humankind, in the realm of a goddess, who takes him by the hand, promising to reveal to him not only the truth about the world, but also all the false notions of reality that humankind holds. This is recounted as follows:

> *It is necessary that you shall learn all things,*
> *as well the unshaken heart of well-rounded truth,*
> *as the opinions of mortals in which is no true belief.*
> (Parmenides, B 1.28ff.)[22]

The poem is divided into three distinct parts: a prologue (or proem), in which the young man recounts his journey to the goddess; the goddess's account of the truth about the world; and finally, an account of the wrong-minded ideas that people hold about the world. The prologue, which we believe to be preserved in its entirety, consists of 32 verses and is generally referred to as fragment 1. The central part, constituting the philosophical core of the work, is also relatively well preserved in the form of several extracts (fragments 2–8), the correct sequence of which is, however, disputed. Relatively little has survived of the poem's final part (fragments 9–19). In the following I shall concentrate on the first two parts: the prologue and the goddess' presentation of truth. The final part of the poem will be discussed in the next chapter.

THE PROLOGUE: THE YOUNG MAN'S JOURNEY TO THE GODDESS

> *The mares which carry me, as far as ever my heart could desire, were*
> *escorting me, when they brought and placed me on the resounding road of the*
> *goddess, which carries through all places the man who knows.*
> (B 1.1ff.)

In these opening verses we meet a self-confident youth who knows what he wants and trusts in his ability and intelligence to achieve his ambitious goal, which is to meet the goddess who can tell him the truth of our existence and all Being. It is no ordinary journey upon which the young man (*kouros*, B 1.24) has embarked. Initially we learn of his expedition through his own words. Let us see what happens in the prologue, which both defines the

themes and provides a perspective for the remainder of the work. Like the
poem as a whole, the prologue also has a three-part structure: verses 1–10
describe the young man's journey 'into the light'; verses 11–21 give a detailed
account of the closed gates in front of which the traveller arrives, and which
are eventually opened for him; in verses 22–32 the young man has entered
the gates and encounters the goddess.[23]

It is not just the poets' masculine hero – the only figure of that gender in
the entire poem – whom we meet in the prologue, but also the daughters of
the sun, who guide his horses in the right direction. The route passes
through 'all places', away from 'the realm of night' and into the light. While
guiding him along this path, the maidens 'pushed back the veils from their
heads'. It is striking how many philosophical themes are introduced in these
first few lines of the poem which were destined to remain among the central
concerns of philosophy for the next few thousand years, with far-reaching
consequences. Here we find suggested not only a metaphor of light and a
notion of thought as a process of unveiling, but also the metaphor of a path,
which Plato would later develop into a concept of methodology. Neither
should it pass unnoticed that the philosopher is portrayed as a masculine narrator surrounded by female figures, who in various ways seem personally
remote from the desire for enlightenment.

Having been given a brief but fairly detailed glimpse of the chariot ride
towards the light, we suddenly find ourselves at a crucial location, which is
pointed out with a demonstrative 'there' (*entha*). 'There are the gates [separ-
ating] the ways of Day and Night', where the philosopher is brought to a halt
by Dikē, the divine gatekeeper.

Dikē is the Greek goddess of justice, which means she is a 'goddess of
boundaries'; she marks off yours and mine, for instance by setting marker
stones between our respective territories. But Dikē also watches over cosmic
boundaries, and this is the function she assumes in, for example, Heraclitus:
'Sun will not overstep his measures; otherwise the Erinyes, ministers of
Justice [Dikē], will find him out' (fragment 94).[24] And in Hesiod's *Works and
Days*, Dikē is said to distinguish people from animals; she sets limits to
human behaviour in forbidding them to eat one another.[25] As we shall see,
the portal in Parmenides' poem functions as such a decisive boundary. It is
located on the border between the mortal and the divine realms, between
existence and non-existence, and Dikē is the one who watches over this
border.

The gateway is described as ethereal and 'enclosed by a lintel and a
threshold of stone'. This is strikingly reminiscent of the decisive location in
Hesiod, where his three fundamental genealogical principles are resolved into
a single *archē* that transcends all oppositions. Hesiod visualised his new, uni-

fying principle as a portal that rests on a bronze threshold, and, as in Parmenides, he described his gateway as 'there', at the meeting point of the paths of Night and Day. There can be no doubt that this is one and the same place.[26]

The description of the gates provides substance for the entire middle part of the prologue and is therefore also located between two 'worlds': the world of humankind on the one side, through which our hero has already passed, and the residence of the goddess on the other, the goal of the philosophical journey. The gates define the limits of the latter realm, and there is evidently something extraordinary in the fact that the young man is permitted to cross this line. But there is also a hint of something ominous in the opening of the gates. The daughters of the sun 'knowingly persuade' Dikē 'with gentle words ... to push back quickly from the gates the bolted bar', whereupon the road is left behind and instead a 'gaping chasm' is disclosed, which evidently alludes to Hesiod's description of Tartarus and Chaos. It is as if the world is surrounded by a bottomless pit, full of chaotic, destructive forces. The description of the gates and the place it defines is abruptly interrupted, just as the young philosopher is traversing this void. From this point onwards there is no more description, and we find ourselves in another, divine universe.

For the final section of the prologue, we are at our journey's destination. The young man is received by the nameless goddess, and henceforth it is her voice that is heard:

And the goddess received me gladly and took in her hand
my right hand and addressed to me the following words.
(B 1.22f.)

The remainder of the poem consists of the goddess' speech to the young man, who retains a significant role as the poem's familiar 'thou'; everything the goddess says is addressed explicitly and directly to the youth, who can be said to provide her utterances with meaning. Numerous verbs are in the second person, thus presupposing the presence of the addressee. On several occasions the goddess also uses the imperative. The communicational situation, in which a divine speaker faces a mortal audience, is therefore of central importance.

What is it the goddess wishes to convey? She says:

It is necessary that you should learn all things,
as well the unshaken heart of well-rounded truth
as the opinions of mortals in which is no true belief.
(B 1.28ff.)

The knowledge about 'all things' is conveyed in exclusively *verbal* terms, which in this case means the words of the goddess, such as they are reported in Parmenides' text from fragment 2 onwards. Nevertheless, she does not deal with 'all things'; for one thing, she tells us nothing about herself. The goddess constitutes the locus from which everything is told, but that locus itself is not discussed. We have to assume that she is extraneous to what Parmenides regards as 'all things'. By allowing the young man to cross the threshold, which we can regard as the outer limit of the human world, and enter the realm of a nameless goddess who stands beyond 'all things', Parmenides takes us beyond the limits of the world with which Hesiod's reflections were concerned. Since this happens already in the poem's prologue, we can assume that Parmenides is looking for a more radical starting point for his reflections, a point that allows us to leave behind Hesiod's genealogical project and its attendant problems.

It is important to note that the nameless goddess has nothing in common with the traditional Greek deities as portrayed by Homer and Hesiod. The latter are always named and associated with specific aspects of the world, or realms of experience, and each has his or her peculiar attributes. Poseidon, for example, is the god of the sea and governs the way mankind relates to that element. Aphrodite is the goddess of love, and so on. In contrast, Parmenides' goddess seems remote from anything we could designate as the 'real world', an impression that is reinforced by her lack of a name. By using such a figure as his mouthpiece, Parmenides achieves a holistic perspective, one that allows us to see the world from the outside, as it were. The goddess describes mankind's finite universe from a divine point of view; she provides an immortal angle on mortal circumstances. We might say that this privileged perspective provides the philosopher himself with a glimpse of immortality. Seen from this vantage point, the world – referred to in the poem as Being – is conceived of as something quite dissociated from birth and becoming, decay and death.

Implicit in the poem is the conception that, by means of his reflective activity, his thought, the philosopher partakes of something immortal. This notion is not exclusive to Parmenides, but is in fact fundamental to much of Greek philosophy. It is crucial to Plato's thought, as we shall see later. But it also occurs in Aristotle, who, in the first book of his *Metaphysics*, distinguishes philosophy from all other human activities as a 'divine science' (983a). For Plato and Aristotle, philosophy's privileged access to immortality affords it a clearly spiritual dimension, due to its ambition to purge the soul of all things corporeal. Whereas the body is subject to decay and destruction, the soul subsists in another dimension. Correspondingly, that which is eternal and immutable can only be grasped by means of intellectual activity. In contrast, the bodily senses can only grasp transient aspects of the world.

Although Plato and Aristotle follow Parmenides in thus idealising immortality and the divine dimension, they differ from him in linking this dimension to the spirit and the soul, while leaving the body unambiguously in the realm of the ephemeral. It is hard to say whether Parmenides intended a clear distinction between body and soul, or alternatively between the body and reason, or between sense and thought. Personally I would claim that such distinctions are not his main concern. I consider this an important point and it will become essential to my interpretation of Parmenides' philosophy. I shall briefly explain the drift of my argument.

Concerning the mortals in whose opinions 'there is no true belief', that is those who have not found the path of truth, Parmenides has the following to say:

> For helplessness guides the wandering thought in their hearts. They are carried deaf and blind at the same time, amazed, a horde incapable of judgment, by whom to be and not to be are considered the same and yet not the same, for whom the path of all things is backward-turning.
> (B 6.5ff)

Here there is no juxtaposition of thought and sense, such as is often ascribed to Parmenides. On the contrary, he explicitly claims that these people think, but do not sense; they are both deaf and blind. This must of course be understood as irony. The 'two-headed', as he also calls them, both think and sense, but they do neither thing correctly. Their thoughts are guided by helplessness, their senses of sight and hearing by confusion. Since they are two-headed, they look in different directions at one and the same time, yet are unable to tell the one from the other. If they wish to think of anything essential, namely that which *is*, and if they wish to keep such things distinct from Not-Being, indeed from all kinds of change and plurality, they must learn to collect their thoughts and their senses. The principle distinction in Parmenides' ontology is, in my opinion, the distinction between Being and Not-Being, between unity and plurality, between immutability and change, a distinction which in his case does not involve a clear separation of mind and body.[27]

Parmenides' ontology therefore does not seem fundamentally irreconcilable with human bodily existence. However, the point I wish to stress is that it does indeed seem irreconcilable with the human's existence as a sexual being. As we have seen, for Hesiod it was woman's body, and the sexuality associated with it – hence not the body as such – that led to human decay and destruction. For the philosopher to grasp the eternal dimension of human life, assuming of course that he subscribes to the Hesiodic line of argument, he must first strive to imagine a world without sexual reproduction, and in which there is no requirement for two distinct sexes. And this indeed is Parmenides' project: to establish a concept of existence divorced from sexuality, and hence remote from birth and death.

BEING AND THINKING: A MUTUALLY DEPENDENT RELATIONSHIP

The main theme of Parmenides' poem is 'to be' (*einai*), or 'Being' (*to on, to eon*). Abstract as this might sound, his concern is evidently to grasp something utterly fundamental: what does existence entail? What does it mean to say that something exists? Parmenides' concept of 'Being' implies first and foremost something like 'that which there is', 'that which exists'. But it also has a far broader sense. 'Being' relates to the word that links a subject to a predicate; the little word 'is' (*estin*) assumes a crucial role in Parmenides' thought.

There is no indication that Parmenides made a clear distinction between what we would call the ontological (or existential) and the logical (or grammatical) meanings of the verb 'to be'. He did, however, ascribe considerable importance to another distinction, namely that between Being and Not-Being. Indeed, his entire argument builds on this opposition: 'there is Being, but nothing is not' (B 6.1f.). Or, as he puts it on another occasion: 'Concerning these things the decision rests in this: is or is not' (B 8.15). For Parmenides, Being and Not-Being are evidently mutually exclusive contraries, meaning that Being excludes in an absolute sense anything that has the merest hint of Not-Being about it. Parmenides' poem can be read as an investigation of the consequences of making radical deductions from the principle of contradiction.

These consequences are not easy to live with: Parmenides' Being excludes not only all kinds of change, but also plurality, and the existence of all things of different nature. These phenomena – change, plurality and difference – all imply Not-Being. When something changes it *is not* what it was before. Or conversely, it *is* something which it *was not*. A plant changes from being a shoot to being a flower. The shoot that was *is not* any longer, and that flower that is *was not* before. In other words, there can be no change without Not-Being sneaking into the process. Also the existence of things that are different from one another can only be explained in ways that acknowledge Not-Being. A person *is not* a tree, a man *is not* a woman. For Parmenides this would imply that these extant objects – the person and the tree – both are and *are not*, and to his rigorous way of thinking this is not possible.

Parmenides pictures Being – or that which exists – as an absolute and self-identical entity, without plurality and difference of any kind. Only thus can anything be said to exist, or to *be*, in a strict sense. If there are differences, then they must occur on another, more superficial level, and in such a way that true thought can conceive of them together as a fundamental unit, since that which exists 'is now altogether, one, continuous' (B 8.5f.). In Parmenides' poem, thought and Being are remarkably closely related. True thought is the thought that grasps what *is*, whereas false conceptions are unable to get a hold on the fundamental distinction between 'is' and 'is not', and consequently cannot get a hold on true existence. This relationship between thought and Being, meaning here between language and reality, will be crucial in my analysis of Parmenides' concept of reality, and we should therefore look at it more closely.

In the poem, reality is presented in the words of the goddess. There is nothing arbitrary in this. For Parmenides, reality is mutually dependent on language, on *logos*. It is language – meaning here words, speech or thought – that determines what can be considered true. And the interdependence is mutual: in thinking, a person must be thinking of some*thing*, meaning something which *is*, something that exists. This mutual dependence between language and reality is expressed in one of the best-known fragments:

for thinking and being are the same. (B 3)[28]

To grasp what Parmenides means by this it is useful to know that 'to think' (*noein*) is in this case a transitive verb, in other words, it takes a direct object. Grammatically speaking, there is an analogy between 'to think something' and, for example, 'to observe something', or 'to see something'. For Parmenides there is no crucial difference between thinking and talking, expressing, or speaking (*legein*), a verb which he also uses transitively. In the activity of speaking one does not simply speak *about* something, but the speaking has the effect, as it were, of calling that something into being. By means of the words, or the names of things, reality is effectively made present in language. One of the words Parmenides uses in this context (*phrazein*, B 2.8) means not just 'to say', 'to tell', or 'to show forth', but also 'to point out'.[29] In other words, someone who speaks reveals something to his listener. This 'something', which is said, or thought – that which by means of thought is rendered verbally present and evoked – is for Parmenides that which exists in a true sense, in other words, Being:

It is necessary to say and to think Being. (B 6.1)

Not only is the extant thing an object of thought, it is also *necessary* to think that thing; it is necessary to make reality present in thought, or rather, to name it. For something to exist, it must do so in language.

Elsewhere Parmenides calls that which exists 'that for which thinking is' (B 8.34);[30] thought is there for the sake of existence, of reality, or of that which is. This can only be interpreted as meaning that reality needs thought, or language, if it is to exist at all. The fragment just mentioned – 'It is necessary to say and to think Being' – can be understood as a philosophical imperative. What the goddess is saying is that the philosopher has a job to do, namely to evoke and maintain that which exists by means of language.[31] By giving reality a name, thought imbues it with meaning and existence. Things that are not brought to expression in language remain nameless, and will consequently fade away and vanish into nothingness. In this regard we can say that for anything to have Being, it is in need of thought and speech.

The distinction between Being and Not-Being is perhaps not so absolute as it first appeared: Being has to be held continually in thought so as not to vanish into Not-Being, which thereby poses a constant threat to Being. This unstable relationship between Being and Not-Being seems implicit throughout Parmenides' poem. Having made it clear that the philosopher's legitimate concern is with Being, Parmenides devotes considerable energy to persuading the reader (in fragment 8) to keep Being distinct from Not-Being. As we might expect, the purity of Being can only be preserved by means of thought, or language. And preserving the purity of Being is one of Parmenides's prime objectives. Let us study this more closely.

BEING: SECURELY HELD IN UNYIELDING BONDS. MYTHOLOGY AND LOGIC IN PARMENIDES' POEM

Parmenides describes truth as an 'unshaken heart' (B 1.29). The metaphor has military origins and brings to mind the soldier who stands firm in the face of the enemy despite dangers. If we take the metaphor seriously, then we have to conclude that the apparently well-defined, restfully poised and self-identical reality[32] does in fact have external enemies, against which it has to be defended. The external enemy can hardly be anything other than Not-Being, the only conceivable threat to the identity of Being. In its differentiation from Not-Being, the self-identity of Being is comparable to a sovereign state; its condition is not secured once and for all. It is an entity that has to be defended and constantly maintained.

Parmenides' poem reinforces the analogy between Being and the city state by means of numerous allusions to borders. The limits of Being keep out Not-Being in the way that city walls keep enemies at bay; and just as such walls afford protection to the citizens of the *polis*, so too does the 'furthest limit' (B 8.42) of Being ensure that Being remains 'inviolate' (*asylon*, B 8.48).[33] A place would be called inviolate when it offered foreigners refuge from attack. In describing Being in similar terms, Parmenides is suggesting that Being is threatened and requires protection. In fact Parmenides makes every effort to emphasize that Being is well defended. One of the words he uses to describe the borders that surround Being is *pedai* (B 8.14 and 8.37), meaning literally 'fetters'. Being is guarded by mighty goddesses like a prisoner. One of the guardians is Dikē, whom we have already met as the gatekeeper that blocked the approach to the menacing 'chasm'.

By comparing Being to a fettered prisoner, Parmenides suggests not only that Being needs to be defended, but also that there is a danger of its breaking out of confinement. According to this interpretation, Being needs various forms of protection if it is to remain self-identical. Thus the self-identity so vital to the maintenance of Being hardly seems a 'natural' condition.

In fragment 8 we are presented with numerous characteristics (*sēmata*) of Being. Curiously, many of these are couched in negative terms; in other words, we are told what Being is *not*. The negative attributes of Being include 'ungenerated', 'imperishable' (B 8.3) and 'immovable' (B 8.4), 'it was not once nor will it be' (B 8.5), 'without beginning and never-ceasing' (B 8.27), 'motionless' (B 8.26), 'not divisible' (B 8.22), 'not in need' (B 8.33). It would therefore seem that we know a lot about *Not*-Being, which Parmenides warned us to avoid as something that language cannot grasp or render present. To find out why Not-Being is seen as threatening, we must take a closer look at these negative attributes and their attendant arguments.

The word Parmenides uses for the first characteristic of Being is *agenēton*. This is translated here as 'ungenerated' but it can also mean 'not born'. It is no coincidence that he starts with this: 'Being ungenerated is also imperishable', or, as it might also be rendered, 'Being unborn is also without death.' Parmenides seems to regard death/destruction as resulting from birth/becoming. That which is born must also die. Or alternatively, if we wish to avoid death, we must first avoid birth. In arguing against birth and becoming, it would seem that Parmenides wants to clear the ground for a concept of Being that excludes decay and death.

> *For, what origin could you search out for it [Being]? How and whence did it grow?* (B 8.6)

The question would seem to open for two possibilities: Being can originate either in something non-existent, or in something that already exists. Parmenides pursues his investigation systematically. He considers both options, and dismisses each in turn. It seems self-evident that Not-Being – or nothing – cannot be the source of anything that *is*, and the goddess categorically forbids the young man even to consider the possibility:

> *Not from Not-Being shall I allow you*
> *to say or to think, for it is not possible to say or to think*
> *that it is not.* (B 8.7ff.)

Having so forcefully denied that anything can come from Not-Being, Parmenides nevertheless feels it necessary to distinguish between past and future becoming, both of which are disposed of with a rhetorical question:

> *What need would have made it grow,*
> *beginning from Not-Being, later or sooner?* (B 8.9f.)

This elaboration is, to say the least, unnecessary. It merely underlines Parmenides' determination to deny that anything can come from nothing.

But Parmenides also rejects the second possibility:

> *Nor will the force of conviction permit anything to come to be beyond itself;*
> *wherefore Justice [Dikē] looses not her fetters to permit [Being] to have come*
> *into being or to perish, but holds [it] fast. Concerning these things the decision*
> *rests in this: is or is not.*
> (B 8.12ff.)

The distinction between Being and Not-Being is adduced here to explain why something that exists cannot be the source of some other thing that exists (something new, different). Becoming necessarily entails Not-Being; some new thing that exists *is not* the same as the original thing that existed. But here it seems that logic alone is not enough to persuade the listener: Parmenides invokes the goddess of boundaries, Dikē, to reassure us that the fetters on Being are so secure that any kind of becoming is out of the question. This is a recurrent theme in fragment 8; in the final analysis it is the goddesses of boundaries and their chains that make sure that Being never becomes greater or smaller than it currently is. For the 'father of logic', logic and mythology work hand in hand, and it is intriguing to note the roles that the mythical figures assume in the poem.

Dikē (B 1.15 and B 8.13), Ananke (B 8.16 and B 8.30) and Moira (B 8.37) are three goddesses mentioned by name who strive to hold Being securely in its fetters.[34] Their function is twofold. On the one hand they appear as personified goddesses, while on the other they stand for logical inferences. This is most evident in the case of Ananke. The basic meaning of *ananke* is 'power', 'force', 'necessity' or 'fetter', and the term occurs both as the name of a virginal goddess of destiny and as a designation for logical 'necessity'. This combination of mythology and logic should not be lightly dismissed. It is hardly coincidental that the divine guarantors of logical stringency are female figures. Neither is it a coincidence that they all use *fetters* to keep Being in check; what seems to matter here is not so much that Being is clearly delimited, as that so much effort goes into keeping it intact. By alluding to fetters Parmenides emphasizes the unnatural, or violent, aspect of the task. Ananke, the guardian of logic, leads our thoughts on to slavery.[35] The fact that Parmenides' appoints Moira, the powerful goddess of fate, as an additional guardian of Being (B 8.37) suggests that even death has to be kept from Being by means of force. Ultimately, Being seems inaccessibly isolated from every form of Not-Being, both logically and ontologically.

BEING: LIFE WITHOUT DECAY AND DEATH

In describing Being as something kept in place by harsh and unbreakable chains, Parmenides implies that Being possesses an inner potential that seeks to overcome its own limits. Of course, we are not obliged to interpret these images as literally as I have done here. It could be argued that Parmenides employs them as mere rhetorical devices to point up the contrast between Being and Not-Being. My reasons for laying such emphasis on the compulsion metaphor are, firstly, that it is employed with such remarkable consistency, and secondly, that it is quite in keeping with the picture of Being that would emerge from Parmenides' work even if the metaphor were ignored. The best way to illustrate this interpretation will be to look at another of Being's negative characteristics, viz. 'never-ceasing' (*apauston*, B 8.27).

I shall begin by taking a rather bold leap forward to Aristotle, who uses the verb 'to cease' (*pauesthai*) in a way that might also throw some light on Parmenides' notion of Being.[36] One passage in which the word is used occurs in Book IX of the *Metaphysics*, in a discussion of the meaning of *praxis*, which is the Aristotelian term for human action (1048b 18–36).

Aristotle explains that an action consists in an endeavour to achieve a certain goal, the action's *telos*. Thus an action does not end when its goal is reached, but is rather thereby completed, or perfected. To put it another way, the action consists in the achievement of its purpose. As examples of actions Aristotle mentions 'to think' and 'to live well' (1048b 24f.). A person who thinks is someone who has already perfected a thought act. And it is only possible to say that someone lives well who has already experienced what it is to live well. To accomplish an action therefore implies, not that one dismisses it as finished, but rather that one is involved in it. Aristotle further illustrates the point by comparing an action with a movement (*kinēsis*): whereas an action carries its purpose within itself, the aim of a movement is something external to the movement, and the movement is concluded (*pauesthai*) once its aim has been achieved. It has been suggested that *kinēsis* can be described as 'incomplete activity' and *praxis* as 'completed movement',[37] a description that seems very apt.

We could say that *praxis* is a 'never-ceasing movement', that is a movement that is constantly being perfected. However, in speaking of 'perfected movement' there is also a suggestion of a state of rest; it is a kind of action that does not involve progress towards some other state, but which rather rests in itself. Consequently, in its strictest sense, *praxis* can also be described as *energeia*, or pure activity, pure reality without any form of potentiality and alteration.[38] This reminds us that the highest form of *energeia* is the Aristotelian godhead, the unmoved mover, which is pure thought, or *nous*.

In *De Anima* Aristotle discusses the relationship between movement (*kinēsis*) and activity (*energeia*) in a similar spirit. Whereas movement is characterized as 'imperfect', activity is described as 'perfected' (*tetelesmenon*; *De Anima* III 431a), and this is a word Parmenides uses to characterize Being (B 8.42). It is therefore possible to compare Aristotle's concepts of *praxis* and *energeia* with Parmenides' concept of Being. The latter is analogous to the former in being 'never-ceasing'; Being is a kind of unceasing, perfected activity; 'to be' is the same as 'to have been', the condition of having perfected the 'act of Being'. Such an interpretation of *apauston* corresponds well with uses of the word elsewhere in Greek literature; it invariably signifies an *action* that does not cease. The point I wish to make here is that Parmenidean Being does not denote a state of inertia, but rather an activity or process.

Let us venture a little further. One of the most fundamental meanings of *praxis* and *energeia* in Aristotle's writings is 'life' (*bios*), which can be ascribed to all living organisms. For Aristotle, 'life' is in the vast majority of cases synonymous with 'growth', implying that the living organism is subject to change and ultimately death. In other words, living things are mortal. Yet there are exceptions. God, the unmoved mover, is also accredited with life, but in this case it is 'never-ceasing' life – life that is being continuously perfected and which rests in itself (*Metaphysics* XII 1072a19–1073a13). We find the same conception in Plato's *Timaeus*, where the world-soul is described as 'never-ceasing life' (*bios apaustos*; *Timaeus*, 36e). The subject is the same: divine life, a thing of which also humankind can partake, to the extent that they succeed in emulating God.

I shall attempt to transfer this to Parmenides. 'Being' has to be grasped as an active verb denoting an unceasing, consummate activity or event in which people participate by thinking what is. The fact that Being is not a static, lifeless entity is further confirmed towards the end of fragment 8. At one point Being is described as a movement reaching from the centre of a sphere out towards the periphery, where it is halted by the fetters that hold Being:

> *But since there is a furthest limit, it is in every direction complete; like the body of a well-rounded sphere, from the middle everywhere of equal strength; for it need not be somewhat more here or somewhat less there.*
> (B 8.42ff.)

Being is described as a sphere, or perhaps more appropriately as that which constitutes a sphere. It begins as a point (the centre) and emanates outwards in all directions until – constrained by its fetters – it meets its spherical limit. This 'activity of Being' should not be understood as a movement with a beginning and an end, but as a self-contained process, a 'perfected movement'. If it were not for the 'furthest limit', this 'activity of Being' would continue outwards towards Not-Being, where it would be annihilated. Thus it is still the fetters of the goddess of boundaries that keep Being distinct from Not-Being and thereby prevent its destruction.

PARMENIDEAN BEING: CEASELESSLY VIRILE ACTIVITY?

From the foregoing analysis Parmenidean Being emerges as a kind of activity, action or life that retains its self-identity thanks to an array of unyielding fetters, which are partly logical and partly mythological in nature. This activity is being continuously perfected, thanks to that very protection against destructive forces. We have seen that the self-identity of Being is highly vulnerable since the chains that protect it are forever in danger of being broken. If Being were a motionless, lifeless entity, it would hardly require such durable defences to ensure that it remains 'whole and immovable' (B 8.38). The fact that it is described as 'immovable' (*akinēton*) does not preclude a state of constant activity. 'Immovable' is in fact an unfortunate translation for *akinēton*, since it immediately suggests a state of rest. 'Unshakeable' comes closer to Parmenides' meaning. According to Nicole Loraux, the fundamental sense of *kinēsis* is 'shaking'.[39]

The divine guardians, Dikē, Moira and Anankē, have a vital role to play. By keeping the fetters perfectly secure on the sphere of Being they ensure that nothing can escape from it and nothing can find its way in, and thus maintain it intact. Knowing that it is birth – and consequently death – against which Being has to be protected, it is perhaps not irrelevant to mention the

following: for the Greeks, both the virgin and the pregnant woman represented, each in her own way, *closed* bodies. A virgin had to be kept intact so
as to retain her purity. Nothing was to enter her, and the proof that nothing
had entered her was that nothing came out of her.[40] The body of a pregnant
woman was regarded as closed to an even greater degree.[41] Due to her condition, nothing – not even menstrual blood – comes out of her. In order to
signify that her body was closed, a woman would wear a belt. This was the
practice among both unmarried and pregnant women. The expression 'to
loosen the belt' was a euphemism for sexual intercourse. The pregnant
woman would remove her belt as the moment for birth became imminent.[42]

Let me risk the following conjecture: the Parmenidean sphere of Being can
be regarded as a masculine (virile) parallel to virginity and pregnancy; it is a
closed system, active – or animate – and well-nigh explosive, but nonetheless
such that nothing can escape from it. By means of powerful bands (or
perhaps belts[43]) the goddesses constrain this masculine Being to make sure
that it remains 'inviolable' (*asylon*, B 8.48).[44] In contrast to the woman's
pregnant body, Being knows neither past nor future, but merely a complete
and perfected present:

> *It was not once nor will it be, since it is now altogether,*
> *one, continuous.* (B 8.5f.)

Such a sexualized interpretation of Parmenidean Being might at first glance
seem a little far-fetched, but when we read Parmenides' poem – as I have
done here – as an answer to Hesiod's stranded genealogical project, this
reading immediately becomes more plausible. The line just quoted can also
be seen as a direct polemical attack on Hesiod, who in the introductory lines
of his *Theogony* praised the muses for their ability to describe

> *things which are, things to come and things which were before.*
> (Hesiod, *Theogony* 38)

Whereas Hesiod describes the plurality of everything that has come into existence through the sequence of generations, Parmenides focuses on that which
is now. Not only does he reject birth and becoming, but also all forms of
plurality. For Parmenides the One is itself not an *archē* for anything else, nor
does it have any *archē*, since every *archē* implies becoming and birth. For him
this is a crucial point. Since his project is to refute Hesiod's genealogical
hypothesis, it should not surprise us that he adopts a sexualized understanding of the fundamental categories of Being. He takes over such a picture
while at the same time trying to negate it. He replaces fundamental feminine

categories with fundamental masculine ones, which can more easily be dissociated from all kinds of genealogy.

*

In this chapter I have endeavoured to show that Parmenides' poem manifests the philosopher's yearning for eternity. In conceiving of death as a consequence of birth, birth becomes something he feels compelled to attack. In order to do without birth, one must evidently do without two sexes, and without sexual difference. Or to put it another way: in order to comprehend existence from a divine, non-temporal perspective, we have to *think* it in other than the traditional genealogical terms. This is what Parmenides attempts to do. He establishes Being as something constituted explicitly by thought, not by the becoming associated with birth, or by some mingling of elements. One could say that, for Parmenides, thought takes on the function that birth has in the myths and which the mixing of elements had for earlier philosophy (for example, for the Pythagoreans). Parmenides seeks to establish what we can call a 'pure' concept of Being, that is a concept of existence that excludes the possibility of Not-Being, and hence also becoming and destruction. He succeeds in this aim, insofar as life is conceptualized as 'ungenerated and imperishable' (B 8.3). This is not human life, but Parmenides imagines that one can partake in it by complying with the goddess's command:

It is necessary to say and to think Being. (B 6.1)

By means of thought – philosophy – people gain an inkling of the immortality of which sexuality has deprived them.

Parmenidean Being therefore transcends sexual difference. It is 'perfected' and 'not in need', and as such it knows nothing of the limitations that go along with sexual difference. Plato teaches us that defect is a prerequisite of love,[45] but we should not rule out the possibility that Parmenides had already said as much. In the opening verses of the poem we encounter something reminiscent of the Platonic Eros: a young man with an aspiring spirit, and a thirst for knowledge, which is ultimately fulfilled. Whereas for Plato Eros is the model or ideal for each and every human, the youth in Parmenides' poem is more ambiguous, if not indeed paradoxical in nature. His journey to the goddess is hardly intended as an example for us all to follow, but is presented rather as something exceptional. There is something unprecedented in the way the gates are opened to the young adventurer, and something unnatural – or supernatural – in his passage through the 'gaping chasm'.

The goddess teaches the young man that such journeys should not – indeed cannot – be undertaken; limits are not to be transgressed. The young man's desire for knowledge can thus be described as illegitimate. One implication of this reading is that Parmenidean Being will not even accommodate desire, but only narcissistic love. In its utter self-sufficiency it can tolerate nothing other than itself. There is something paradoxical in this: the transcendence of the outer limit is presented as a condition for the realization that such transcendence is in fact impossible. Perhaps Parmenides is hinting here at the limit of the principle of contradiction. My reading of the poem would suggest as much.

Parmenides also alludes to the boundary between human and divine existence. Even if the ideal that he sketches is of life independent of sexuality, birth and death, he does not of course mean to deny that we are all born or that each of us has a mother. On the contrary, this is part of 'mortal knowledge', which, although it has no power to convince us, must still be regarded as valid on the empirical level (cf. B 1.28ff.). Even so, Parmenides makes no attempt to hide his distaste for this kind of biological fact, which he too conceives of as quite fundamental:

> *In the middle of these is the goddess who governs all things. For everywhere she is the beginner of union and of abhorrent birth, sending the female to unite with the male and again to the contrary the male with the female.*
> (B 12.3ff.)

The birth that the nameless goddess commands the philosopher to reject in thought occurs here on the empirical level, where the divine purview has been lost from sight and things are looked upon as isolated phenomena (cf. B 8.51ff.). Here coming-to-be is a fact, caused by 'birth' and 'mixing'. The word Parmenides uses to characterize birth, and which is translated here as 'abhorrent' – *stygeros* – is used both by Homer and in the tragedies about that which is terrible in human fate: death. We must assume that Parmenides is using the word in the same sense. What is terrible about human 'mixing' and birth, in effect about human sexuality, is simply that it leads to death. This returns us to the starting point for my analysis: by means of his concept of Being, Parmenides seeks to envisage the world without sexuality and sexual difference, and thereby to evade death.

CHAPTER 3

The Logic of Exclusion and the Free Men's Democracy

An analysis of the notions of equality and balance in Anaximander and Parmenides

INTRODUCTION

It is well known that the Greeks were fond of thinking in analogies, that is they equated certain structures in different areas of experience, and used the same concepts in analysing them. The most striking and best-known example of this tendency is provided by Pythagorean philosophy, which proposed that all aspects of reality could be understood on the basis of musical harmonies; not just the soul and the body, but also society and the universe were built on musical structures. One characteristic of Greek philosophy as it emerged in the sixth- and fifth-centuries BCE is that it often conceptualized the most disparate phenomena by means of one and the same relatively simple intellectual device. It should not surprise us that things which we today regard as very different intellectual activities, such as astronomy, town planning and legislation, could all be practised by one and the same person.[1]

Neither should it surprise us that the majority of early Greek philosophers were active in the political life of the communities where they lived. The earliest philosophical theories, some of which strike us today as highly abstract, can to my mind only be understood against the background of the expanding city states. The first Greek philosophers rarely made a clear distinction between what we would call ontological speculation – thoughts concerning existence as such, for example how things came into being and what all things consist of – and cosmological theories about the origins of the heavenly objects, their movements and positions relative to one another. When we look more closely at these theories, we find they also contain an idea – or an ideal – about how society should be organized. Or to put it another way, the earliest philosophical speculations – with ontology and cosmology as the most important 'disciplines' – can best be understood as a part of a broader intellectual project: to put the idea of the city state into practice.

If we wanted to find what the early Greek philosophers had in common, one way to proceed would be to isolate the intellectual model that served as a foundation for the democratic Greek city state. In a number of books and articles published in the 1960s and 1970s, the so-called Paris School, centred around the anthropologist, historian and mythologist Jean-Pierre Vernant, argued that there was a close link between the geometric way of thinking – which takes the *circle* as a central motif – and the archaic and classical city state. The circle can serve first and foremost as a symbol for the democratic attitude, which entails that power is distributed among equal citizens who, in a figurative sense, are all equidistant from the centre of power. In a democracy the citizens hold power together, and this communality is symbolized by the point at the centre of a circle, while the citizens themselves balance one another on the circle's periphery. In the democratic city state no citizen has the right to monopolize the position at the centre (that is, the position of power); this is a position which citizens can only hold in turn. From the perspective of Greek democracy, the circle serves as an image of political equality, or balance, between the citizens.

The idea that some kind of geometric concept underlies the democratic city state has proved highly fruitful in several fields of inquiry. It can be argued, for example, that the circle played an important role in the physical development of the city state, which tended to be organized around an open market place. This is most evident in the case of Athens. Here the public buildings of the city state were located around the marketplace, at the centre of which stood the *prytaneion*, a circular building where the highest power of the state had its seat. The symbolism of this is clear: power is focused at the public centre, which collectively belongs to the citizens.

According to Vernant, a geometric model also underlies the earliest Greek philosophy. In his opinion the growth of philosophy and the development of a geometric understanding of the world are two aspects of one and the same thing. From this point of view it is Anaximander, and not Thales whom we have to regard as the first philosopher. For Anaximander proposed that the universe is geometrically ordered: for him the earth was situated at the centre of the universe, while the planets, the moon and the sun occupy concentric circles around the earth. Vernant interprets for example the earth as an image of the city state's central organ of power, which is physically placed at the centre of the state itself. If this is correct, it implies that Anaximander's philosophy contains the seeds of a political model.[2]

Among the other Presocratics, it is in the ideas of Parmenides that we find the clearest geometric pictures, of which the most significant – and the best known – is that of the 'sphere of Being'. In his poem he describes the One as 'a well-rounded sphere'. Within this sphere of Being, such as Parmenides imagined it, everything is in a state of equilibrium. In due course we will see that his account of this equilibrium employs some politically loaded words, and that political and military metaphors occur also elsewhere in his poem. Truth, for instance, is said to have 'an unshaken heart', a quality that was ascribed to the city state's courageous soldiers. The unbreakable bonds that enclose the sphere of Being also suggest the formidable city walls of a city state. As a metaphor of the early Greek city state it therefore seems that Parmenides' image of the sphere of Being alludes both to its architecture and its political institutions.

Whereas Anaximander's notion of equilibrium is comprehensive and all-inclusive, Parmenides' poem establishes balance and equality by means of exclusion. The analogy between the Parmenidean sphere of Being and the democratic city state is warranted insofar as exclusion is also a definitive feature of the latter. The community of politically equal citizens is constituted first and foremost through the exclusion of women and slaves. Or put another way, the democratic city state is dependent on nothing less than the mechanisms of exclusion.

In this chapter I shall argue that the unity and balance of Parmenides' sphere of Being depend on the exclusion of Not-Being, and that this strategy can be regarded as analogous to democracy's dependence on those groups that were excluded from it. To my mind the ontology that Parmenides developed proved a powerful ally to the political attitudes that entailed the exclusion, not least, of women.

There is, however, another aspect of Parmenides' philosophy which has been given far less attention. In his exposition of what he refers to in the poem as 'the opinions of mortals', opinions that apparently contain 'no true belief', Parmenides seems to describe a world in which the two sexes are equal in status. Unfortunately most of that part of the poem that deals with this theme has been lost, but the surviving verses still convey a sense that in Parmenides' day, that is in the fifth century BCE, there were the rudiments of an attitude that presupposed no hierarchical order among the sexes.

I do not intend to go into the relation between slaves and Greek democracy. But as Moses I. Finley has argued, this also involved a kind of dependency.[3] Finley suggests that, as an integral feature of the Greek *polis*, slavery was a prerequisite for the development of democracy. Slaves participated in all but two aspects of society, the exceptions being the political and the military, both of which were the preserve of citizens. Nietzsche also emphasized the significance of slavery, which he called 'a necessary disgrace'.[4] The dependence of Greek democracy on slaves and its exclusion of them are two aspects of one and the same thing. In this regard there is no difference between the city state's attitude to slaves and its attitude to women.

The aim of the present chapter is twofold. Firstly I wish to deepen the philosophical aspect of Vernant's interpretation of Anaximander. And having established this as the background, I will endeavour secondly to present the political aspects of Parmenides' philosophy. I wish to show how Parmenides' seemingly abstract ideas can be read as a contribution to a politically charged intellectual debate. This will help us appreciate the far-reaching consequences of the fact that later Greek philosophy – led by Plato and Aristotle – chose to build on Parmenides' exclusive principle of unity, rather than either Anaximander's all-inclusive philosophy, or Parmenides' theory of the untrue beliefs, which regarded the sexes as equal in importance.

To prepare the ground for this analysis let us first take a look at the role played by geometry and notions of equality in the thought of ancient Greece. My point of departure will be the theories of Vernant and his colleagues Pierre Lévêque and Pierre Vidal-Naquet, from which I shall attempt to draw further philosophical inferences.[5]

THE DEMOCRATIC POLIS: CIRCULARITY AND BALANCE

According to Herodotus, democracy was introduced into Athens following the radical political reforms of Cleisthenes around 510 BCE.[6] Lévêque and Vidal-Naquet tell us that this represented the first systematic organization of a *political space* (*espace civique*). The foundations of this political space were manifest realities: first and foremost, Cleisthenes' radical reforms established territorial divisions, which for their part were quite obviously organized on a geometric model. Attica, which comprised the urban centre of Athens plus the town's surrounding land areas, was divided into three main geometric regions approximating to three concentric circles: the outer coastal area, the inner area and the urban area itself, which formed the core of the city state.[7] Each of these three regions was further divided into ten smaller areas called *trittyes*. Attica therefore consisted of 30 small land areas, distributed in three roughly circular regions.

These new territorial divisions provided the basis for radically new political divisions. The people were divided into ten tribes, each of which encompassed the inhabitants of three *trittyes*, one from each of the three main regions. Thus each tribe included members from the outermost coastal area, from the intermediate land area, and from the city itself. The idea behind these new territorial and political divisions was in part to break up the traditional bands of loyalty within, and the allegiances between, the larger noble families. The tribe, called a *phyle*, was the new political unit, and as such it was no longer based on any kind of 'natural' affiliation, either geographical or consanguineous. Cleisthenes' political reforms were if anything what one could call an intellectual project, a construction based on a geometric model – the circle.

Attica's innermost circle, the city, was for its own part built around the marketplace, or Agora, where the official buildings were located. The Agora belonged to the city state as such, in other words, it belonged to everyone and no-one. It was here that the state authorities had their seat, and here that the citizens met to exchange their produce and their news and views. Encircling the Agora were the citizens' private houses. From the point of view of the geometric model, the centre therefore symbolizes the *community*, whereas the surrounding area represents the private, or the individual. Lévêque and Vidal-Naquet tell us that, in conjunction with Cleisthenes' reforms, a circle of boundary stones was erected for the first time around the Agora. This can be seen as a clearly political symbol: the aim of the political and geographical division of Attica was not to destroy the unity of the state, but rather to consolidate it by giving it a clear focus at the geometric centre of the city state, in the Agora.[8]

Even the Agora had its central point, namely the Prytaneum, where the prytaneis assembled. The prytaneis was the council that governed the city state at all times. It consisted of 500 councillors, 50 from each tribe. Thus the city's power was solidly gathered at the centre, which itself represented the community: power belonged to the community. But the symbolism does not stop there. Even the Prytaneum had a centre. In the middle of the building stood a circular hearth where the 'fire of the state', also known as the 'communal fire' (*hestia koinē*)[9] was tended. This is where guests of honour were received on behalf of the *polis*. Once again, the symbolism should be clear: the city state as a whole is represented by its centre.[10] The same relation is clearly expressed in language: the expression 'at the centre' was synonymous with 'in common', a use that Vernant illustrates with many examples.[11]

The city state's *calendar* was also organized according to the geometric model. It was no longer the heavenly bodies or the gods that provided the basis for temporal rhythms, but the political distribution of administrative posts. The year was defined as encompassing 360 days, divided into ten *prytanies* of 36 days. This was a crucial feature of Cleisthenes' reforms; no single citizen nor a single group could monopolize the central position, which was occupied on a rotating basis. In this sense the prytany was not just the administrative group of the moment, it was also the unit of time for which power was allotted to any one person or group. Not only space but also time had become political, or rather: both time and space would henceforth be organized according to an intellectual project. There was no talk of a 'natural' organization of space or a 'natural' organization of time.

In order to convey the political significance of the centre it can be helpful to employ a model that represents physical balance in addition to purely geometric aspects. If we imagine all enfranchised citizens around the edge of a circular disc, all equidistant from the centre, then the centre is also the point on which the disc would balance. Political stability and balance are maintained because in this figurative sense no individual citizen is any closer to the centre of power than any other. Stability is inherent; it is secured without the need of any external force.

One of the writers who uses such a metaphor of physical balance in relation to democracy is Herodotus. For example, he understands democracy as a constitutional system in which the power of the separate citizens is in balance, insofar as all have similar access to government (*isokratia*; cf. Herodotus, 5.92). Whereas in a tyranny power is concentrated in the hands of a single person, in a democracy it is distributed among the people. Thus Herodotus describes democracy as the type of constitution in which 'all questions are put before the community (*to koinon*)' (Herodotus, 3.80.2). This displacement of power from one man at the top to all men corresponds to a further displacement. Whereas in the seventh century BCE the focus of the city state was the Acropolis, the highest point of the town, in the sixth century, when democracy began to take shape, this focus shifted to the Agora, a flat, open space.[12] The analogy between the geometric and the political should be clear.[13]

The circular structure of the city state, in both the figurative and the concrete senses, is therefore closely connected to its democratic constitution based on equality and balance among male citizens. Insofar as the city state was effectively a closed and independent entity, it is hardly surprising that this notion of balance was further associated with concepts of self-sufficiency (*autarkeia*) and liberty (*eleutheria*).

'The basis of a democratic state is liberty (*eleutheria*),' writes Aristotle in his *Politics* (VI, 1317a40). One thing that 'liberty' implies in this context is that the city state was independent of other states and that its citizens had the freedom necessary for personal participation in government, that is, the citizens were not subject to inner despotism. A democratic form of government therefore entails the freedom of both the city state as such and of its individual citizens. Accordingly, Aristotle stresses that self-sufficiency is an essential attribute of both the city state and the free man: 'The state is independent and self-sufficing, but a slave is the reverse of independent' (*Politics*, IV, 1291a10). Aristotle seems here to regard independence and self-sufficiency as two aspects of the same thing, thus suggesting that independence is also related to concepts such as power and domination. Only those who are not governed by others and who participate in government can be said to be self-sufficient.

Thanks to Cleisthenes' reforms, the citizen did indeed become independent in this sense; by rotating responsibility for government, the individual citizen could avoid being ruled over and instead – whether potentially or actively – be among those who ruled. Aristotle expresses it thus: 'One principle of liberty is for all to rule and be ruled in turn' (*Politics*, VI, 1317b2f.). In other words, power should be held by the community.

In the ideas I have reviewed so far, two words in particular are used to denote different forms of power: *kratos*, which appears in terms such as 'democracy', and *archē*, which we find in terms like 'monarchy'. As it happens, these words play a crucial role not only in political thought, but also in Greek cosmology and ontology. I shall delve into the meaning of *kratos* a little later when I turn to the philosophy of Anaximander. At this point I will look more closely at the meaning of *archē*, with the aim of illuminating the connection between the earliest ontological and cosmological speculations on the one hand, and political ideas on the other.

It appears that Greek thought never managed to free itself from the inherent ambiguity of the word *archē*, an ambiguity that made it especially suitable as a fundamental concept of both political theory and metaphysics: *archē* implies not only 'power' (or 'dominion'), but also 'beginning' (or 'origin'). The corresponding verb *archein* was apparently a military expression meaning 'to lead' (soldiers to the battlefield).[14] In this case 'dominion' and 'beginning' are obviously two aspects of the same thing. He who goes first, or takes the lead, is also the one with power.

We find a corresponding double-meaning in Homer's *Iliad*, when Hector characterizes the rape of Helen as the *archē* of the Trojan war (*Iliad* 22.116). Paris's abduction of Helen not only causes the war to begin at a specific point in time, it is also a decisive factor in the war's continuation. Were Helen to be returned to the Greeks, they would lose their reason to make war on the Trojans.

Thus the *archē* of a phenomenon does not belong merely to the past, but is present in the phenomenon for as long as it exists. In defining *archē* in this way, it begins to look like a philosophical principle, which is indeed what it became for Aristotle: 'It is common, then, to all beginnings (*archai*) to be the first point from which a thing either is or comes to be or is known; but of these some are immanent in the thing and others are outside' (*Metaphysics*, IV, 1013a17ff.). In other words, a phenomenon is imbued with its origin, which also determines ('has dominion over') its existence (Being).

These two aspects of *archē* seem to have acquired significance both for Greek political thinking and for philosophical cosmogony. Or to put it another way, reflections on the freedom and self-sufficiency of the democratic state are closely linked to the question of origins. To my mind this point is crucial, and I shall attempt to explain it further. Again, the obvious starting point is Aristotle, insofar as he employs the word *archē* with a broad range of meanings.

Aristotle uses *archē* as a metaphysical term to denote the cause or principle of a thing, and for him this also entails the thing's origins or its essential source. In his biological writings it is important for him to show that the man – or more generally the male – is the sole source of offspring, a position that Aristotle interprets metaphysically: the male is the proper and determining *archē* of the offspring.[15] Thus the man is effectively self-sufficient in both a biological and a metaphysical sense. Apart from the matter required for growth, which the woman contributes to the process – although in Aristotle's opinion it plays no part in determining the nature of the offspring – the man does not require anything extraneous to himself in order to continue his line. I wish to claim that Aristotle's explicit linkage of the concept of the citizen's freedom with that of his self-sufficiency is closely related to his endeavour to justify the man as the sole origin of the child.[16]

In common with a number of other researchers, I regard the term *autarkeia* to imply the ability of an object to maintain its own existence by means of its own resources alone.[17] If we pursue this radical self-sufficiency to its logical conclusion – something which I consider Aristotle to have attempted – we would have to conclude that the fully self-sufficient person is also his own origin; anyone whose origin is someone (or something) other than himself owes his existence to that other. *Autarkeia* is thus an unachievable, indeed, a divine, ideal: ultimately only God is self-sufficient, for only He is His own cause. For Aristotle this further implies that only God is absolutely free. The democratic ideal of freedom therefore entails not just a conception of political self-sufficiency and independence, but ultimately also a concept of the potential to be one's own origin.

It is against the background of such a radical desire for self-sufficiency that we have to interpret the various political and social strategies used in explaining that the man (that is the citizen) was the sole source of the child.[18] In this spirit, the notion of being one's own *archē* found clear expression in the myth of Athenian origins. As we saw in Chapter 1, this myth portrays the Athenians as identical descendants of the single ancestor Erichthonius, who himself grew from the earth like a plant when the seed of his father, the god Hephaestus, was spilt on the ground. The ability of the city state to perpetuate itself, and hence be its own *archē*, was assured in virtue of its identical citizens.

Evidently, the problem of origins also plays a part in the institution of the *hestia*, another theme we discussed in the first chapter: the offspring of the family are regarded as the produce of the male head of the house and his *hestia*, which together ensure that the children constitute a pure and unmixed continuation of the man's *oikos*. Just as each family constantly reproduces itself in pure and unmixed form, so too does the city state, as is symbolized by the central fire.[19] As a radical form of self-sufficiency, self-reproduction is undoubtedly related to the idea of perpetually self-identical existence. This connection between self-reproduction and immortality is also evident in Plato, and above all in his *Symposium*, which we will return to in Chapter 5.

At this point I shall attempt to bring together the threads, if only rather loosely. We have touched on a number of interrelated concepts, all of which can be linked to the circle as a geometric model underlying the concept of the Greek city state: democracy and equality, balance and stability, centre and community, power, freedom and self-sufficiency, self-identity, self-reproduction and immortality. Some of these notions are advocated by Anaximander, others by Parmenides, who also links them to a geometric way of thinking.

But before considering Anaximander in greater detail, we should pose the following question: are we justified in regarding the cosmological speculations of Anaximander of Miletus as an expression of the kind of ideas entailed in the democratic reforms that Cleisthenes' introduced in Athens many decades later? We are fortunate in possessing a contemporary report about Thales that makes it reasonable to answer in the affirmative: 'Thales ... advised the Ionians to have a single deliberative chamber, saying that it should be in Teos, for this was in the middle of Ionia; the other cities should continue to be inhabited but should be regarded as if they were demes' (Herodotus, 1.170).[20] In other words, Thales, who was an elder contemporary of Anaximander, suggested the establishment of a substantial Ionian *polis* along the lines of Cleisthenes' Athenian reforms: 'Since this is located at the geometric centre of the Ionian world, Teos was to be a communal hearth (*hestia koinē*) for the new state.'[21]

This implies that the earliest Ionian philosophy of nature and later Athenian democratic thought belong to the same intellectual environment. Of course, this is not to say that Anaximander's philosophy directly influenced subsequent political developments in Athens. It is merely relevant to point out that the theoretical structures apparent in Anaximander's cosmology are similar to those that underlie the ideology of the Athenian city state.

COSMOLOGY: FROM THE HIERARCHICAL WORLD-VIEW OF MYTHOLOGY TO ANAXIMANDER'S MODEL OF COSMIC STABILITY

In order to illuminate the peculiarly 'democratic' aspect of the earliest philosophy, it may be useful to compare the cosmologies of those first philosophers with the speculations about the nature of the universe that occur in Homer and Hesiod. For Hesiod the universe was divided into a number of physical levels, each of which was clearly personified: uppermost was Heaven, the dwelling of the immortal gods; below this was Earth, the realm of humankind, among others; beneath Earth, or rather inside it, was Hades, the realm of the dead. In Hesiod's cosmogony, the most significant role is accorded to Earth: she is a 'secure seat for all' (*Theogony* 117). As I argued in the preceding chapter, Hesiod is concerned to establish a firm foundation for the universe, and there are good reasons to suppose that this is the principle theme of the *Theogony*. At this point I shall review only one of these.

In the latter third of Hesiod's poem, Earth literally opens herself towards Tartarus, which is described as a 'vast chasm, whose floor a man would not reach in a whole year if once he got inside the gates' (*Theogony* 739–741). This place 'is a cause of fear even for the immortal gods', and the reason for this seems to be that this realm lacks both firm ground and any kind of direction on which one can depend for orientation. Nevertheless, Hesiod provides a solution. Tartarus, which he seems to imagine with the form of an inverted vase,[22] is sealed at the base and secured with 'continuous roots, self-grown' (*Theogony* 821f.), which ensure in turn that Earth has an unshakeable foundation. This might seem a mere figurative device, but the intention is clear: it is the roots that make Earth a 'secure seat for all'.

Hesiod describes the various physical levels of the universe as strictly separate from one another, and there is no straightforward way to pass from one to the other; this can only be done under special circumstances. Thus the universe consists of qualitatively distinct spheres that give meaning to concepts such as 'up' and 'down'. The gods dwell 'up there', whereas the dead are 'down below'.

In the philosophy of Anaximander, this conception of the universe is utterly absent. Indeed, his ideas allow us to speak of philosophy's radical break with the mythical world-view: in his philosophy it is no longer 'up' and 'down', but geometric relations that guarantee, among other things, the world's stability (Anaximander, A 11.6f.). In this regard, Anaximander is a 'purer' philosopher than either Thales or Anaximenes, the first of whom imagined the earth to rest on water, the latter on air.

According to Aristotle, Thales said that 'the earth rests on water ... that it stays in place through floating like a log' (*De caelo* II, 294a). Evidently Thales does not see any problem in postulating water to be the guarantor of the earth's status as a 'secure seat'. It is possible to imagine the ocean continuing downwards to infinity. By contrast, he imagined the earth to be limited and therefore incapable of supporting itself. Without some fundamental substance, or principle, to fix it in space it would be in danger of falling. Water is just such a principle. Diogenes Laertius tells us that Thales called water 'the strongest' and 'that which carries all'.[23] This supporting principle must of course be the source (*archē*) of all things, since it is not in need of anything other than itself as a foundation. This is also how Anaximenes pictured things. Anaximenes was a generation younger than Anaximander. In his view, the principle that supported the world was air: 'The earth is ... borne upon the air, and similarly sun, moon and the other heavenly bodies' (Anaximenes, A 7.11f.). Evidently the earth is not self-sufficient, and neither is it master (*archē*) of its own condition; such attributes can only be ascribed to the source (*archē*), to that which is in need of nothing to 'hold itself up'.

For both Thales and Anaximenes there is just one dominant power, or force: water for the former and air for the latter. Most of the 'physicists', as Aristotle called the early Ionian thinkers, shared this way of thinking. Translating this into the language of politics, we could say that these philosophers still exemplify a monarchic mindset.[24] The problems that seek articulation here can effectively be reduced to the question of which physical element is the strongest, yet the language is still clearly political in character. Nature is regarded as characterized by a power struggle in which the strongest has dominion. The strongest element dominates insofar as it encompasses everything.[25] And for some Presocratics, Anaximenes[26] among them, since that which is all-encompassing cannot itself be encompassed by anything else, it must be infinite. Bearing in mind these few remarks about the philosophy of Thales and Anaximenes, let us now take a closer look at the cosmological theories of Anaximander.

The earth is on high, governed by nothing. (A 11.6)

Such was the view of Anaximander, as passed on to us by Hippolytus, a Church Father of the third century. The Greek original uses the word *kratein*, which is here translated in the sense of 'to govern', but can also mean 'to hold up', or 'support'.[27] In contrast to Thales and Anaximenes, it is explicitly claimed here that the earth is not held up by any kind of supporting element. It floats in the air, but without being governed by the air. How is this possible? Anaximander's immediate explanation is that the earth remains where it is *on account of its similar distance from all things* (A 11.6)

that is, it is equidistant from all points of the heavenly perimeter.

This explanation is very different from those given by Thales and Anaximander. The earth's stability is explained exclusively in terms of geometric considerations: the earth remains at rest because of its central position, its equidistance from everything else.[28] The stability of the earth is unique in Anaximander's universe, for this is a place where everything else is in motion. Even if the earth is 'not governed by anything', clearly it is not itself the all-encompassing, primary element. On the contrary, it is bounded as a result of its situation at the centre of the cosmos. So what is it that governs the universe in Anaximander's view?

Like Thales and Anaximenes, Anaximander uses the concept of a single principle underlying all else, and this he calls the 'boundless', or in Greek *apeiron*. At first glance *apeiron* seems to play much the same role as water does for Thales and air for Anaximenes.

On closer examination, however, we begin to suspect that Anaximander stands for a very different way of thinking. Even if *apeiron* is said to 'surround all things and steer all' (A 15), and although it is infinite, this does not prevent the earth from being 'governed by nothing'. If the 'boundless' were an element similar in essence to water or air, we would be faced with a paradox. No element can be boundless and have all power while some other element remains ungoverned by anything. In fact, what Anaximander calls the 'boundless' is not simply one element among others, rather, it is not an element at all. Nevertheless, the 'boundless' still constitutes the *archē* of all things, the source of all elements and physical forces.

In describing the thoughts of Anaximander, Aristotle writes that 'opposites are separated out' from *apeiron*.[29] In this context, 'opposites' refers to distinct elements such as warm and cold, or wet and dry. It is interesting that Anaximander should have classified these elements as opposites. For in doing so he establishes them as relational entities: 'cold' is what it is in relation to 'warm' (and vice versa), 'wet' is what it is in relation to 'dry', etc. And this is how all extant things are to be conceived. The essence of each thing is determined by its relation to an opposite. Here the term 'opposite' should not be understood as a neutral characterization, but rather as an antagonistic disposition. Each and everything that exists is conceptualized as a force (*dynamis*, *kratos*) antagonistically disposed towards some other extant thing.

A good illustration of these ideas will be found in the field of ancient medicine, in which the concept of force played a central role. The body was regarded as the sum of a number of forces all contending for power, each against its own specific contrary (warm against cold, dry against wet etc.).

The body's health was a matter of the balance (*isonomia*) between qualitatively different but equally important (*homoioi*) forces. This approach to medicine, which itself can be viewed as closely analogous to democratic thinking,[30] seems to overlap significantly with the ideas of Anaximander. For him as well, what mattered was the balance between contraries. Let us see how he imagined this balance might arise.

No more than a few lines have survived of what we believe to be Anaximander's own words. These occur as a quotation in a work by the Neoplatonist Simplicius, in a passage that translates as follows:

> *And the source of coming-to-be for existing things is that into which destruction, too, happens, according to necessity; for they pay penalty and retribution to each other for their injustice according to the assessment of Time.* (B 1)

This is not the place for a detailed examination of this fragment, which has been described as 'the most controversial text in Presocratic philosophy'.[31] At this point I shall merely suggest an interpretation, most of which ought to be widely acceptable.

It is reasonable to understand the quoted words as implying that each and every extant thing stands in debt to other things, and that these debts have to be repaid if justice (*dikē*) is to be restored. In the fragment this debt relation is linked to time. It is difficult to make sense of this other than by suggesting that Anaximander conceived of time as distributed among the various 'extant things' (*ta onta*), that is, that each thing has been allotted a time in which to exist, and that they have offended against their fixed time limits. They have quite simply existed too long and thus hindered other things from coming into existence. Putting this together with what we know of Anaximander's theory of opposites, we can interpret the fragment as follows: where, in a relationship of opposites, one of the elements has dominated for a longer time than is 'permissible', then that element has to pay retribution to its contrary element by letting that element become dominant in its turn. In this way the various elements and forces are forever contending for their places, constantly offending against one another and constantly paying out measured reparation. For instance, 'wet' struggles with 'dry', and having outstayed its rightful time, it must step back and surrender its place – or time – to 'dry'.

What is the penalty in such a system? An answer is given in the first sentence of the above passage. Once the time of each extant thing (each element or 'force') is over, it returns to its origins, to the common source of all things. And this, as we have already seen, is the 'boundless', *apeiron*.[32] The parallel to democratic institutions should now be obvious: citizens are allotted a certain time to govern, each in turn, and once this period has elapsed, they have to step down and hand over their mandate to others. There is no pre-established and natural harmony either in democracy or within the world as Anaximander pictures it. Justice, which is understood here as a state of balance, must constantly be reestablished according to a common law, a common *dikē*.

In the philosophy of Anaximander, *apeiron* ensures that no force becomes supreme, but guarantees instead a (democratic) balance of power. *Apeiron* is not associated with any particular governing element or force, but is rather the shared foundation of all forces and that which mediates between elements.[33] Consequently, *apeiron* is what encompasses all other things, and also what they all have in common, that is, it accounts for the entirety of extant things and is so to speak inherent in them all.

As already mentioned, Anaximander's universe is in constant motion. It is a universe where each extant thing must in due course surrender its dominance to its opposite. Only one entity remains at rest relative to the rest of the universe, and that is the earth. The earth is in a privileged position due to its location at the centre of the universe, a location that precludes the possibility of an opposite. This means that the earth is exempted from the universal struggle for power and is therefore 'governed by nothing'. In this sense it seems to be on a level with *apeiron*, which itself governs, or steers, everything. But whereas *apeiron* is boundless, the earth is the universe's bounded centre-point, implying that the earth and *apeiron* are certainly not identical. How are we to understand the relation between the earth and *apeiron*?

Vernant suggests a symbolic interpretation of the earth's function in Anaximander's universe: 'Because it is central (. . .) it is not particular but common (. . .), and in this sense it is like the whole itself. On the political plane, the same applies to the public hearth, which, similarly, is not a "private" hearth like the others, since its function is precisely to represent every hearth without being identified with any particular one' (*Myth and Thought*, p. 208). The earth is representative of *apeiron*, just as the Prytaneum at the centre of the city state is representative of all citizens in the democratic order of things. For Anaximander the earth is a picture of the central fire, which does not stand for any single private home, but rather for the common home, or the community, of citizens.

Evidently Vernant sees a direct and almost self-evident analogy between Cleisthenes' geometric model of the city state and Anaximander's cosmological speculations: 'Not only are the terms 'centrality', 'similarity', 'absence of domination', to be found in Anaximander's cosmology, but they are clearly linked together there in the same way as they were in political thought. The geometric character of the new conception of the world thus seems to have been modelled on the view that the city state had of itself' (*Myth and Thought*, p. 192).

This analogy between the city state model and Anaximander's cosmology is, however, somewhat dubious. Whereas Anaximander's universe is unbounded and therefore all-encompassing, the city state is clearly bounded in relation to the world beyond. Cleisthenes' picture of Athens approximates to a circle, with clear outermost boundary. The sharp distinction between *polis* and non-*polis* is a crucial necessity to the city state, for its self-sufficiency and self-identity. By contrast, the universality implicit in *apeiron* is not based on any dichotomy of inclusion versus exclusion.

We could revise the terminology by saying that the city state concept is essentially nationalistic, whereas Anaximander offers something more like a model for a universal state in which individual differences – whether between the sexes, between nations or races – are of no political relevance. Whereas it is essential to the ideology of the city state that the 'purity' of the *polis* be maintained – it has to be kept unmixed and self-identical – no such problem can afflict the world as imagined by Anaximander. For in the latter there is no distinction between 'inside' and 'outside'. This difference is articulated for the first time in full-blown form by Parmenides, and it is also in his writings that we first encounter the problems that arise from the idea of self-identical reproduction.

In the philosophy of Anaximander, sexual difference is unproblematic, since it amounts to a relation between two conflicting but equally endowed forces. For Parmenides, on the other hand, it poses a significant problem, since his system cannot accommodate any kind of difference.

There is another reason to question the analogy between the city state ideology and Anaximander's philosophy. Unlike the city state, which only recognizes the 'equals' (*hoi homoioi*), the 'boundless' includes utterly disparate entities, namely pairs of things with opposite properties, which are nonetheless equal in status. In the city state there was of course a clearly hierarchical distinction between the citizens on the one hand and the non-citizens on the other. Paradoxically, we could say that the city state's ideal of equality was founded on a hierarchical model: on the one side stood the (fully franchised) citizens, on the other the (unfranchised) women and slaves. In contrast, Anaximander's universe precludes hierarchic thinking.

This also entitles us to regard the city state's self-image as illusory. Strictly speaking, the institution consisted only of free male citizens, and hence it was evidently not self-sufficient, in terms of either material production or the reproduction of its population. The self-image of the *polis* as one and self-identical – qualities symbolized by the central fire – depended on its belief in a pure and unpolluted reproductive capacity. For this reason both slaves and women had to be kept out of sight in the state established by Cleisthenes. In being both invisible yet essential elements of society, women and slaves were in fact similar. Nevertheless, we find it easier to imagine the city state getting by without slaves than without women. And indeed it is the latter that feature most prominently in the various paradoxes that afflict philosophical thought from the time of Parmenides onwards. Despite the fact that these paradoxes did not arise in Anaximander's philosophy, it is far from coincidental that his *apeiron* concept failed to take a hold on Greek philosophy. His model of universal balance might well have provided a basis for democratic political theory, yet his idea of the boundless and all-encompassing remained fundamentally alien to the Greek democratic city state.

We also find this confirmed when we look more closely at the *apeiron* concept. So far I have translated this term as the 'boundless', meaning that which is without limits in space or time. Other common translations of the term are the 'infinite' and the 'indefinite' (that is, without definite qualities). These translations all assume the adjective *apeiron* to consist of the negational prefix 'a-' plus a word stem derived from the noun *peirar* (or *peras*), meaning 'boundary': accordingly, *apeiron* is that which lacks both quantitative and qualitative boundaries. Charles Kahn, however, has argued that *apeiron* more probably derives from a root that is also shared by the verbs *peraō* ('to drive through') and *perainō* ('to accomplish').[34] *Apeiron* therefore implies a negation of these terms, viz. that which cannot be traversed, the unaccomplishable. In Homer, for instance, *apeiron* is used to describe the earth, which in this case means that, no matter how far one travels, one will never reach its limits (*Odyssey* 1.98).

As a translation of *apeiron*, 'boundless' is by no means inaccurate, but it does not convey the aspect of movement implicit in the Greek. Neither does it bring out the sense of activity that we find in 'unaccomplished'. *Apeiron* is all of these: boundless, infinite and unaccomplished. We could describe it as a picture of the divine – and hence of perfection – as seen from a human and hence imperfect perspective; for the human mind, *apeiron* is unfathomable and incomprehensible. It is not a defined and manageable unit like the city state. The latter, as conceived by for example Cleisthenes, is a perfectly rational (and therefore transparent) entity, something which *apeiron* could never be.

Vernant has celebrated Anaximander as a theorist of the city state. But if among the early philosophers there is anyone who deserves to be seen as such, it is in my opinion Parmenides. His philosophy hardly corresponds to the city state's self-image, insofar as the assumptions behind the city state seem so carefully thought through in his work that even its starkest paradoxes are brought to expression. It is not so much the self-image of the *polis* that we find in Parmenides, but its truth – in the sense of something that is unwittingly exposed therein.

PARMENIDES: THEORIST OF THE POLIS?

It is common to regard Parmenides as rather remote from the political realities of his day. He is seen as an essentially abstract philosopher, the 'father of logic', and it was during the period in which he lived that philosophy became autonomous relative to other disciplines, with its own peculiar subject matter and its own vocabulary. According to the traditional interpretation of Parmenides' work, it contains no clear analogy between the philosophical and the political, such as we found in Anaximander.[35] One person who breaks with this tradition is Gregory Vlastos, who in his essay of 1947, 'Equality and Justice in Early Greek Cosmology', portrays Parmenides as an almost explicit political thinker.

In the following I shall pursue a few threads of Vlastos' argument and attempt to show that his hypothesis, 'that Parmenides' justice is grounded in equality', is correct,[36] but only with the qualification that the equality Parmenides imagined presupposes the radical exclusion of the 'unequals'. This is not to say that Parmenides considered politics to be the theme of his poem, nor of course that he was in any way influential in the establishment of democracy in Athens. My exclusive aim is to show that there are clear parallels between his ontology and theory of knowledge on the one hand, and the contemporary political discourse on the other. In other words, I wish to situate Parmenides' poem within the masculine geometric-political discourse of the period in which he lived.

My claim is that Parmenides conceives of equality in two fundamentally different ways. One of these gives structure to his *ontology*, which also underlies his theory of truth. The other provides the foundation for his *cosmology*, or what he refers to in his poem as 'the opinions of mortals'. Parmenides tells us that these latter are based on misguided concepts, which he wishes to review in order to expose them as untrue. Thus he acknowledges both a 'true' and an 'untrue' notion of equality. His idea of 'true' equality is based on exclusion, whereas 'untrue' equality is if anything inclusive. Parmenides' ontology therefore amounts to a clear expression of the city state's radical and brutal mechanism of exclusion. In contrast, his cosmology operates with a non-hierarchical view of reality, in which antagonistic but equal opposites hold one another in check, much as they do for Anaximander and the medical theories of the time. But unlike Anaximander, Parmenides refers explicitly to the issue of sexual difference, and this makes his cosmology of particular interest.

In the following I shall attempt to show, firstly, that Parmenides' concept of reality – that is, that which he regards as true – can be read as a picture of the city state, and secondly, that he provides philosophical legitimation for the paradoxes implicit in what I here refer to as the ideology of the city state, although those paradoxes are by no means thereby resolved. In other words, I shall contend that Parmenides' abstract, logically oriented thought lays philosophical foundations for a view of humanity that puts sexual difference beyond the pale. He establishes a notion of reality that is independent of reproduction, coming-to-be, growth and change, and which entrenches the ideal of a one-sex world. This line of thought, later taken up by Plato, acquired decisive significance in determining how the relationship between the sexes would be viewed throughout subsequent European history.

My point of departure is once again Parmenides' rejection of coming-to-be, change and death. My intention is to show how these concerns, along with the associated ideal of a one-sex world, connect up with the masculine ideology of the city state. I shall begin by returning to the main philosophical part of the poem, that is the fragments that present the truth about what exists, before taking a closer look at the *doxa* section, in other words, the discussion of mankind's 'misguided notions'.

Similar to Anaximander, who explained the earth's stability in terms of its position at the centre of the universe, Parmenides claims that Being – reality, that which exists – is motionless because it is

> like … a well-rounded sphere, from the centre equally balanced in every direction. (B 8.43f.)

In addition to such geometric imagery, Parmenides also employs various political and military metaphors. As we have seen, there is no great originality in such a linkage of geometry and politics; indeed, it accords with a well-established tradition of describing the city state in geometric terms. But this being so, it might seem unreasonable to claim that Parmenides divorces philosophy from the political discourse.

His most prolific use of geometric and political metaphors occurs in fragment 8. At 61 verse lines this is the longest surviving fragment of Parmenides' text and hence our principle source for his philosophy. In this passage he describes the characteristics of Being. The first 21 lines of the fragment argue boldly against the assumption that birth and death, coming-to-be and destruction are in any way compatible with what Parmenides regards as 'true Being'. This argumentation, which we have already looked at in some detail, concludes that existence cannot be attributed to the phenomena of coming-to-be and destruction ('So coming into being is extinguished and perishing unimaginable', B 8.21). From this point onward the tone is far less polemic. The subsequent section consists of 28 verse lines and can be regarded as the conclusion of the poem's 'truth' part, and it is here we find most of the geometric and political metaphors.

THE SPHERE OF BEING AS METAPHOR FOR THE DEMOCRATIC CITY STATE. THE UNITY, EQUALITY AND SELF-IDENTITY OF BEING

This is how the section begins (B 8.22–50):

Nor is it divisible, since it is all alike (homoion). Nor is there somewhat more here and somewhat less there that could prevent it from holding together.

Parmenides is claiming here that Being, or what he regards as the true reality, is of equal strength in all places. Such variations, were they to be there, would constitute a fault in the unity and continuity of Being. Within these few lines we find a series of terms typical of the political discourse of the time, and which more than hint at an analogy between Parmenidean Being and the democratic city state.

The analogy is of course implicit in the concept of equality, or sameness (*homoion*), but the words he uses here for 'more' and 'less' (*mallon, cheiroteron*) are also politically loaded, since they signify differences in power and honour. Differences of this kind should occur neither in democracy, nor in Parmenidean Being. Another word with clear political connotations is *synechein*, used here to express the unity and continuity of Being. *Synechein*, which means literally 'to hold together', is used elsewhere in the literature to emphasize the necessity of cohesion within the city state to prevent it from falling apart.[37] Just as the city state requires its citizens to display solidarity, so too must there be something that holds Being together. And just as it would contradict the fundamental notion of democracy if some citizens had more power than others, so too would the self-identity of Being be contradicted if one part were to gain power over others. This is a thought that Parmenides repeats several times in the ensuing passage.

In addition to the political power metaphor, Parmenides also uses words reminiscent of the language used in the medicine of the time. For example, Being is said to be

From the middle everywhere of equal strength; for it need not be somewhat more here or somewhat less there. (B 8.44f.)

The expression 'of equal strength' (isopales) is applied both to the healthy body, in which the various forces hold one another in check,[38] and to power struggles in which the contenders are so perfectly matched that neither can overcome the other.[39] Comparable to the healthy body, Being can be said to have a democratic rather than a monarchic constitution: it involves no hierarchy, but only a constant confrontation between equally powerful forces.

Seen in this light, we can hardly interpret Parmenides' concept of unity in an absolute sense, since it seems if anything to entail a certain multiplicity. Being would seem to consist of a closed unity of equal parts, an indissolubly integrated community with no inherent inequalities:

Therefore it is all continuous, for Being is in contact with Being. (B 8.25)

The latter expression – 'Being is in contact with Being' – suggests not so much an accidental contiguity of parts, but rather an encounter, or even a confrontation. The Greek word *pelazei*, translated here as 'in contact with', often involves a hint of antagonism. Herodotus, for example, uses the word to denote a meeting between two warring armies (9.74.1). We can therefore describe Parmenidean Being as a tightly integrated unity in which a number of component elements come into contact with one another.

In the realm of truth, however, Being has no variety of manifestations. Here there is only one difference, namely that between Being and Not-Being. It is not possible for one part of Being to be big and another small, since, if it were so, the latter would be not-big and thus imply Not-Being; it is simply not possible for one part of Being to have a property that excludes others. On the contrary, Being is 'from every point ... equal to itself' (*ison*; B 8.49) and consequently 'the same and in the same, it lies by itself' (B 8.29). Despite consisting of parts, the self-identity of true reality is in other words absolute.

Evidently there are logical difficulties here that Parmenides' system fails to resolve. How can a plurality, or a single entity consisting of separate parts, lack internal differences? How can one claim that 'Being is in contact with Being' without implying that one part of Being *is not* the same as (identical with) another part of Being? What Parmenides faces here is a problem that acquired central importance in later ontology and political theory: what is the relation between identity and difference, between unity, entirety and multiplicity?[40]

Compared with Parmenides' ontology, which implies paradoxes of which he was unaware, the egalitarianism of the city state seems somewhat more flexible, or rather less stringent: people do not have to be exactly equal in power and honour at all times, since responsibility for governing passes from citizen to citizen. The city state acknowledges political differences between citizens, but these are relevant only for limited durations.[41] This is very different from Parmenides. He pursues the notion of equality to its logical conclusion; the self-identity of Being is consummate at all times. His philosophy can accommodate neither past nor future, but is rather an enduring present:

> It was not once nor will it be, since it is now, altogether, one, continuous. (B 8.5f.)

THE SELF-SUFFICIENCY OF BEING AND THE IMPOSSIBILITY OF REPRODUCTION

We have already examined the connection between the notion of the city state's self-sufficiency and the problem of its reproduction. The city state can be said to be self-sufficient insofar as its male citizens constitute the true source of offspring. This connection between the ideas of self-sufficiency and of being one's own origin is also implicit in Parmenides' reflections on the nature of true Being. For him the perfection and self-sufficiency of Being presuppose the rejection of all forms of coming-to-be. If Being were to have an origin in anything other than itself it would imply that it lacked something, that is that it is neither perfect nor self-sufficient. Parmenides stresses that Being has no extraneous *archē* (cf. *anarchon*; B 8.27), but 'abides so firmly where it is' (B 8.29), and is therefore 'not in need' (B 8.33).

We can regard the self-sufficient, well-bounded sphere of Being as analogous to the self-sufficient and well-bounded *polis*. The freedom and self-sufficiency of both depend on exclusion. Whereas the perfection of Being presupposes the rigorous exclusion of Not-Being, the self-sufficiency of the *polis* presupposes the political exclusion of non-citizens, a group that includes women, slaves and foreigners.

The combination of absolute exclusion with the absolute equality of what is included gives rise to problems on both the political and the ontological levels. Since the traditional political notion of equality applies only to men, the ideology, when strictly interpreted, is unable to account for the city state's self-reproduction. Evidently the Greeks themselves were aware of this problem, for their culture included a range of mechanisms, the purpose of which – if not always conscious – was to suppress or minimalize the issue, by suppressing or minimalizing the role of women in reproduction. Having discussed this theme at some length in Chapter 1 it need not detain us here.

What I wish to do at this point is clarify how Parmenides resolves, or rather evades, the difficulty. For he makes no attempt to explain how reproduction is possible within a self-identical unity. Indeed, he chooses to pursue an opposite course. Faithful to his original and fundamental dichotomy between Being and Not-Being, he denies all possibility of coming-to-be and reproduction. Whereas the traditional ideology of the city state sought to safeguard its continued existence – and, we might add, its immortality – by postulating the possibility of one-sex reproduction, Parmenides attempts to guarantee the continued existence of Being by demonstrating the impossibility of becoming and growth. But what both the ideology of the city state and Parmenides' ontology have in common, despite their different strategies, is an aspiration to immortality through the exclusion of the other (that which is foreign, or 'unequal'), which was woman for the former and Not-Being for the latter.

BEING AND POLIS: THE ACTIVE EXCLUSION OF THE UNEQUAL

In describing the exclusion of Not-Being from Being, Parmenides reverts to surprisingly violent language. One would think his prime concern ought to be the logical relation between Being and Not-Being, and that Not-Being should be a fairly harmless phenomenon since it is not actually there. But in Parmenides' poem Not-Being is described as something threatening which has to be constrained at all costs. The work suggests fear at the possibility that Not-Being might infiltrate Being, or perhaps rather, that Being will become receptive to Not-Being. I shall briefly examine some of the metaphors of war and violence used in the text.

In the preceding chapter I discussed what is perhaps the most obvious political metaphor in the poem, which occurs at the close of the prologue. The 'well-rounded truth' is said there to have an 'unshakeable heart' (B 1.29). As we have seen, this expression has clear military connotations; it is used of soldiers who stand firm in the face of an enemy onslaught despite all danger.[42] For Parmenides the best defence for Being seems to lie in thought: true thought is, as it were, armed against the attacks of 'the opinions of mortals', which regard Being as something that both is and is not, that is as something that has both come to be and will cease to be. Thanks to its unassailable defences, Being need not fear the incursions of Not-Being, which would effectively threaten its continued existence. Instead, like a courageous and well-armed soldier, or a well-defended *polis*, it maintains its poise and meets the enemy with 'a fearless heart' – another possible translation for *atremes ētor*.[43]

Nicole Loraux has described Homer's depictions of fear in the *Iliad* as 'the thing that no one but Zeus can avoid' (*Les expériences de Tirésias*, p. 76). Fear is associated with the trembling of the body, which the epic hero strives to overcome. This he does by holding his ground, by not fleeing, by fighting on until either he or his opponent falls. This is what it means to be a hero. But even a hero is no more than human; the hero trembles above all at the thought of the day when he might succumb to his fear (ibid., p. 86f.). There is a clear parallel in this to the Parmenidean concept of Being. Above all else Being is 'fearless', or 'unshakeable' (*atremes*, B 8.4), and holds its ground. But in contrast to the hero, who is no more than mortal, Being will never allow fear to take hold and will therefore never give ground and never be defeated. By comparing thought to the 'fearless heart' (*atremes ētor*) and describing Being as 'unshakeable' (*atremes*; B 8.4), Parmenides implies an analogy between Being/thought and the soldier. We should recall that, in the Greek city state, the heavily armed soldiers known as hoplites were considered citizens par excellence. The military analogy helps underline the parallel between Being and the *polis*.

Not only is Being 'unshakeable', it is also 'motionless' (*akinēton*; B 8.26; 8.38), that is, not affected by any form of *kinēsis*, which can be translated as 'shaking'.[44] Also in the Greek city state there was a fear of *kinēsis*, in the form of *stasis*, or civil war. *Stasis* was a condition of deadlock in political conflicts that made it impossible to declare one of the contending persons or groups the winner. The danger in such cases was that they might undermine the unity of the city state and even lead to its breakdown.

The fear of civil war was a recurrent theme in Greek politics and probably found its best expression in Thucydides (2.20), who was particularly concerned by the possibility of the total failure of order that might result from such conflict. Thucydides tells us that, when the unity of a state breaks down, not even words retain their meaning – even language is lost. Parmenides' emphasis on the 'motionlessness' of Being has to be viewed against this background. The implication is not that Being is totally inert, but rather that it is so well secured that it cannot be shaken. The unity of Being is so solid that it will never fall apart.

Yet neither the unity, the balance, nor the self-sufficiency of Parmenidean Being, all of which are preconditions for its existence, can be taken for granted. It seems incessantly threatened by contact with Not-Being, that is, with something alien to itself. Active exclusion of everything *other* (than Being), or of everything *unequal* (to Being), is therefore of vital importance to its integrity and continued existence. The fact that Being needs protection from what is alien is best expressed in Parmenides' use of the phrase 'everywhere inviolable' (*asylon*). We should note that for Parmenides the meaning of *asylon* was almost diametrically opposed to that of our word 'asylum'. For Parmenides what matters is not that the community protects what is alien, but rather that the community (Being) is protected *against* the alien (or Not-Being).

Elsewhere in Greek literature *asylos* is applied to both people and places. A person who is granted protection on foreign soil is called 'inviolable', and correspondingly, a place becomes 'inviolable' when designated as a place of refuge from attack.[45] The hearth of the city, like that of the home, is just such a place of refuge, where the community accords protection to people who would otherwise have been a prey to all. Within the framework of Parmenides' geometric model, however, this kind of symbolism proves untenable. Being (which is spherical) is a single entity for as long as it has neither the scope to accommodate differences nor the need to regard one part as a privileged representative for the whole. At any one time the whole is present in any of its parts: '... it is now, altogether, one, continuous' (B 8.5f.). In describing Being as *asylon*, Parmenides can only mean that Being as a whole has become an asylum, albeit exclusively for itself.

The mechanism of exclusion is therefore even more blatantly apparent in the ontology of Parmenides than it was in the Greek *polis*. In states based on a high degree of exclusion, such as ancient Greece, the right to asylum was of vital importance. Asylum amounted to an exception from the rule that only the 'equals' had rights within the community. We do not find this exception in the philosophy of Parmenides. Indeed, he makes no exceptions of any kind. He pursues the notion of equality to its logical conclusion, and in my opinion this is what allows us to view his ontology as a rigorous investigation of the theoretical foundation of the *polis*. But although Parmenidean ontology seems to lead us to the true face of the democratic city state, we could start from the other end and say that the democratic *polis* also had a far more human face.

THE OPINIONS OF MORTALS: AN ALTERNATIVE IDEAL OF EQUALITY

In conclusion I shall survey the other side of Parmenides' thought, namely his cosmology, which does not belong to what he himself calls 'the truth', but is rather an example of what he regards as the false conception of reality (*doxa*). This latter seems nonetheless to entail some kind of necessity. The subject here is still reality, but seen now from a human perspective, which will always be inadequate and will never be capable of grasping the whole in a single, all-encompassing glance, such as the one afforded us by the goddess in the preceding section. The view is now fragmented, and it no longer allows us to discern the inner bands that hold things together.

The surviving fragments of this part of the poem (B 9–19) are far fewer and less continuous than those dealing with truth. Nonetheless they are sufficient to provide an insight into the original lines of argument.

The cosmology is introduced immediately after the goddess has given her account of Being and explained how it has to be defended against everything alien:

> *Here I end my trustworthy account and thought concerning truth. From now on learn the beliefs of mortals, listening to the deceptive order of my words.* (B 8.50ff.)

Although the 'beliefs of mortals' are false, they possess their own logic, even if it is, as the goddess says, 'deceptive'. In other words, it is not always easy to discover where they go wrong. There is nothing inconsistent in their logic. As long as one accepts the basic premise, then the rest follows of necessity. This is expressed in the poem as follows:

> *Nevertheless you shall learn these [opinions] also, how the appearances, which pervade all things, had to be acceptable.* (B 1.31f.)

It is the premise itself that Parmenides rejects. He rejects a non-monistic conception of reality, or rather, any view of reality that does not assume the self-identity of reality.

The starting point for the Parmenidean *doxa* is a theory of cosmic stability in the form of a balance between two antagonistic principles:[46]

> *... they divided form contrariwise and established characters*
> *apart from one another; for the one the ethereal flame of fire,*
> *gentle and very light, everywhere identical with itself*
> *but not identical with the other; but that one too by itself*
> *contrariwise obscure night, dense in body and heavy.* (B 8.55ff.)

Parmenides is operating here with a kind of dualistic theory, in which everything can be reduced to two fundamental principles (here called 'forms'). According to this fragment each principle is self-identical and related to the other as an opposite. The one is characterized as gentle, light in weight, ethereal, and is referred to as Light, or Fire. The other is dark, heavy and dense and referred to as Night. There is no hierarchic relation between these two. As he says in another fragment (B 9) they are entirely equal.

These two fundamental principles – light or fire, and night – form the basis of Parmenides' cosmology. As in his ontology, he imagines the universe to be circular, possibly spherical. The two self-identical, equal and mutually exclusive principles are pictured as concentric 'rings' that successively overlay one another and which collectively surround a core of dense night:

the innermost ring is of pure fire, followed by a ring of night, followed by
another of fire, and so on. Here as well there is an outer limit, which consists
of pure, unmixed night. At some point in time, these cosmic rings came into
contact with one another, with the result that some part of each contributed –
curiously enough – to a 'mixture':

> *For the narrower [rings] are filled with pure Fire and those which come after*
> *them with Night, and a portion of flame is discharged. In the middle of these*
> *is the goddess who governs all things. For everywhere she is the beginner of*
> *union and of abhorrent birth, sending the female to unite with the male and*
> *again to the contrary the male with the female.* (B 12)

The mingling of the various elements is presented as a kind of cosmic birth,
which is evidently how any form of coming-to-be begins. Far from being
pleasant, this experience is characterized as 'abhorrent'. It is another reminder that Parmenides is not especially fond of the processes of generation and
birth. Yet they cannot be avoided in the building of a cosmos.

From this point on everything is in motion, and in the ensuing lines of
verse the goddess explains the details of the universe's construction (the disposition of the earth, the moon, the sun etc.), which I shall not look at
further here. What we should note, however, is that the male and female
principles are not subject to any kind of hierarchy.[47] Empedocles, who was
somewhat younger than Parmenides and an astute critic of the latter's ontology, held a similar view of the relation between the male and female elements, whereas for other non-hierarchical thinkers, such as Anaximander and
Heraclitus, the relation between the sexes does not become an explicit issue.
The Pythagoreans also advocated a theory of principles organized into
dichotomous pairs, in which all generation was regarded as a mingling of
contrary principles or elements. For the Pythagoreans, however, a hierarchical relation did obtain between the elements in each pair of opposites;
light was superior to dark, the good was (naturally enough) superior to the
bad, and the male was superior to the female. Parmenides' rigorous egalitarianism, with its explicit discussion of the gender relationship, suggests a
shrewd philosopher: if coming-to-be is to have a place within the model of
cosmic stability, then the relation between the sexes has to be acknowledged.
The fact that it is characterized as non-hierarchical is worthy of note.

The political analogy seems to recur in this part of Parmenides' poem as
well, as we can see from an indirect fragment (A 37), in which the outer ring
of the universe is referred to as a 'wall', or 'fortification'. Nothing lies beyond
this wall, which seems to encompass 'everything'. In other words, the universe is not defined by exclusion.

*

Both the ontology and cosmology of Anaximander and the cosmology of Parmenides offer a model of cosmic stability that is very different from the latter's ontology, one that depends not on exclusion, but on universal inclusion. This model can accommodate – or rather, requires – not just difference, but also opposites, which hold one another in check. Admittedly, there are considerable differences between Parmenides' cosmology on the one hand and the ontology and cosmology of Anaximander on the other. The former does not involve anything equivalent to Anaximander's all-encompassing *apeiron*. Consequently, coming-to-be is also conceptualized differently. Whereas for Parmenides coming-to-be results from a mingling of opposites, which themselves do not seem to have any origin, Anaximander thinks of coming-to-be as a separating out of contraries from *apeiron*. In other words, Anaximander does not conceptualize generation by analogy to sexual reproduction, as does Parmenides. The reason why I nevertheless consider the two cosmologies worthy of comparison is not just that they both make use of the inclusion concept, so much as that they share a certain concept of equality. In neither of them does equality imply identity, but rather the equivalence of opposites.

The Greek political theory of the classical period – with Plato and Aristotle as its foremost representatives – built on the legacy of identity theory. The fact that Plato and Aristotle adopted this approach meant that the concept of the equality of opposites was unable to gain any significant influence in subsequent philosophy. As we might expect, this had consequences for the way people viewed the relation between the sexes. Since the time of Plato and Aristotle much philosophy has been permeated by what we can call a one-sex model: in reality there exists only one sex, the man, who constitutes the norm of all human life.[48] Within this model, the specifically female could only be defined negatively. Woman was characterized primarily in terms of what she is not (or does not have). These developments have also had implications for how we define differences between people in general. Difference of any kind came to be regarded as aberration from the norm. Just how the relation between man and woman would have been conceptualized in the history of European thought if Anaximander's inclusive philosophy had won the day, must of course remain a matter of speculation.

PART II

Plato, Love and Sexual Difference

CHAPTER 4

Tragic Conflict or Platonic Harmony?
Two views of gender in antiquity

There is broad agreement that the origins of the misogyny that prevails in our philosophical tradition are to be found in ancient Greece. In that culture, such prejudices were betrayed not only in many philosophical and literary works; the social and political institutions were also deeply marked by them. Moreover, most people would agree that it is the philosophy of Aristotle that must bear much of the responsibility for the fact that the man has survived up until our own day as the exemplar of the human condition, and that the woman is correspondingly – and by definition – relegated to a subordinate position.

When Sartre, for example, describes slime and mucus as symbols of the feminine, or of that aspect of the world from which we must dissociate ourselves in order to achieve authentic life, he locates himself firmly in a metaphysical tradition that stretches back to Aristotle, and which defines the fundamental principles of existence in sexual terms. Aristotle refers explicitly to matter, potentiality and passivity as feminine principles, whereas form, actuality and activity are for him masculine principles.[1] Even Simone de Beauvoir, who encouraged women to strive for a more authentic life, fails to rid her language of what are in effect misogynous metaphors. She regards the woman's body and female sexuality as symbolic of the category of immanence. The female body is that which receives the man's seed and, through the processes of pregnancy and parturition, stands for the perpetuation of the species. The body of the man and his sexuality are visible signs of the human potential to transcend one's given circumstances; the man ejects his sperm like an existential projectile and is free to move on to new authentic projections.

For de Beauvoir, masculine sexuality represents free and authentic existence, and thus serves as an ideal for women as well. In *The Second Sex*, a work in which she analyses the peculiarities of the woman's social situation and contrasts it with that of the man, her discussion of sexual differences is impaired by the metaphorical models of the tradition to which she belonged.

Although the goal of her work is unambiguous – to show that the status of women as the second sex is a result of our sexist culture – her use of traditional metaphors leads to a number of contradictions.[2]

In short, people have found it difficult to dissociate themselves from what I have characterized here as our misogynist tradition of metaphors. Among the Greeks this tradition had a metaphysical foundation in one-sex attitudes, such as we find in various forms in Aristotle and Plato. Similar to their view of a hierarchical world structure, they conceptualized also human life according to a hierarchical scheme, with the man representing what was highest. For them the man was, as it were, the true human, whereas the woman could only be defined as a negation of the man (Plato)[3] or as a defective man (Aristotle).

In Part I of this book I attempted to show how this tradition could be traced back to Parmenides. But I also wanted to show that there was another thread to Greek philosophy, even if it failed to make any significant mark on later thought. Anaximander's non-hierarchic philosophy offered a framework that could accommodate man and woman as different but equal entities. Among the non-hierarchical thinkers, the most important is undoubtedly Heraclitus, who regarded the world as a battleground for conflicting forces. The same conception occurs in what Parmenides calls 'the opinions of mortals', although these he considered to lack all credibility.

In this chapter I shall briefly allude to Empedocles, a sharp critic of Parmenides, whose reflections nevertheless have much in common with the latter's theory of untrue belief. It is important to note that, whereas the Platonic tradition focused on immortality as the ideal of human life, death itself was a central theme of much non-Platonic, non-hierarchic thought (Anaximander, Heraclitus, Parmenides' theory of untrue belief, Empedocles). The view of human life conveyed by Greek tragedy seems to accord with the latter tradition. In the following I shall juxtapose these two intellectual trends, focusing especially on the distinct views of sexual difference to be found in Plato and the dramatists.

TRAGIC AMBIVALENCE

In one of Plato's early dialogues, *Euthyphro*, Socrates aims some sharp criticism at the traditional, mythical grasp of the world. One of the things he finds incongruous is the propensity of the gods for internal conflict and disagreement. He makes the point that the gods seem to differ in their opinions about what is right and wrong, what is noble and base, and good and bad (*Euthyphro* 7b).[4] The hunter goddess Artemis, for instance, rejoices in things that are very different from those that please Aphrodite. Where the one calls for chastity, the other demands love. Mortals cannot satisfy all the gods at once, and this gives rise to conflict not just between one person and another, but also within one and the same person. We are familiar with such conflicts from the Greek tragedies. In Euripides' *Hippolytus* it is just such an insoluble conflict between Artemis and Aphrodite that triggers the tragic events. Aphrodite punishes Hippolytus' preference to worship Artemis, which amounts to a rejection of sexual love, by encouraging his stepmother Phaedra to fall in love with him, with fatal consequences. This situation results in the death of Phaedra and the banishment of Hippolytus. The former commits suicide, since she prefers to die rather than live with her forbidden, incestuous desire.

It is impossible for mortals to satisfy the absolute demands of the gods. Only the gods can live according to their one-sided, 'pure' natures. A mortal who attempts to live in the same way is likely to incur the ruin not only of himself but of his family as well, and sometimes even of his entire ancestral line. Even so, each of the gods *demands* of the tragic hero that his or her one-sided and absolute requirement be honoured exclusively. It is the conflict between such demands that constitutes the tragedy.

The point to be made is simple: the Greek tragedies investigate the fundamental conflicts of human life that often unfold with disastrous consequences. They aim to show us that the potential for insoluble clashes of interest is an aspect of our existence. Most of the Greek tragedies are built around gender disputes, on both the literal and symbolic levels. In the *Oresteia* trilogy, Clytemnestra struggles against her husband Agamemnon, whom she kills, whereupon their son Orestes kills his mother to revenge his father, reflecting a conflict on the symbolic level between the masculine principle of community on the one hand, and feminine principles of love and blood-ties on the other. In the final scene, Apollo and the masculine virgin Athena throw their support behind the man and all that is manly, whereas the avenging Erinyes, related to the darker forces of the earth, speak for the woman and womanly interests.

The sexual conflict is equally evident in *Hippolytus*, and many further examples could be given. In each case little effort would be needed to demonstrate that the drama grew from a conflict between man and woman. What is at issue in these works is not so much a neutral sexual *difference*, but a *conflict*. The insolubility of the tragic conflict indicates that sexual differences are regarded as irreducible, that the contending interests cannot be traced back to some unified point of origin. The tragic universe acknowledges no condition of original harmony, either between the sexes or between anything else. On the contrary, the beginning itself is the conflict of different principles.

I have already suggested that it is not just in the tragedies we encounter this view of human life and the world. Some of the early philosophers regard the world as a whole as a battleground of opposing forces. Empedocles, who to the best of our knowledge was a contemporary of Sophocles, took the four elements – fire, air, earth and water – as the basic principles of existence. For him, these were not so much neutral, inanimate substances, as natural elements with sexual characteristics that determine how they relate to one another. He associated the elements with mythical figures in a way that help us visualize their mutual relations. The relation between earth and fire, for instance, can be interpreted as the relationship between Zeus and Hera;[5] at times they succumb to mutual attraction and are united in love, at others they quarrel and go their separate ways.

Empedocles tells us that love between opposites is the cause of birth and death. Normally the unions of love create life, but a union that is too close will destroy the individuals involved. Both love and contention, agreement and disagreement are therefore necessary forces of existence. Empedocles puts it as follows:

> *Double is the birth of mortal things and double their passing away; for the one is brought to birth and destroyed by the coming together of all things, the other is nurtured and flies apart as they grow apart again. And these things never cease their continual interchange, now through Love all coming together into one, now again each carried apart by the hatred of Strife.* (B 17.3–8)

The relation between the sexes functions as a model for irreducible opposites, whose mutual love and conflict are the source of both fertility and death.[6] It is only a short step from here to the world of the tragedies: even if love between man and woman is a divine requirement and a condition for continued life, it can also result in death and ruin. The union of Oedipus with his mother is a prime example of this. Their union is too close. The coupling of mother and son incurred a danger of total collapse; it represents a threat that 'all becomes one', as Empedocles puts it.

Love is the foundation of all fertility and growth, but also of decay and death. The tragedies place greater emphasis on the latter; sexual difference is an aspect of humankind's tragic condition. In their focus on sexual difference, the tragedies illustrate the fundamental and insoluble conflicts that result in death. The tragedies emphasize the fragility of human existence, of the individual's finiteness and vulnerability to death and misfortune. But why should sexual difference be so critical? What has sex to do with death and misfortune? I have already hinted at an answer, but will attempt to make it clearer.

One of the themes of tragedy seems to be the apparent impossibility for mortals to harmonize the many conflicting demands of their existence. The human is limited and imperfect and can never represent any form of wholeness and totality. This is true not only of the individual, but also of social groups, such as the family, the ancestral line and the *polis*. In *King Oedipus*, for example, the entire house of Cadmus falls victim to the anger of the gods. The members of this clan have attempted to emulate the gods; they have tried to overcome the difference between the human and the divine, or between the mortal and the immortal. Among the gods themselves, incest is permissible, but for mankind it signifies an attempt to make both the individual and the race into a self-sufficient unity. But humans are not self-sufficient; they are neither self-identical nor whole.

Each human being, each ancestral line, each *polis*, has its own unavoidable deficiency, and is therefore reliant on something *other* than itself. Man depends on woman in order to propagate, and one family must form alliances with others for its self-perpetuation. By the same token, no *polis* is a self-identical unit, but is founded on differences, first and foremost on sexual difference. And sexual difference is a reminder that people are limited and imperfect.

Throughout Western history, human sexuality and mortality have been regarded as two aspects of one and the same thing. Humans are mortal thanks to their sexuality; those who come into being by sexual means must also die. But this is true only of humans, not of the gods. Only *human* sexuality, only the sexual difference of *humans*, has mortal consequences. This insight seems to have been of primary significance for much of Greek literature, from Hesiod to the Presocratics, the dramatists, and ultimately Plato and Aristotle. Admittedly, very different conclusions can be drawn from this premise. In the tradition that goes back to Parmenides, there is a tendency to see humankind in a divine perspective: the human strives to be like god, to overcome his mortality, that is, to transcend the radical difference of sexuality as a defining factor of human existence. In Empedocles and the tragedies, on the other hand, the focus is rather on the aspect of mortality, which means in this context that the focus tends to rest on sexual difference and the mortal conflicts that arise therefrom.

The point I wish to make here is both general and specific. Within the universe of the tragedies there is scope to reflect on *differences*, not just on those that can happily coexist, but also those that clash head on. This worldview is not founded on any single, unified set of values, but rather on a range of norms represented by various gods, which individual people are unable to reconcile at any one time. And among the differences and conflicts that constitute the themes of the tragedies, one in particular stands out as irreducible:

the sexual. In this setting, the woman is not just the negation of the man; she is something *other* and *distinct* from him.

Since the tragedies treat all people – both woman and man – as imperfect, they do not imply a view of the woman as an imperfect man, which is what she is in the tradition stemming from Plato and Aristotle. Although the tragic universe regards the two sexes as eternally dependent on one another, this hardly implies that the one achieves completeness via union with the other. The one needs the other but even in coming together they are not perfected. And it is in this that the tragic condition of mortals lies: imperfection is inherent in existence itself. This being so, the scene is set for conflict; nowhere do the tragedies describe a clash of interests that resolves in harmony. The tragic universe is a battleground, and the option of with-drawing to 'a room of one's own' is out of the question. But even so, the per-spective of the tragic dramatist is hardly neutral. If there is one person who can in any sense be described as the winner in these struggles, it is the man, or what the man stands for.

PLATONIC CONCORDE

Let us now return to Plato's *Euthyphro*, where Plato discusses the ambiva-lence of myths on the matter of morality, or more precisely, the gods' lack of agreement about what is good and just. In order to introduce his arguments, he has Socrates report on the accusation that has been levelled against him, to the effect that he has introduced new gods and abandoned the old. In other words, he has been accused of impiety (*Euthyphro* 5c). As we might expect, Socrates asks what impiety and piety really are. His conclusion is that, within a mythical perspective, the question cannot be answered, since 'the gods revolt and differ with each other, and ... hatreds come between them' (*Euthyphro* 7b).[7] In this manner he makes the case against him seem absurd. In Socrates' opinion, ethical questions about what is good and what is bad, what is just and what unjust, can only be answered if there is a common norm that applies to all.

One consequence of this aspect of the Platonic tradition is that it precludes all form of conflict or disagreement. The ideal is the conflict-free mind and the conflict-free society, total peace, agreement and unambiguousness. In the tragedies, conflicts are fundamental and permit no kind of 'solution' other than the ruin of a person or even an entire family. The Platonic vision, on the other hand, is eternal agreement and peace on both the collective and indivi-dual levels. Let us see what this implies.

Plato does not of course deny the occurrence of conflicts. On the contrary, we would be justified in saying that no one made greater efforts to character-ize the world as a place of conflict than he did.[8] Moreover, he tells us that oppositions and conflicts are a characteristic not merely of empirical reality. Also the ideal, non-empirical and insensible world is strongly marked by contraries. In *Phaedrus*, for instance, he depicts the soul as something in con-flict with itself (*Phaedrus*, 253c-255a). According to the image he uses, the soul consists of three parts: two steeds and a charioteer. One of the horses is good and obeys its driver, whereas the other is evil and pulls in various directions. What this image is meant to convey is that the human soul is by nature in conflict with itself. Similarly, Plato claims that political states will also entail self-conflict: their very nature presupposes the clash of different social classes – peasants, soldiers and philosopher-kings.

According to Plato's vision of the ideal state, the task of the peasants is to produce food for the entire population, and assuming this class serves the state as a whole, its members will have to work more than they wish to. What this means is that the need for their labour will be at odds with their natural appetite for sensual gratification. Supported by the soldiers, or guardians, the philosopher-kings have the task of ensuring that the peasants curb their desires. But the restraint of the peasants is important not just for the well-being of the state as a whole. The peasants need the philosopher-kings also for their own sakes. Their sensual natures are so dominant that, if left to their own devices, they would never be able to manage their lives. Without help from 'above' they would slide into a state of total chaos, and the result would be the ruin not just of the state, but also of the individual.

But although the peasants' sensual nature needs to be suppressed, it cannot be done away with entirely, for this would lead to the end of the state itself. Even the ideal state has to depend on people who crave the gratifications of food, drink and love. And herein lies one of Plato's many dilemmas: if the conflicting forces within the ideal state can neither be left to their own devices nor totally eliminated, then they must be controlled. And this indeed was Plato's project: oppositions need to be reined in, there has to be order, and in the case of the state, the only people able to manage such a task are the philosopher-kings. Correspondingly, in the case of the individual human soul, it is only the faculty of reason that can establish order.

According to the spatial order of Plato's ideals, reason is *higher* than sensual appetite, just as the philosopher-kings are *higher* than the peasants. Spatially speaking, this order and its axes are therefore not value-neutral; the 'highest' means here the 'best', and it is only natural that the best should govern over what is inferior; reason should govern the senses, the philoso-pher-kings the peasants. Plato does not imagine that this will put an end to conflicts, but he argues that, by conceding a single standard, rather than allowing several mutually contradictory norms to hold sway simultaneously, it should be possible to restrain or mitigate further oppositions. The degree of control required is, however, total; the reins cannot be slackened by so much as an inch, or for the briefest moment. Ideally speaking, the suppression should be so total that it is not even experienced as suppression. The peasants must be made to believe that the limits on their sensual desires are set by themselves rather than, as is in fact the case, by the philosopher-kings; they desire, so to speak, their own repression.

There is nothing self-evident in the notion of reason being better than the senses, or of up being better than down. So how does he justify his preferences? Why does he see reason as the best? At this juncture I shall merely suggest an answer, which will certainly be far from exhaustive: reason is the human capacity capable of providing the highest possible assurance of self-sufficiency. When, in the first book of the *Republic*, Socrates asks the aged Cephalus whether he is capable of sleeping with a woman, the latter answers with a quote from Sophocles: 'Hush, man, most gladly have I escaped this thing you talk of, as if I had run away from a raging and savage beast of a master' (329b–c).[9] Physical desire turns us into the slaves of some other master; it is not just that we are unable to control our own appetites, but also that we are in thrall to someone else, the person we desire, whose behaviour is beyond our direct control.

Our sensual appetites are a sign of our insufficiency; satisfaction depends on things outside oneself. Even if my beloved is beside me now, and even if I have enough food and good wine today, still I cannot know what tomorrow will bring. Where sensual appetites prevail, so too does arbitrariness. In contrast, reason demands nothing extraneous to itself for the satisfaction of *its* appetites. Only where reason rules can the individual be master of himself and exercise full control over his life. Socrates is the best example in this regard. He is so thoroughly ruled by reason that he seems liberated even from his own body; neither cold nor alcohol nor naked flesh seem to have the slightest effect on him. Socrates is the most self-sufficient person one can imagine. He needs neither food nor clothes nor the love and care of others. All he needs is the satisfaction afforded by reason.[10] And reason approves only of what is clear in sense and free of conflict. The Good cannot be partially good and partially bad, but has to be good in its entirety. The Good and the Just are self-identical, and therefore harmonious entities. But for Plato the body is something very different; it is the locus of arbitrariness, plurality, conflict and change.

The Platonic aspiration to unity and harmony is simultaneously an aspiration to immutability and self-sufficiency.[11] Within the Platonic vision, there is no scope for fundamental *differences*, but only for absence and lack. There are no competing norms. It is therefore hardly a coincidence that the Platonic system cannot accommodate sexual differences either. There is only one human standard, which the individual can embody to a greater or lesser degree. There is nothing imperfect in the notion of the human as such; what is imperfect is the individual who fails to achieve that standard – who fails to be governed by reason. For the true human, which happens to be the philosopher, sexual difference is irrelevant; sexuality is of no consequence and neither is physical reproduction. In claiming to have overcome his imperfections, the Platonic philosopher also claims to have overcome his body and the mechanism of reproduction. For Plato this also means he has overcome death: 'if ever it is given to man to put on immortality, it shall be given to him' (*Symposium* 212),[12] says Diotima, having just described the lover-philosopher who has attained a glimpse of ideal beauty (the idea, or form, of Beauty), and thereby given birth to the true and eternal progeny of thought.

It is against this background that we must seek to make sense of Plato's birth metaphors. Regarded as a kind of birth, thought represents a more perfect way of immortalizing oneself than bodily reproduction. But this is not all. The foregoing discussion should also shed some light on Plato's derogation, not just of women and the female, but of heterosexuality as such. Throughout his works, Plato tends to associate the female with the body, and heterosexuality with an enslavement to the body, its urges and to reproduction. Consequently, the only kind of love capable of overcoming physical desire and reproduction and of attaining fulfilment on the purely spiritual level is homosexual. Only homosexual love can dissociate itself entirely from the other, from the beloved, and thus achieve the freedom necessary for union with the form of beauty. In effect, only homosexual love can serve as a picture for the philosophical eros. For Plato this means that, in its ideal state, the human would be one-sexed and not dependent on anything other than the form of which it is itself a copy. If we were then to ask what that form of the human is, the answer would have to be the soul, for the soul is essentially sexless, although on closer analysis it will turn out to be characterized by masculine ideals. All the themes touched upon here will be examined in detail in the ensuing chapters.

In trying to place Plato's texts in literary terms, we could distinguish them from the tragedies by calling them comic; they aim to eliminate all conflicts. Whereas in the tragedies people are regarded as imperfect – meaning among other things limited by their sex – and as mortal, Plato regards humans as potentially self-sufficient, and therefore potentially capable of overcoming death. Sex is no limitation, since it does not exist in the realm of the real, that is, the realm of forms.

Let me risk the following generalization: those Greek thinkers and poets

who regarded the capacity for conflict and disagreement, and the suscept-
ibility to accident and death, as fundamental aspects of human existence were
also able to accommodate sexual difference in their intellectual universe. But
those who adopted unity, harmony and self-sufficiency as their standard
invariably sought to eliminate, or overcome, sexual difference. In another
formulation we could say, wherever the divine is taken as the standard for
human existence, as it is in Plato, we also find an attempt to negate sexual
difference and sexuality. But where the human is defined as a creature blatantly different from the gods, wherever people are defined as fundamentally
mortal, then sexual difference is accommodated in thought.

*

To my mind there are good grounds to distinguish two principle currents in
Greek philosophy. The one is the Platonic tradition, dominated by hierarchic
thinking. This can be traced back to Parmenides, who, as I aimed to show in
Chapters 2 and 3, sought to do away with the sexual difference and the
finiteness – indeed, the very humanity – of human existence. I believe it
would require some effort to demonstrate that Aristotle was also of this
school, and the scope for disagreement is greater in his case. The second tradition can be traced back to the Ionian philosophers. Here we find names like
Anaximander, Heraclitus and Empedocles. These philosophers do not divide
the world according to a hierarchic system, where up is good and down is
bad. Instead they regard existence as a battleground for distinct and opposing
forces. The norms that govern their world are not one but many. Of these,
some will win, others will lose; conflicts will arise, harmony will be restored,
and harmony will be followed by further conflicts. Such is the universe of
tragedy. There is no logically necessary reason why misogyny should be any
less acute in this universe than it is in the Platonic-Aristotelian tradition, yet
in many cases it is. I consider it important to bear in mind that in antiquity
there was in fact an intellectual perspective capable of accommodating sexual
difference. This, however, was not destined to become the dominant current
in European philosophy, which has largely preferred to regard – and has
remained faithful to – Plato and Aristotle as its origins.

CHAPTER 5

Sexuality and Philosophy in Plato's *Symposium*

ABOLISHING THE FEMALE, OR, THE ABSENCE OF SEXUAL DIFFERENCE IN PLATO'S PHILOSOPHY

One does not have to study the *Symposium* in detail to notice the numerous sexual connotations and the repeated sexual metaphors that Plato uses in this dialogue. Socrates' claim that love (*ta erotika*, 177d[1]) is the only thing in the world he understands must of course be read as irony. He employs a word that has sexual implications in everyday life, but which in the course of the dialogue is given a new content, one purged of all sexuality, until Platonic love ultimately emerges as a purely spiritual phenomenon.

It is certainly true that in this dialogue the words *eros* (love) and *erotika* (matters of love) acquire a new, more spiritual – or 'Platonic' – meaning. But although Plato's intention is to equate philosophy with a form of love, we should be careful not to lose the everyday sense of these words entirely from view. Admittedly, what Plato has in mind is love of wisdom, but in his effort to explain what he means by love, he has Socrates claim that the aim of love is reproduction and birth (206e).

If love is directed towards reproduction and birth, and philosophy is a form of love, then philosophy must also have reproduction and birth as its aims. The fact that Plato uses precisely these two words – reproduction and birth (*genesis kai tokos*) – makes it reasonable to assume that he is referring to the respective contributions of the man and the woman in reproduction, such as he understood the process: the man's fertilization of the woman and female parturition. In other words, Plato explains love and philosophy in terms of sexual love. By taking a closer look at the images Plato uses so frequently in the *Symposium*, I believe we will achieve a more astute understanding not just of what an expression like 'Platonic love' entails, but also of the general aims of Plato's philosophy.

I shall begin by drawing attention to two aspects of the *Symposium* of particular significance in this regard. This will also demonstrate the scope of the imagery used in the dialogue. Firstly, similar to a number of other Platonic dialogue's, the *Symposium* is situated dramatically in a homoerotic context. Several friends of the tragic poet Agathon have gathered at the latter's home to celebrate his victory the previous day in Athens' annual theatre festival. The erotic tension that prevails among these men, reclining together around the table, is almost palpable. Indeed, the dialogue as a whole is shot through with homoerotic metaphors. But there is a further aspect to the dialogue. Although the Platonic *eros* is sketched with clearly homoerotic contours, very different images are adduced when Socrates describes the proper and highest goal of love, for he adduces the specifically female contribution to procreation, namely pregnancy and birth, as characteristics of the philosophical *eros* (206b–207a).

How are we to understand this description of Platonic love, which combines masculine homosexuality, with its implied exclusion of the feminine, on the one hand, and a purely feminine aspect on the other? This will be the crucial question in my analysis of the dialogue, and already here I shall indicate an answer.

In the *Symposium*, metaphors of male propagation and female childbearing are brought together in the description of the personified Eros, a figure that Plato adopts from traditional mythology, which regarded Eros as a masculine god of love. In Plato's text Eros is both a lover and a philosopher, or rather, he is the Lover and the Platonic philosopher *per se*. But despite his male nature, Eros also manifests female functions, such as pregnancy and giving birth. Thus he represents something 'complete', a being without the sexual limitations that each and every man and woman is obliged to live with. Eros – the Philosopher – is more than human. He is a *daimon*, as it says in the dialogue. In other words, he is not entirely divine, but rather a being halfway between god and man. Eros transcends sexual difference, not because he lacks gender, but because he embraces both male and female sexuality.[2]

This exposes a fundamental ambiguity in Plato's notion of sexual difference. On the one hand, since sexual differences are purely bodily in nature, and thus of no consequence in the realm of forms, they could be characterized as insignificant for Platonic philosophy. But in describing philosophy in terms of sexual love, and Eros as a masculine being of androgynous sexuality, Plato has effectively absorbed the feminine into the masculine, and thereby forfeited any position of neutrality with regard to gender. This ambiguity is the starting point for my analysis of the *Symposium*. But before turning to that particular text, I shall briefly review some of Plato's other dialogues, in order to illustrate my claim that the apparent gender neutrality of Plato's philosophy in fact entails the negation of the feminine.

In Book V of the *Republic*, Plato develops a kind of equal opportunities programme. In this well-known passage, Socrates demonstrates the basic insignificance of sexual difference by means of a simple illustration. He maintains that the difference between the one who gives birth and the one who 'begets' is as trivial as the difference between short hair and long hair. Physical differences of this nature are of no consequence for a person's spiritual qualities, and it is the latter that constitute what is uniquely human. Thus it seems that Socrates regards the sexes as equal, at least where ability to govern the state is concerned. But the way in which he presents his arguments is likely to leave us in doubt as to whether his subject really is equality of opportunity, or whether here as well the real concern is the negation of the feminine. This point requires some clarification.

At an early stage in the *Republic* (Bk II) the inhabitants of the ideal state are divided into a class of workers and a class of guardians. At a later stage in the work (in Bk III), Plato separates out from the latter also a governing class. Thus his ideal state consists of three quite distinct social groups: the workers, the guardians and the rulers. Strictly speaking, the discussion of sexual equality in Book V of the *Republic* is concerned only with equality within the ruling class. Even so, Socrates' argument refers repeatedly to the functions of the guardians, and the way it does so is worthy of particular note. Like the workers and the rulers, the guardians also have a special virtue (*arēte*), namely courage, or rather, manliness, which is a more literal translation of the Greek word *andreia* (from *anēr*, meaning 'man'). Reasonably enough, courage and manliness were regarded as masculine virtues, and when Plato has Socrates advocate that the 'best of all the women' (*Republic*, 456e) should participate in governing the state, he is in fact speaking of the most masculine of women.[3] By the same token, love and eroticism also are all but absent from this text, in which Plato finds it appropriate 'to go through with the female [drama]' (*Republic*, 451c).

Another thing worth noting is that, in the very passage where he claims that women and men are fundamentally the same, Socrates indirectly betrays an assumption of their essential difference. Whereas the male guardians are characterized as the best citizens (*politai*), the female guardians are described quite simply as the best women (*gynaikes*). In other words, the man belongs to the political community – which is what defines his nature as a human being – whereas the woman belongs to her sex. In this context, 'the best women' means – paradoxically – the women that have most successfully overcome the fact that they belong to their sex. Thus what we find in Book V of the *Republic* is not a proposal for equal empowerment of the sexes, as is often claimed, but rather an attempt to cultivate masculine qualities within the ruling class.

The conclusion cannot be avoided that, for Plato, the ideal person – that is, the person who is guided in all things by *logos*, or reason – is masculine in character, whereas woman and the feminine tend rather to represent the body. We will see examples of this attitude in the *Symposium*. At this stage I should also mention *Timaeus*, where the relation between the immaterial realm of forms and the material world is compared with the relation between the father and the mother (*Timaeus*, 50). In other dialogues, not least in the *Republic*, women are frequently mentioned in the same breath as children and slaves, which in this context means they are equated with people whose capacity for reason is regarded as imperfectly developed (for example *Republic* 395d–e; *Gorgias* 502; *Laws* 669).[4]

Clearly there is an ambivalence in Plato's view of women: either the woman is entitled to be regarded as a human being because she resembles a man, or she is merely a woman and as such of lower value than her male counterpart. This ambivalence in Plato's philosophy can also be illustrated with an anecdote. In his *Lives of Famous Philosophers*, Diogenes Laertius relates that among the people who attended Plato's Academy there were also two women, albeit dressed as men. From this we learn that the Academy was accessible to women, but only insofar as they abandoned their womanliness.

In regarding the man as the true representative of human nature and the woman as something qualitatively inferior, Plato was echoing the common attitude of his day. It is therefore tempting to dismiss his outlook as excusable on historical grounds, but even if we do so it cannot be denied that his views in this regard tell us something about his own way of thinking. In our context it is important not to miss what is peculiarly Platonic about his discussion of equal status in the *Republic*. As already mentioned, the aim of his attempt to include women among the rulers is not to place woman on an equal footing with man, but rather to negate sexual difference. And it is here we find the significance of the strongly homoerotic element of the Platonic dialogues. When the discussion turns to the theme of love, the focus is not on the love between sexes but rather on the cultivation of a single sex.

Although almost unthinkable in historic terms, from an intellectual standpoint Plato might just as well have treated Eros as a female figure and taken love between women as the starting point for his philosophy, instead of love between men. On the other hand, the philosophical impossibility for Plato – in other words, the utterly un-Platonic option – would have been to regard the highest form of love, and hence the highest form of insight, as a spiritualizing of love between the two sexes. For Plato, the philosophical *eros* can only find sustenance in the love between two people of the same sex. His thoughts on this subject are given shape not just in the *Symposium*, but also in his other great love dialogue, *Phaedrus*.

One of Socrates' objectives in *Phaedrus* is to account for the diversity of human types and their desires, and to this end he recounts a myth about human souls before their birth. Some people become warriors, others philo-sophers; some are most preoccupied with carnal love, others with spiritual love. The myth is meant to show what it takes to become a philosopher, and what kind of love the philosopher manifests. In order to illuminate the various types of desire to which all people – philosophers included – are subject, Socrates depicts the human soul as follows.

The soul is like a team of two horses pulling a chariot and steered by a charioteer. One of the horses is noble and obedient and goes where the char-ioteer wishes, whereas the other is a rather more wretched creature and follows its own immediate urges. The two steeds represent different types of desire – the spiritual and the carnal respectively – while the charioteer repre-sents reason. In these terms, the human soul is depicted as a battleground, where noble desire – the desire for true goodness and beauty – struggles to gain the upper hand over the 'bad', or physical, type of desire.

Few passages in Plato devote so much attention to sensual love as this one. Although sensual urges are portrayed as something inferior to spiritual plea-sures, the text clearly suggests that the desire for sensual beauty is a neces-sary precursor to the desire for the true Beauty, that is, for the form of Beauty itself, which lies beyond all form of sensuality. Moreover, sensual pleasure is presented as a natural concomitant of the highest form of love: the very climax of the myth describes a point at which the lover and his beloved jointly desire the form of Beauty and have thus become philosophers, but here as well they find pleasure in looking at one another, in touching and kissing and in lying together (*Phaedrus* 255e). Not even the force that guides and guards the two lovers, namely reason – the charioteer in the myth – feels any shame about these sensual pleasures.

Literally speaking, the word translated here as 'lying together' means 'to have intercourse', but the one thing the charioteer tries to hinder is con-summation of the sensual love (*Phaedrus* 255e–256b). If it happens that the bad, characterless horse nevertheless disobeys the charioteer, thus over-coming the good advice of reason, then the soul is no longer master of itself. It has become enslaved to passion and is thus no longer able to devote itself to the philosophical life. Those who not only dream of sensual love, but also consummate their dreams (cf. *diaprattein*, 'to do it'; *Phaedrus* 256c) have opted for sensual pleasure as the goal of love. For Plato this means they have lost sight of love's proper goal, namely Beauty itself, which lies beyond all things sensual. True lovers, that is philosophers, must under no circumstance abandon themselves to carnal lust; on the contrary, they must restrain them-selves and guide their souls towards the form of Beauty.

Plato's *Phaedrus* presents us with the following train of thought: sensual desire and carnal lust are needed to point the soul towards philosophical insight, but for this goal to be achieved, care must be taken not to satiate sensual desire. From this it should be fairly clear why Plato avoided hetero-sexual love as the starting point for his philosophical love. As something required for the continuation of the human species, sexual intercourse between a man and a woman can be seen as a simple 'function of nature'. Plato's argument suggests that, by contrast, homosexual love cannot be dis-missed so easily. To put it another way, the love between a woman and a man has its 'natural' conclusion in coitus and does not in itself point towards any-thing beyond the purely physical. For this reason, heterosexuality hardly offers a suitable parallel to philosophical love in the Platonic sense. This purpose can only be served by unconsummated physical love, which Plato's text represents as an ideal of homosexual relationships. Homosexual love is therefore more independent of sensual gratification, which in Plato's opinion is generally so delightful that it jeopardizes the lovers' self-control.

It is worth noting that women simply do not figure in the intense discourse about love that makes up most of *Phaedrus*. Neither does the woman play a part in Plato's account of the birth of the soul in various human types: the soul is planted directly into a man's seed (*Phaedrus* 248d), which seems potentially capable of producing a human without the assistance of a woman. This rather curious absence of women supports my contention that, in the framework of Plato's ideal of love, the woman is an element of inconvenience. It should not surprise us therefore that there is hardly any talk of love in Book V of the *Republic*. For this periodic absence in the Platonic dialogues, sometimes of women, sometimes of love, seems to follow a pattern. Where the theme is love, the woman is conspicuous in her absence,[5] and where the subject is the woman, love is excluded from the discourse.

PHILOSOPHY AS MASCULINE BIRTH: AN ANALYSIS OF THE SYMPOSIUM

THE PROLOGUE (172A–180B): RHETORICAL PRESENTATION OF THE DIALOGUE'S THEME

Like Plato's other writings, the *Symposium* is generally classified as a dialo-gue, although in this case the text is not clearly dialogical in character, con-sisting rather of a series of monologues in dramatized form. The situation dramatized in the work is a social gathering – in Greek, *symposion*, meaning more literally a drinking party – at the home of the tragic dramatist Agathon, where the people have come together to celebrate his victory at the Athenian theatre festival the previous day. The host and his guests, with the exception of Socrates, are more or less hung over from the day before. Consequently, they agree to refrain from the otherwise obligatory drinks (176e) and to entertain themselves instead with speeches (*logoi*). In other words, they wish to intoxicate their thoughts rather than their bodies, to get drunk on words (*logoi*) rather than wine.

The person who suggests this diversion is the physician Erixymachus, and he elaborates his proposal with the following suggestion: 'I also propose that we dispense with the services of the flute girl who has just come in, and let her go and play to herself or to the women inside there (. . .) while we spend our evening in discussion' (176e). Out with the women, in with the words. Barbara Freeman has remarked that the flute girl only appears in the dialogue so that she can be sent out again.[6] Thus a vital contrast is suggested at the very outset, even before the dialogue's theme has been disclosed: the contrast between *logos* – which can be translated as word, speech, reason or thought – and woman, or the feminine. This tension will be seen to run through the entire dialogue. It is typical of Plato to indicate the principal theme of his dialogue by means of such a seemingly innocuous remark.

Erixymachus is also ready with a suggestion for the theme of the discussion. The subject is admittedly not his own inspiration but that of another guest, the beautiful Phaedrus, who is said to have complained that, although there are hymns and anthems to all the other gods, no poet has yet paid homage to Eros. Thereupon they agree that each and every one of them should hold a speech in praise of Love, or Eros. The addresses are to be delivered according to the order in which the men are arranged around the table. Phaedrus begins, since he is, as we are told, 'father of the thought' (*patēr tou logou;* 177d). Here we should note that Plato is craftily inverting what was a well-known verse from a (lost) tragedy by Euripides (*Melanippe*): 'The word is not mine, but my mother's. In Plato's text the source of the words is not the mother, but the father. This subtly suggests the notion of spiritual, masculine reproduction.

The homoerotic context of the dialogue is obvious: the men around the table are linked by lover-like relationships – in some cases rivalrous. Agathon, the host and 'the handsomest man in the room' (213c), is the lover of the older Pausanias, although he is also a source of attraction for Socrates and Alcibiades, who enters the scene late in the work. Then again, Erixymachus pays court to the beautiful but shy Phaedrus. The erotic game reaches its climax towards the end of the dialogue, when the drunken Alcibiades lurches into the company and tells about his many ill-fated attempts to become the focus of Socrates' affections.

The thematic horizon suggested early in the dialogue, before the speeches in praise of Eros begin, applies to the dialogue as a whole: the women have been sent out, and the men, variously in love with one another, settle down to concentrate on words and thoughts rather than bodily pleasures, although, as one might expect, the thing they want to talk about is love. Homoerotic, masculine, spiritual reproduction and the absence of women – these are essential components of the Platonic love discourse presented in the *Symposium*.

Plato's claim – contained in Erixymachus' report of the words of Phaedrus – that Greek poets have never eulogized Eros, is simply not accurate, and of course Plato himself is aware of this. I shall therefore take the claim to imply that Plato intends to focus on an Eros that is *different* from the traditional one. In the literature prior to Plato, Eros was portrayed primarily as a divinity of heterosexual love. For Hesiod, Parmenides and Aristophanes, Eros is a cosmic power that unifies the female and male elements of the universe, thereby providing the conditions for all kinds of generation and growth;[7] for Sophocles and Euripides, Eros is a power that unites man and woman.[8] When, in the *Symposium*, Plato has Aristophanes present a theory about the homosexual Eros and this figure's superiority to the heterosexual, we have to understand it as a conscious rewriting of the literary tradition. Phaedrus' complaint about Eros' absence from literature can be interpreted as a criticism that no poets have paid homage to the homosexual Eros.[9] Whereas both Aphrodite and Eros serve in Greek mythology as gods of the love between man and woman, there was no separate divinity to preside over love between men, despite the fact that such relationships were both common and accepted. We can say that, in the *Symposium*, Plato creates just such a god.[10] It seems reasonable to suppose that this transformation of the traditional Eros is of philosophical significance.

Plato's *Symposium* thus describes a purely homosexual ideal of love, one that is not structured according to a heterosexual model. Plato wishes to establish a love that is different in kind from one based on the attraction of opposites. For him the ideal love could be represented by the attraction one might feel on seeing a beautified version of one's own reflection. The attraction is that of what resembles oneself, or more accurately, of what resembles one's own ideal. For Plato, ideal love is the attraction between elements that are masculine, good and unifying. Like is attracted to like, where 'like' is synonymous with 'good'. Adopting Plato's way of thinking, we could characterize such love as an impossibility, as an ideal in the utopian sense. Erotic striving, which he regards as the aspiration to partake of something one lacks in oneself, will cease once unity and wholeness (sameness) have been attained.

Full consummation of the Platonic *eros* would entail the end not just of love and philosophy, but also of humanity. It is not immediately clear whether Plato would have regarded such a result as paradoxical. Whereas in

Phaedo Socrates describes philosophy as a 'preparation for dying and death' (*Phaedo* 64a), in the *Symposium* he claims that the aim of love is immortality, meaning transformation to the divine. The *Symposium* seeks to achieve this aim by eliminating the sexual distinctions associated with love, which it does partly by negating the feminine, and partly by assimilating certain feminine attributes among the masculine. This does not mean that Plato denies sexual difference as such. He does not deny the world's 'bad' feminine aspect – for this would ultimately entail a negation of the material world itself – but love is established as a domain for the exclusive cultivation of what is masculine. This ideal finds its most refined expression in Socrates' speech, although the ground is well prepared in those that precede it. Let us now look at those speeches in greater detail. I shall begin with that of Pausanias, then turn to Aristophanes' well-known myth about the origins of sexual desire, and conclude by reviewing Socrates' account of his discussion with Diotima about love.

PAUSANIAS' SPEECH IN PRAISE OF THE HEAVENLY, PEDERASTIC EROS (180C–185C)

Eros, the masculine love god, is commonly thought of as a companion of Aphrodite, the goddess of love in Greek mythology. Pausanias begins his speech by pointing out that there are two versions of Aphrodite, one of which is heavenly (*Ouranian*) and the other of which is earthly, or 'vulgar' (*Pandēmos*). Corresponding to each version of Aphrodite is a different version of Eros. The heavenly Aphrodite is claimed to be of purely masculine origins. She has no mother, but rather – as we learn from Hesiod's *Theogony* – sprung from the foam that developed when her father's genitals were thrown on the sea close to the island of Cythera (*Theogony* 190ff.). The vulgar Aphrodite, on the other hand, was of more natural birth; she is the daughter of Zeus and Dione and is therefore of double parentage. She partakes of both the masculine and the feminine. And it is precisely this double origin that Pausanias finds so characteristic of the men who follow the vulgar Eros:

> *For, first, they are as much attracted by women as by boys; next, whoever they may love, their desires are of the body rather than of the soul; and, finally, they make a point of courting the shallowest people they can find, looking forward to the mere act of fruition and careless whether it be a worthy or unworthy consummation. And hence they take their pleasures where they find them, good and bad alike. For this is the Love [Eros] of the younger Aphrodite, whose nature partakes of both male and female.* (181b–c)

These vulgar lovers, devotees of the Aphrodite who was herself a product of sexual reproduction, are interested exclusively in the bodily aspect of love, which effectively means the sexual act. The background to Pausanias' thought is a range of analogous polarities: man-woman (alternatively man-boy), soul-body, intelligent-unintelligent, good-bad. Reflecting the vulgar Aphrodite's origin in various elements, the vulgar lover seeks that which is different from himself, or rather, that which differs from the masculine element within himself. For this reason he loves women or young boys and is obsessed with their bodies rather than their souls, and thus he prefers the unintelligent to the intelligent and has little appreciation of what is noble and good.

Evidently it will make little sense to describe the vulgar Eros as heterosexual if we take the word in its everyday sense. Even so, it still seems reasonable to use the term: the man who follows the vulgar Eros is attracted by what is different (*heteron*) from himself (or more precisely, what is different from his own manfulness and reason), namely, the feminine aspect in another person, whether that other be male or female. The text makes it clear that when these vulgar lovers turn to their own sex it is the very youngest of the boys whom they select, and these are in effect the ones that have least to offer other than their still childlike – meaning for the Greeks, their feminine – bodies. A boy's development towards manhood was commonly looked upon as a development away from female qualities towards the male. Characteristic of the vulgar Eros is his two-sided nature, since he encompasses both female and male elements. Correspondingly, it is a characteristic for the vulgar lover to crave that which differs from his own masculine nature.

By contrast, the Eros associated with the heavenly Aphrodite 'springs from a goddess whose attributes have nothing of the female, but are altogether male' (181c), and his essence is therefore purely masculine. The adherents of this Eros

> turn rather to the male, preferring the more vigorous and intellectual bent. One can always tell – even among the lovers of boys – the man who is wholly governed by this elder Love [Eros], for no boy can please him until he has shown the first signs of dawning intelligence, signs which generally appear with the first growth of beard. (181c–d)

What this more noble type of pederast desires in young men is not their feminine so much as their masculine qualities: the stirrings of intelligence and the bloom of a coming beard, corresponding to the spiritual and the physical aspects of a man. The heavenly Eros is homoerotic in the literal sense of the word: the man who is driven by this type of love desires what is masculine in a man, in other words, that which is similar to (*homoion*) himself.

In his speech, Pausanias tells us that this purely masculine pederasty, which in theoretical terms is uniform and in some sense 'simple' (cf. German: *einfach*), is in practice the most complex of all. He describes in detail the intricate, manifold (*poikilos*), and contradictory moral rules for pederasty in Athens. But why should contradictory practices develop around an *eros* that is simple and uniform? The answer to the question is simple: there is a tendency to try to combine the purely masculine *eros*, which on its own is self-consistent, with the moral standards of heterosexuality, which are based on a relationship between an active, masculine agent and one that is passive and feminine.

Pausanias' description accords with what we know of Greek pederasty from other sources,[11] for example that young boys were forced to play a feminine role in relation to their lovers, even though it was precisely this kind of behaviour that would be forbidden him throughout his later life once he himself had become a citizen. For a citizen only one thing was morally acceptable, and that was of course to play an active, masculine role. The young Greek boy therefore faced a dilemma: how was he to have an erotic relationship with a citizen – something that was expected of him – without losing his dignity as a prospective citizen?[12] The Athenians of the time found a pragmatic solution to the problem by adopting a complex set of rules to govern pederastic relationships. For example, there were detailed descriptions of the positions permissible for the boy during the sexual act.[13] Above all, anal coitus was to be avoided. The youngster should stand upright, look straight ahead, and show no signs of sexual arousal. In this way he could avoid identifying himself with the feminine role that he was in fact fulfilling.

Pausanias does not explicitly discuss the problems associated with pederasty. Nevertheless, his speech includes a suggested solution, even if not quite as practical as the one cited above. His answer to the problem is rather more abstract in nature. By putting together new, unfamiliar combinations of terms, and thus constructing new conceptual polarities, he avoids the traditional contradictions that afflict pederasty.

What was special about the traditional pederastic relationship between a young boy and his lover was the fact that both had their full freedom, and there was therefore never any reason – ideally speaking – why the one should dominate the other. Whereas a wife was quite simply and utterly subject to the authority of her husband, the young boy was free to choose his lover. It was also expected of young boys that they should not throw themselves into the arms of the first to come their way, but rather keep their suitors at a certain distance. This meant that the older lovers had to ingratiate themselves with their favourites, and to endure a complex game of rejection and encouragement, which might not always have been easy to interpret. Pausanias' speech can be read as a sympathetic commentary on the difficulties faced by the older lovers, while at the same time containing a philosophical analysis of their situation. The lover is described as

> *urging his need with prayers and entreaties, and vowing vows, and sleeping upon doorsteps, subjecting himself, in short, to a slavery* (douleia) *which no slave* (doulos) *would ever endure.* (183a)

Taking this at face value, the lover accepts a kind of voluntary slavery in order to win the favour of his beloved. The relationship between the lover and the youngster is one of master and slave, where the boy is master and the citizen the slave. Pausanias uses rare combinations of ideas to explain this relationship. He describes it as one between an active and free slave (the lover as such is active, while as a citizen he is free) and a passive and free master (the beloved plays a passive sexual role, but as a prospective citizen is free).

Pausanias tells us that the lover's aim is to secure the youngster's devotion, meaning he should persuade the beloved to place his body at the man's disposal. Yet the youngster will not allow the lover to enjoy his body unless he gets something in return; for his physical favours he demands spiritual compensation, in the form of philosophical instruction. At this stage in the pederastic game, the roles become inverted. For now it is the lover who is intellectually dominant over the boy, who for his own part voluntarily accepts subjugation for the sake of developing his character.

In Pausanias' opinion, the moral dilemma afflicting this tradition can be resolved by combining 'the law of pederasty' with 'the law of philosophy', such that the voluntary slavery is practised on both parts, by the one on the physical level, and the other on the spiritual level. In this case the relation is no longer between a passive – or seemingly feminine – agent and one that is active and masculine, but rather between two free, active and hence masculine partners. In this way Pausanias seeks to resolve the pederast's dilemma, and the conclusion is that the boy's role in such a relationship is not irreconcilable with his future role as a citizen.

But were we to accept this 'solution', we would have to overlook that it is still a form of slavery, albeit a voluntary one, that the boy and the citizen submit to, and this would mean that the contradictions that Pausanias attempts to avoid have simply cropped up elsewhere in a more revealing guise. Unwittingly, Pausanias has cast both eroticism and philosophy as forms of slavery, and this is evidently incompatible with the citizen's freedom, which is such a vital part of his identity. Plato emphasizes this irony by giving Pausanias' speech a slightly comical tone: Pausanias insists that the heavenly, masculine Eros has nothing to do with sensual lust, despite the fact that, in the course of his speech, it becomes steadily clearer that the peder-ast's aim is precisely this kind of pleasure, even if its justification is the reward of philosophical education.

In his own speech, Socrates makes it his aim to do away with all such unworthy master-slave relationships, whether in the field of love or of phi-losophy (cf. 210c–d). But in order to achieve this end, he has to abandon the fundamental polarities of active-passive and masculine-feminine in terms of which traditional pederasty was structured. This implies that ideal love – that is, philosophical love – involves a structure that does not consist essentially of polarities. And it is just such a model that Socrates attempts to describe in his own speech, in which he develops a metaphysical founda-tion for love. What the philosophical lover desires is not just – or rather, not primarily – another person resembling himself, but rather sameness and unity *per se* (211b). This is a point I shall return to in due course.

ARISTOPHANES' SPEECH (189C–193D): ON THE ORIGINS OF EROTIC DESIRE

Unity and sameness, the ideals of love introduced by Pausanias, and which will prove so decisive for Socrates, are also developed in Aristophanes' speech, albeit in a very particular way. When Aristophanes discusses human sexuality and reproduction, he refers to an ideal that was by no means unfamiliar to the Greeks. The ideal is that of vegetative propagation, which presupposes no sexuality; in other words, propagation by a *single* parent. In order to appreciate Aristophanes' ideas, we must first take a closer look at his magnificent and well-known myth about the original, spherical people.

The purpose of Aristophanes' fantastic tale about the original human con-dition is to account for the various forms of erotic attraction that people experience. Originally, he tells us, there were three sexes

> *that is to say, besides the two sexes, male and female, which we have at present, there was a third which partook of the nature of both, and for which we still have a name, though the creature itself is forgotten. For though 'androgynous' is only used nowadays as a term of contempt, there really was a man-woman in those days, a being which was half male and half female (anēr = man, gynē = woman).* (189d–e)

These original people were self-sufficient and lived independent of one another, also in the sense that they 'begot and conceived not upon each other, but ... upon the earth' (191c). In other words they propagated like plants by sowing their seeds or their shoots in the earth. In those early days sexuality was still a thing of the future. Not only did they greatly enjoy their perfect autonomy, they were also so content with themselves and of such strength and energy that, in their arrogance, they even threatened the hegemony of the gods. Zeus felt himself compelled to reduce their strength and hit upon a cunning plan. He sent Apollo to cut the people in two, turning their faces towards the side on which they were cut, and closing the skin 'over what we now call the belly' and to tie it up so as to form 'what we call the navel' (190e). Henceforth, each half of a bisected body would use all its strength and energy searching for its counterpart, to which – if found – it would cling until both died of hunger.

This embrace evidently had no sexual function, since the sexual organs remained on what was now the back of each halved body. For a while, the human race was in danger of dying out, but then Zeus shifted the sexual organs round to the front, thereby introducing sexuality into the lives of humans. Sexuality is characterized as 'another mechination' (*allēn mēchanēn* 191b), that is, a remedy for human immortality. Aristophanes explains that this remedy functions in two ways. Firstly, the reproduction that results from the embrace of a man and a woman ensures the continuation of the race. Secondly, gratification from the sexual act allows people to return to the mundane affairs that are so necessary for their day-to-day survival (191b–c). But in continuing his account of human sexuality, Aristophanes simply forgets to return to the former of these functions. What we are left with as the only proper function of sexuality, and as Eros' rightful domain, is gratification:

> *The man who is a slice of the hermaphrodite sex, as it was called, will naturally be attracted by women – the adulterer, for instance – and women who run after men are of similar descent – as, for instance, the unfaithful wife. But the woman who is a slice of the original female is attracted by women rather than by men – in fact she is a Lesbian – while men who are slices of the male are followers of the male. (191d–e)*

This passage alludes to three types of erotic desire: the heterosexual, and those of female and male homosexuality, whereby the latter is intended in the narrower sense of pederasty. From the Aristophanic point of view, the sexual function of the two latter types of desire is unproblematic; the purpose of homosexual desire is nothing other than gratification. But also the heterosexual form of desire is only discussed in terms of sexual gratification. Aristophanes talks exclusively about extra-marital eroticism and avoids mentioning the marital form, which for the Athenians was the only one that was seen as serving reproduction.

The reason why Aristophanes ignores reproduction in the remainder of his discussion of sexuality seems clear. Once gratification has been isolated as the only legitimate function of human sexuality, then no further argument is required to justify pederasty as an ideal, despite the fact that the practice is evidently incapable of perpetuating the human race. The sense of that ideal is that the pederast demonstrates the 'most virile constitution' (*andreiotatos*; 192a), and hence the typical qualities – or virtues – of manly character, such as 'daring, fortitude and manhood' (*tharrous kai andreias kai arrenopias*; 192a). The masculinity of these virtues is obvious, in that the Greek words for two of them – fortitude and manhood – are derived from *anēr*, meaning 'man'. Owing to their uniform, masculine nature, such men 'tend to cherish what is like themselves' (*to homoion*; 192a) and are 'always rejoicing in [their] own kind' (192b).

Having set up masculine love as an ideal, Aristophanes is then in a position to narrow down its requirements still further. The aim is not carnal pleasure, but eternal spiritual companionship between the lover and his beloved (192cff.). Eros is thus portrayed as a yearning for one's originally spherical shape, not so much in the physical as in the spiritual sense: 'and now, when we are longing for and following after that primeval wholeness (*tou holou*), we say we are in love (*eros*)' (192e–193a). Towards the very end of his speech, almost by way of conclusion, he briefly returns to heterosexuality, although by this point it is no longer able to threaten the status of pederasty as the supreme form of love. The ideal unity has to be that which is uniform in itself, and which therefore cannot consist of contraries but must encompass parts that are like one another. Unity and sameness are evidently the ideal of erotic desire: 'to live two lives in one' (192e).

Aristophanes' speech changes direction in a curious way. In their primeval condition, humans propagated by non-sexual, vegetative means. The difference between this and their current condition is radical. The ideal is no longer propagation without sexuality, but sexuality without propagation. For it to occur, this reversal presupposes the idealization of unity and sameness mentioned above, and this amounts to an idealization of pure manliness. Plato continues his investigation of this ideal in Socrates' speech, where he adds yet another twist. Unlike Aristophanes, who excluded propagation from the ideal, unitary love, Socrates fetches it back into love's domain: to love means to create and to give birth. But in order to recast the relation between love and birth in an utterly new way, Plato has to bring in a woman: Diotima.

SOCRATES' / DIOTIMA'S SPEECH (199C–212C): PHILOSOPHY AS MASCULINE REPRODUCTION

When at last his turn to speak arrives, the first thing Socrates does is define love in a way that differs entirely from that of the previous speakers. Whereas the others dealt with Eros from the point of view of love's object, of the thing that is loved, Socrates approaches him as love's subject, as the agent that loves. For Socrates, this approach entails that Eros does not represent perfect goodness and beauty – that is, he is not a divinity in the way the other speakers have presented him, but rather a figure who himself desires perfect beauty for the reason that this is something he lacks. In other words, a precondition of love is the *lack* of something. To love someone or something therefore suggests not so much a condition of consummate joy, but rather the activity of striving for such a condition.

Having established the investigation within this new perspective, Socrates introduces the person whom he characterizes as his teacher in 'matters of love', namely the wise woman Diotima of Mantinea. The remainder of Socrates' eulogy to Eros is a report of a conversation he once held with Diotima. Many readers of Plato have been surprised that he should employ a woman to tell a group of intellectual men in the excessively patriarchal city of Athens the truth about their homosexual desires.[14] For it is precisely this that seems to be the core of Diotima's statement about love: she explains how 'loving boys correctly' (211b) can lead to the highest form of love, and it is this which we must take to be Plato's own philosophy.

There has been a great deal of speculation about Diotima's identity. Was she a real person? If she was, is Socrates referring to a conversation that actually took place? Or is she a Platonic fiction? There are good reasons to suppose such a woman really existed, and that she was respected for her wisdom, despite the fact that there is no other mention of her in surviving literature. The most convincing argument for her existence is that Plato was not in the habit of using fictional figures in his dialogues.

The conviction that there really was a woman called Diotima with her own theory about love has prompted some scholars – Luce Irigaray among them – to read a specifically feminine theory of love into the *Symposium*.[15] Although it is important to draw attention to the feminine aspect of Diotima's ideas about love, one should not forget that the *Symposium* is a work of literature, in which the various voices participate in a unified text composed by Plato. Even if Diotima can be said to speak from a feminine standpoint, this would still be a position allotted to her by a man who knows how to organize his literary means so as best to serve his philosophical aims. For example, in the dialogue *Parmenides*, Plato ascribes words to the person who bore that name, yet it would be rash to take these as representative of Parmenides' own philosophy. That dialogue contains various Parmenidean elements, but these are employed in a Platonic context to illuminate philosophical points that we know to be different from those of Parmenides himself. Not even Socrates, who was certainly authentic, appears in the dialogues 'as himself', but serves rather as a voice within Plato's complex discourse.

Even if we assume that Diotima really existed and had her own theories about love, we still face the question of why Plato chose to articulate the truth about love by means of a woman. In his essay 'Why was Diotima a Woman?'[16] David Halperin makes a valuable suggestion, which, despite its apparent obviousness, has received only scant consideration: Plato introduces into his dialogue a realm of female experience, in which pregnancy, labour and delivery are the focal elements, and a woman is far better placed than a man to describe this realm with conviction and authority. Even so, Plato makes no attempt to conceal the fact that this female voice does not speak on its own terms, but is used rather as an element in a masculine discourse. Indeed, he uses various devices to emphasize that Diotima has no place at a gathering of male homo-eroticists. For one thing, she does not appear in person among the current company, but is simply discussed and quoted by Socrates. For another, Socrates introduces her as 'wise' (*sophē*; 201d), and this implies that she is aloof to the realm of philosophy: those who are wise already *have* wisdom and therefore do not yearn for it. Philosophy means 'love of wisdom', or, desire for the wisdom one does not personally possess. This idea is indeed one of the principal points in Diotima's discussion of love. And being at a remove from philosophy, she also stands outside the erotic game being played by the participants at the symposium. Thus Plato does not attempt to include Diotima among the circle of amorous, philosophical men, but seeks rather to make a point in terms of her exclusion from the company. She is excluded on account of her sex, which is nonetheless the factor that allows Plato to use her as a means of introducing certain feminine elements into his love discourse.

Like the other speakers, Socrates and Diotima do not distinguish clearly between *eros* as a concept and the personified Eros. Even so, Socrates' account of his conversation with Diotima begins with a discussion of the nature of Eros, and we would be justified in regarding this also as a conceptual clarification of *eros* – that is, love, or desire – as a phenomenon. Diotima explains that Eros' lack of beauty, goodness and wisdom does not imply an absence of these qualities in any absolute sense, but rather that Eros stands between all and nothing. Eros is neither absolutely beautiful nor absolutely ugly, neither absolutely good nor absolutely bad, neither perfectly wise nor perfectly ignorant; rather, he is situated between these various extremes. As it happens, humans also occupy this kind of intermediate position, but by placing Eros half way between the mortal and the immortal, Diotima also situates him in a space between the gods and human beings. Diotima refers to Eros as a *daimon*, and characterizes him in terms of his desire for beauty, goodness, wisdom and immortality.

She illustrates and elaborates this conceptual gloss by means of a story about Eros' birth (203b–e); knowledge of how something or someone came to be is also knowledge about the nature of that thing or person. This is a belief that the vast majority of Greek poets and thinkers, from Homer and Hesiod onwards, seem to share, and one that underlies much of the philosophical speculation about ontological questions, from Thales to Aristotle. It is always a problem, for example, to find an adequate translation for crucial philosophical terms such as *archē*, which connotes both 'origin' and 'principle', but can also be translated as 'essence'. Birth stories therefore have a peculiar status, and we should be careful not to dismiss the tale of Eros' birth as 'merely a myth' with no particular relevance for the dialogue's philosophical analysis. I shall review the myth in brief.

Eros was conceived on the same day as the goddess of love came into the world, during a festival that the gods happened to be holding. Among the guests was Poros, whose name can be translated as 'passage', or 'resource'. As his name suggests, he was a highly resourceful figure, who demonstrated not least an abundance of wisdom and understanding, which he had inherited from his mother, Metis. Having imbibed quantities of nectar, Poros became intoxicated and fell asleep in Zeus' garden. Meanwhile, an uninvited guest, Penia, had turned up at the party, and her name, like that of Poros, also suggests her nature. *Penia* means 'poverty', 'need' or 'want' (cf. 'penury'). Lacking the qualities with which Poros was so richly endowed, she was tempted to lie beside him and allowed him to impregnate her. The result of this union was Eros, who inherited a double, antagonistic nature, corresponding to the contradictory aspects of his double origin.

As a power of desire, Eros' condition is determined by an incompleteness, or lack, which he has inherited from his mother Penia (he is 'always partaking of his mother's poverty', 203d). The goal of Eros' striving is represented by the father, who possesses not merely beauty and intelligence, but also immortality. This myth explains the nature of Eros in terms of the opposition between feminine insufficiency and masculine completeness: 'His father is full of wisdom and resource, while his mother is devoid of either' (204b). Unexpectedly, however, erotic desire does not take the form of a mutual attraction between the feminine and the masculine. Desire is directed exclusively at the masculine perfection represented by the father; as for the feminine, Eros seeks rather to abolish his feminine aspect. In other words, he struggles to distance himself from the motherly side of his origins, and to come closer to the fatherly. It is interesting to note that Plato's explanation of erotic desire is at this point almost the inverse of Freud's.

In the myth of the birth of Eros, sexual difference is presented as a precondition for erotic desire, while at the same time the goal of that desire is the elimination of that very difference. This goal can be characterized as a conscious utopia: a purely masculine reality. Evidently, this implies a paradox: Eros – insofar as he represents the ideal of the Platonic philosophy – seeks to eliminate himself.

In insisting that Eros is the active lover and not the perfected object of love (see especially 204c), it might seem that Diotima is echoing the traditional dichotomy between the active lover (*erastēs*) and the passive lover (*erōmenos*). Yet she has in fact made a fundamental change. Her identification of the active, erotic desire with the masculine aspect of Eros' origins dissolves the traditional and – for the Greeks – fundamental polarity between the masculine and the feminine; she determines both the active and the passive positions in the erotic relationship as masculine. In this context, the masculine-feminine opposition is therefore not analogous to the active-passive distinction. The feminine appears rather as the negation of the perfect, passive object of love, yet without coming any closer to being the active lover.

Having related the story of Eros' birth, Diotima undertakes a detailed, Socratic-style analysis of the concept of love and its mode of activity (204d–209e), an analysis which might at first glance seem to contradict my foregoing interpretation of the myth. Whereas my reading of the myth presents Eros as desiring by nature to identify himself with what is purely masculine, and to negate the feminine, that is, he desires to eliminate sexual difference, Diotima's Socratic analysis of *eros* as a concept reintroduces sexual love, concentrating in particular on its feminine aspect. She proposes that what is unique to the activity of *eros* is birth. To love means 'to bring forth upon the beautiful, both in body and in soul' (206b). But how can this difference be reconciled? In my opinion, the solution lies in the peculiar meaning Diotima attaches to the notion of birth. One thing that forces us to realize that Diotima's explanation of *eros* entails a theory of love quite at odds with the conventional ideas of the time is Socrates' astonished reaction: 'It would take divination to figure out what you mean. I can't' (206b).

'We are all of us prolific,' Diotima explains, 'in body and soul, and when we reach a certain age our nature urges us to procreation' (206c). She does not use birth as an empty metaphor, but invests her entire female experience in her effort to clear up Socrates' confusion: 'the violent birth pangs' (206e) force the pregnant person towards the beautiful, since only beauty can bring his travail to an end. This use of 'his' rather than 'her' is deliberate, since it seems clear that 'all people' in this context means 'all lovers', in other words, the active and traditionally masculine agents in erotic relationships. Even if it is a woman speaking here, and although she is describing love in terms of a wholly feminine image, there is nothing to suggest that Diotima sees her subject as a woman. She has made passing mention of the relationship between man and woman, yet the text makes it perfectly clear that her real theme is the pederastic relationship.[17]

Diotima evidently imagines the active lover as pregnant, even though he has not been fertilized, and accordingly, it is the meeting between the lover and his beloved that promptly results in birth. Diotima illustrates this by alluding to the sexual encounter between the two sexes: 'The union of a man and a woman is a birth' (206c). This seems to be meant quite literally: in making love, the man gives birth to an embryo when he impregnates the woman with his seed. In due course, the woman repeats the man's birth by bearing forth a fully formed child.[18] Thus, in addition to his own procreative function, the man has also assimilated that of the woman.[19] The man gives birth to *his* child, as an extension of himself.

Clearly, the model here is non-sexual, vegetative propagation. The notion of the man sowing his seed in the woman, who is comparable with the earth, has a long tradition in Greek thought, and is articulated among others by Aeschylus,[20] although Plato takes the idea further. Some of the words Diotima uses to characterize the lover and his agency – for instance, 'to bear' (*kyein*), and 'labour' (*ōdis*) – are used elsewhere in the literature exclusively of women.[21] In Diotima's analysis of *eros*, the function – albeit a limited one – traditionally assigned to the woman is made over in its entirety to the man. Sexual difference is eliminated, just as it was in Diotima's mythical account of the nature of Eros.

Love is the desire to reproduce oneself. This can be understood in fairly general terms: love is the desire to create, it is creativity itself, and it was in order to convey this point that Plato required a woman. This would be a sympathetic reading of the love theory in the *Symposium*, but I believe it obscures what is most crucial. The Platonic lover is not interested in procreation in general, but rather on reproducing *himself*, on giving birth to *his child*. This aspect only becomes clear when Diotima introduces immortality as the proper goal of love: 'It follows from our argument that love must desire immortality' (207a). Why is this?

Diotima explains the human longing for immortality as a natural instinct, and it is worth noting how she justifies her point:

... the mortal does all it can to put on immortality. And how can it do that except by breeding (genesis), and thus ensuring that there will always be a younger generation to take the place of the old? (207d)

Diotima's examination of the meaning of this claim is thorough and seems to play quite deliberately on the ambiguity of the Greek word *genesis*. The word can mean 'becoming' as opposed to pure 'being'. Whereas the divine manifests eternal existence for the reason that it never changes, meaning that it is in a state of eternal, unchanging existence, humans can only prolong their existence by means of constant growth and becoming. In this way, humans can attain a touch of immortality – albeit it in a very limited form. For example, the cells of the body's hair and skin are constantly perishing, yet the body continues to exist since those dying cells are replaced by new ones. This is the only way that 'mortal nature' can maintain its existence from moment to moment and from day to day. In other words, the identity of the individual is preserved by means of a constant process of becoming (*genesis*).

But *genesis* can also mean 'birth'. Assuming this sense, the quoted sentences no longer deal with the individual body's regeneration in the course of life, but rather with the possibility for the individual to continue living after death in the form of a new individual. If one's child can be regarded as a continuation – or 'renewal' – of oneself in a similar way to the constant growth and renewal of the body, then birth will represent a means of getting closer to immortality. In claiming that

This is how every mortal creature perpetuates itself. It cannot, like the divine, be still the same throughout eternity; it can only leave behind new life to fill the vacancy that is left in its species by obsolescence (208a–b)

it would seem that Diotima has the birth of an individual in mind, but due to the ambiguity of the word *genesis*, birth also comes across as a phenomenon comparable to the constant renewal of the body. Thus it is not female birth – that is, the birth that results from the sexual meeting of a man and woman – that serves as a model for love, but rather an asexual birth, a kind of vegetative cloning. The progeny that Diotima describes consists not of new individuals, such as would be produced by sexual propagation. The child is viewed rather as the extension of a previous existence, of the 'source', which in this case means the father, insofar as the topic here is effectively childbearing men. In short, Diotima has taken vegetative propagation as her model and applied it to the human situation. We can only make sense of the claim that 'this ... is how the body and all else that is temporal partakes of the eternal;

there is no other way'[22] (208b) by imagining birth by analogy to the growth of the hair, or as a kind of botanical gemmation.

In this way, Plato has used a woman to introduce the female phenomenon of birth, regarded here as the peculiar 'activity' (ergon; 206b) of love, before furtively going on to identify birth with bodily renewal and vegetative propagation. The female aspect is thereby discarded along the way. Let us summarize Diotima's analysis of eros thus far. By means of the tale of Eros' birth, erotic desire is defined as a yearning for what is purely masculine, that is to say, the yearning to eliminate sexual difference. This point is stressed in the subsequent analysis of eros, in which female parturition is metaphorically applied to the man: the man can only achieve immortality by giving birth to children of his own, who will secure his continued existence in much the same way as new hair and new flesh; new habits and new opinions ensure his survival from one day to the next.

In articulating his ideas about love, Plato has no use for a woman, although he does need an old woman, one who is herself beyond the childbearing age; Plato's notion of love excludes sexual propagation. Or to put it another way, the erotic longing for immortality presupposes a desire for a form of vegetative, non-sexual reproduction. In using the word 'immortal', Diotima is thinking first and foremost of the human perspective; 'immortal' refers to the imperfect means by which humans maintain themselves from day to day and from generation to generation. In effect she is talking of what we might call immortality within the bounds of time, and for Plato this presupposes constant renewal. 'Immortality' therefore implies something like 'continued existence and identity by means of constant and unceasing change'. But such immortality is not of a kind that could be deemed 'true' and 'proper' in the Platonic sense. Indeed, it is little more than a semblance of the immortality which itself stands outside time and is immune to all forms of change. But thus far, Diotima's analysis of eros has only moved on what we can call the level of the imperfect, and for this reason she herself dismisses this first account as a mere 'sophistical' (208c) introduction to the subject.

Ultimately, Socrates – through Diotima – is spokesman for a love that has 'true' immortality as its goal. Diotima's speech concludes with an initiation into what she calls love's 'highest mysteries' (210a), and here we find repeated once again the notion that immortality excludes sexual difference, even if it still entails reproduction. But since we are here on the highest level of love, where the immortality is of a very different nature – one beyond all possibility of change – we must also be dealing with a very different form of birth. Indeed, it is here we meet the notion of 'true' birth, which has to be understood as genuine philosophical activity. Here the philosopher is able 'to give birth, not to images of virtue ... but to true virtue' (212a). The highest form of love is thus the creative activity of the philosopher, since he gives birth to thoughts and thereby cultivates true virtue.

At this conclusive point in Diotima's speech, pederasty – and with it all forms of love between people – is left behind. It is no longer the sensuous young man who eases the philosopher's birth pangs by means of his beauty, but Beauty itself – the form of Beauty. Not surprisingly, the form of Beauty is described as something uniform and eternally like unto itself: it 'subsists of itself and by itself in an eternal oneness' (211b). The goal of love is therefore that which is eternally self-identical, that which knows and needs nothing other than itself. According to Diotima, love is consummated when philosophy glimpses truth, which from the Platonic perspective is the very foundation of all existence – including one's own. When the philosopher is described as glimpsing and thereupon being delivered of the truth – which is represented here as perfect Beauty – we have to picture him giving birth to true thoughts. Or put another way, the philosopher is thereby delivered of his 'true self'. In his encounter with Beauty itself, the philosopher gives birth to the oneness and the self-identity characteristic of the highest forms, and these he discovers within himself. The ideal of love that Diotima is made to advocate is something beyond all forms of interpersonal love; it is a love that cannot acknowledge and has no need of the Other, and which is unaware of differences – especially the differences of sex.

What the philosopher desires is therefore no longer the person who resembles him, but Likeness itself, which is how Diotima defines Beauty. In contrast to the love of her 'sophistical' introduction, that which belongs to the 'highest mysteries' is not characterized by a continuity between the goal and the route to the goal. The person who follows the path to its conclusion recognizes Beauty *all at once* (*exaiphnēs*; 210e), and this ideal Beauty is something very different from all the other manifestations of beauty that guided the lover-philosopher along the path towards this ultimate goal.[23] No sooner is the goal reached than the erotic desire that led him hither ceases. The goal itself knows no deficiency or imperfection, which were precisely the things that love strove to overcome. Here there are no differences of either a sexual nature or any other kind. The pairs of contraries that have been instrumental throughout the dialogue have now vanished. The philosopher is no longer subject to the contradiction between mastery and slavery, as was the lover in Pausanias' speech, but stands instead face to face with the liberating One. The person who pursues Diotima's journey of love to its conclusion

> *will see the beauty of knowledge and be looking not at beauty in a single example – as a servant would who favoured the beauty of a little boy or a man or a single custom (being a slave, of course, he's low and small-minded) –*

but the lover is turned to the great sea of beauty, and, gazing upon this, he gives birth to many graciously beautiful ideas and theories in unstinting love and wisdom. (210d)

*

My aim in describing the love discourse of the *Symposium* in these terms has been to show how the kind of metaphoric language that Plato uses in this text – images relating to sexuality and birth – facilitate a particular understanding of philosophy: philosophy as the highest form of reproduction – the reproduction of the One and of Likeness – with immortality as its objective and a radical homo-eroticism as its precondition. Nevertheless, contrary to what one might expect, the birth metaphors are not reserved exclusively for the love dialogues. They also occur in other dialogues where the explicit theme is something other than love. For example, the philosophical climax of the *Republic* – the allegory of the sun – speaks of 'the offspring of the good and most nearly made in its likeness' (506e), and here as well we find the same concept of philosophy as that conveyed in the *Symposium*. But not only here: I would suggest that the same concept underlies Plato's philosophy as a whole, and is possibly one of its principal motives. In the next chapter we will turn to a text which, while not explicitly discussing birth, makes use of the birth metaphor in an indirect way. We will see that this text also builds on a notion of thought as a kind of perfect reproduction – perfect in the sense that it leads to immortality. Let us turn now to the allegory of the cave, which, together with that of the sun, is commonly considered a key to the understanding of Plato's philosophy.

CHAPTER 6

Virginity and Masculine Reproduction:
Plato in a Woman's Looking-Glass
Irigaray's reading of the cave myth

PLATO'S PHILOSOPHY: PORTAL TO OUR MIMETIC CULTURE

In her principal philosophical work, *Speculum de l'autre femme* of 1974,[1] the French philosopher and psychoanalyst Luce Irigaray presents a highly original, detailed, exciting and above all provocative, interpretation of Plato's cave myth. Of all Plato's writings, the text in which he presents this myth is probably the one most frequently cited by teachers of philosophy as an introduction to his theory of forms. The fact that Irigaray's reading of this myth has received barely a nod of acknowledgement, either from Plato scholars, historians of philosophy, or teachers of the subject, is no doubt due, at least in part, to her unorthodox and unacademic style, which many readers of Plato are likely to find somewhat alienating. This unconventional style is, however, inseparable from her unconventional interpretation, and the latter is probably the main reason why her essay has consistently been ignored.

In order to take Irigaray's reading of the cave myth seriously, it is necessary not just to reevaluate the traditional and widely accepted interpretation of this particular text, but also to place the entire gamut of received opinions about Plato in question. According to her reading of the myth, Plato's ontology and epistemology are simply not gender neutral, as the vast majority of Plato scholars have taken them to be, but rather the consequence of highly specific views about the relation between the sexes, sexuality and reproduction. My study of the *Symposium* is largely inspired by the insights on which Irigaray bases her interpretation of the cave myth: Plato's philosophy implies an ideal of propagation that is independent of sexuality, and this ideal is in effect the very foundation of that philosophy.

But Irigaray goes a step further. For her Plato's philosophy is in turn the foundation not just of Western metaphysics, but of Western culture as a whole. She therefore regards the Platonic attitude towards sexual difference as the very core of our Western mindset. And it is because she finds these ideas about sexual difference to be so crucial to the cave myth that she accords this text such an important place in Western culture. Even if we feel disinclined to follow Irigaray in granting Plato such extraordinary status, there are still good reasons to classify the cave myth as one of the most important texts in our culture.

Irigaray's basic tenet is that the cave in Plato's myth is an image, or a metaphor for something else which the image itself in some sense *resembles*. One of her primary concerns is the way Plato uses the metaphor; the question is, what interests govern its use? Her wish to clarify the role played by metaphors and images in Plato's thinking implies an investigation into the role of metaphors in Western metaphysics in general. In her opinion, the way our language functions – namely in terms of metaphors – reflects a very particular view of the relation between the masculine and the feminine, and of the respective roles of the father and the mother in reproduction. Within a Platonic perspective, an image is a kind of offspring, a child of the model.

Irigaray undertakes a remarkably detailed study of the cave myth. The mere four to five pages of Plato's text inspire a discussion that fill more than 150 pages. The title of the relevant essay, 'Plato's *hystera*', is ingenious and indicative of the double-edge that Irigaray intends her text to have. *Hystera*, the Greek word for uterus, is both the key to Irigaray's exposition and an allusion to Freud's theories about female hysteria. As Toril Moi has shown in *Sexual/Textual Politics*, Irigaray regards hysteria as the woman's only means of getting her voice heard within what she calls the logic of the patriarchate: hysteria amounts to an imitation – a mime – of masculine discourse.[2] This is also the method Irigaray herself uses in discussing Western philosophers. Her mimetic text confronts them with a mirror that clearly distorts their conscious intentions, but which in the very process reveals new and unexpected aspects therein. Plato's text also becomes the subject of an ironic imitation, a kind of deformed reflection. In this way Irigaray demonstrates a kind of 'hysterical' relation to tradition. But what should we make of the fact that she also ascribes to Plato a *hystera*, something that is normally seen as unique to a woman?

What this means in straightforward terms is that Irigaray equates the cave from which the cave myth takes its name with the uterus. But her claim goes deeper: by means of this mimetic device, Plato is effectively exploiting the female body and its functions as a source of images and metaphors to explain knowledge. We could say that Irigaray's reading sees the Platonic philosopher as equipped with a metaphoric, male uterus by analogy to that of the female: the true organ of reproduction is not the female body but the one that propagates genuine knowledge, namely masculine thought. But Plato's mimetic – or 'hysterical' – exploitation of the woman's body is not just a mere artistic device; it reveals something about the Platonic method of seeking enlightenment, for this is itself mimetic in character. According to Plato, any phenomenon that we consciously perceive is an imitation of a form, which for its own part can be regarded as an imitation of the idea of the Good. Among the forms, that of the Good – the One – is the only thing that is not itself an imitation of anything else, since it is the model that all other things imitate.

The fact that – in addition to exposing these mimetic traits in the cave myth and indeed in Platonic philosophy in general – Irigaray herself uses a mimetic method, means that her own text becomes an integral element in the overall picture we are left with. Personally, I consider this picture highly challenging, since it reveals aspects of Plato's philosophy to which traditional approaches are blind.

In order to illustrate what Irigaray regards as the fundamental problem of Platonic philosophy, it can be useful to think of the following image: just as the eye is attracted by the source of light, namely the sun, that makes it possible for the eye to see, so our soul is attracted by the source of all knowledge, namely truth. But the sun is paradoxical in nature. It is not just a condition for the eye's ability to see, it also threatens to destroy the sense of sight. The result of staring directly into the sun will be blindness. By analogy, those who open their souls to the light of truth without preparation are also in danger of being blinded, or driven to distraction. How can we receive the blinding light and the consuming flame of wisdom without risking the conflagration of our souls in the process? For Irigaray, this question marks the beginning of philosophy as such. Plato is the first to pose the question and the first to attempt an answer. He therefore represents both the access point and the guide to all subsequent philosophy. Irigaray's analysis of Plato is a quest for the flame that has given life and meaning to our entire culture, including our language and our ways of thinking, since the times of Plato – the flame that has allowed certain phenomena to emerge into the light and others to remain hidden in shadow.

The title of Irigaray's book, *Speculum de l'autre femme*, suggests an answer to this fundamental question: how can we approach the supreme truth without being blinded? Just as the sun can only be observed indirectly, for example by reflecting it from a mirror, the supreme source of truth can only be looked at by means of images, similes, metaphors or analogies. But at the same time the title is ambiguous. For a *speculum* is a special kind of concave mirror used by doctors to examine cavities of the body, such as the female sexual organs. In other words, this mirror is used to illuminate and examine what is usually confined to darkness, also in a metaphorical sense, namely the female. But like any curved mirror, the image that this one reflects is not only inverted, but also distorted. Moreover, the mirror's source of light does not illuminate impartially. The illuminated object takes on the colour of the light, becomes caught up in it and held in its power. And neither is everything illuminated. Something remains in the shadows, and stays invisible.

Irigaray's title thus captures what she considers the essence of the metaphysics that Plato expounds in terms of light metaphors. Not only does she regard the mirror as an adequate instrument with which to view the sole source of light, she also shows that the insights of our philosophical tradition are gained by means of reflection, including knowledge of the tradition's other, such as the concealed feminine – the dark continent, as Freud called it. The sole source of light – reason, or *Logos* – encompasses also this other within its pool, although it inverts and distorts it. Within the Platonic tradition, light and reason – or the Good, the One – represent the masculine. The woman appears as the Other, as a distorted and inverted image in the light of the One. In this masculine light, the thing that characterizes woman is what she does not have. In other words, Irigaray regards Plato to be the source of that particular view of woman promulgated by people such as Freud: woman as deficiency. By returning to the cave myth, Irigaray hopes to gain greater insight into the very foundation of what she considers the characteristic form of knowledge in our masculine, phallic culture, namely reflection, or *mimēsis*.

My presentation of Irigaray's text is of course an interpretation, an attempt to uncover a meaning that seems to elude precisely the kind of interpretation I wish to impose upon it. In this respect I am distorting the text in the light of a simpler, more normalized language than the one Irigaray herself uses. Although her text does not provide direct support for every aspect of my interpretation, I would nevertheless claim that I succeed in finding words for some of her principal points, even if my presentation conflicts with her own attempt to undermine the traditional methods of philosophic argumentation.

PLATO'S CAVE MYTH: A SKETCH

The cave myth appears in Book VII of the *Republic* (514a–517a), and it is immediately followed by an interpretation. Socrates explains it as a picture of people's lives lived in deceit and ignorance, although it also contains the chance of an escape from this condition – from life in the cave, where we are captive to our sense impressions, to the condition where, by means of reason, we recognize the truth.

The presentation of the myth begins with Socrates asking his interlocutor,

Glaucon, to visualize what he describes. Socrates evidently considers it important that Glaucon uses his powers of imagination in this endeavour.

Picture men [said Socrates] dwelling in a sort of subterranean cavern with a long entrance open to the light on its entire width. Conceive them as having their legs and necks fettered from childhood, so that they remain in the same spot, able to look forward only, and prevented by the fetters from turning their heads. Picture further the light from a fire burning higher up and at a distance behind them, and between the fire and the prisoners and above them a road along which a low wall has been built, as the exhibitors of puppet shows have partitions before the men themselves, above which they show the puppets.

All that I see, he [Glaucon] said.

See also, then, men carrying past the wall implements of all kinds that rise above the wall, and human images and shapes of animals as well, wrought in stone and wood and every material, some of these bearers presumably speaking and others silent.

A strange image you speak of, he [Glaucon] said, and strange prisoners. (514a–515a)

The prisoners who sit facing the inner wall of the cave can of course see nothing of the puppet show going on behind their backs. All they get to see, and the only thing they have ever seen, are the shadows cast on the wall by models of people and animals as they pass in front of the fire; and all they hear – apart from their own voices – are echoes of the voices of the people carrying the figures that protrude above the wall. The prisoners, who can see neither themselves nor one another, take the shadows to be the things themselves, and the echoes for the voices of those things. In many ways, the meaning the prisoners impose on their impressions of these things is a construction of their own minds. It seems, for example, that there is no particular plan or logic behind the sequence in which the puppeteers carry the objects back and forth, nor any clear connection between their chatter and those objects ('some of these bearers presumably speaking and others silent'; *Republic* 514b). For the prisoners, reality – in the form of the shadow play on the wall of the cave – is therefore a complete illusion. And this is precisely the point the picture is intended to convey.

Outside the cave shines the light of day, and it is there that the things exist of which the prisoners merely see *shadows of imitations*, namely, the real animals and people. Outside, the light comes not from some feeble bonfire, but from the sun itself. This makes things visible and allows us to recognize them for what they really are. Moreover, the sun provides the conditions for the life of all animate nature in the form of light and warmth. In other words,

Plato presents the sun as the ultimate source of both true knowledge and all existence.

For the prisoners in the cave to become aware of their situation, they must free themselves from their chains, turn around, and acknowledge that what they have been seeing is nothing more than shadows and imitations of real things, and that the ultimate source and origin of all things is the sun. One of the prisoners is freed from his chains and forced out into the daylight, so that, after a period of painful acclimatization, he is able to see the sun. This aspect of the allegory is an image of the one and only source of truth, the form of the Good. Thus the cave myth presents a picture of the individual's progress (*paideia*) from ignorance to knowledge.

If we attempted to draw the cave according to Plato's account of it, we could probably view the resultant picture as reminiscent of a uterus, or alternatively, an inverted penis. I find it surprising that many scholars merely shake their heads at this interpretation, especially when it is acknowledged that birth metaphors are of crucial importance in Plato's works, and when we also realize that the Greeks regarded the woman's sexual organs as an 'outside in' of the man's, a point persuasively argued by Thomas Laqueur in his book *Making Sex*.[3] It is therefore refreshing to read what Margaret Whitford says in her own book about Irigaray's philosophy: 'It is obvious, even banal, that the cavern presents a womb; this in not a reflex, stereotypical Freudian reading – in the Platonic dialogues themselves Socrates is described as a midwife, his method as a maieutic method, and his role to assist the birth into knowledge of the truth.'[4] In other words, Plato's own extensive use of birth metaphors invites us to interpret the cave as a womb. When, in his account of the cave myth, Socrates describes the liberation of one of the prisoners, it does not need much fantasy to interpret his words as the description of a painful birth, in which the child is retrieved by means of forceps. The prisoner, who is hauled 'by force up the ascent which is rough and steep', will 'find it painful to be so haled along, and [will] chafe at it' (*Republic* 515e–516a).

From other dialogues – for example, *Phaedo* – we know that Plato operated with two concepts of birth: the physical birth, whereby the soul is unified with a body, and the spiritual, which signifies the soul's emancipation from physical bonds. It is just such a spiritual birth that is described in the cave myth. On emerging into the daylight, the unfettered prisoner is liberated from (corporeal) sense experience and becomes capable of insight on the level of reason alone. We will see that Plato's characterization in *Phaedo* of the death of the body as the birth of the soul into another reality adds further support to Irigaray's reading of the cave myth.

Our corporeal existence is described in *Phaedo* as a prison, from which we must attempt to free ourselves in the course of our lives. One way to achieve this liberation is by means of what we call death, which thus amounts to a kind of birth. In the cave myth it is in effect a prison from which the prisoner is released. Socrates describes the cave as a prison in a literal sense and interprets it further as a place where sensory experience is held captive. If we read the cave myth in the light of the central theme of *Phaedo*, it will seem not unreasonable to interpret the cave as a picture of man's dwelling place prior to his birth into another and truer reality. Moreover, when we consider that, for the Greeks, the earth was a birth-giving goddess (*Gaia*), then it does not seem too far-fetched to regard the 'subterranean' (*katageios*; 514a) cave of Plato's myth as a uterus. In Irigaray's reading, prison, body, death and birth are just some of the metaphors that are interwoven with a complexity similar to that of *Phaedo*.

In the cave myth we find a number of images and analogies that depend for their effect on inversion or mirror-like reversal. Whereas the cave is an image that stands for the (illusory) reality that we perceive through our senses, the space outside the cave is analogous to the (true) reality that we are capable of perceiving by means of reason. This means that the dark interior of the cave represents the reality that appears to us like that which Socrates describes as lying *outside* the cave: the world of our everyday sensory experience, where things – such as trees, animals and people – are visible to us thanks to the light of day. In contrast to the dark cave that represents daylight and the visible world, the daylight of the myth stands for something that lies beyond the realm of quotidian experience, namely a reality that we get to know by means of thought, a world that is in itself not visible. Thus the meaning of both the darkness inside and of the daylight outside the cave is the negation of these images; darkness stands for light, and light for what is not visible. These inversions are reminiscent of one that figures in *Phaedo*: death as a picture of the true birth. We shall see how Irigaray herself makes use of such inversions in her interpretation of the cave myth.

PLATO'S TEXT MIRRORED BY IRIGARAY: A GAME OF INVERSIONS, DISTORTIONS AND MYSTIFICATIONS[5]

Irigaray more or less agrees with traditional interpretations insofar as she regards the cave myth as a metaphor for Plato's discourse of the One. All things derive from a single source – the One – and everything that exists is in some sense an expression of the Same. All things that exist are more or less adequate imitations of one and the same model, the form of the Good. For there to be an Other, something that remained untouched by the power of the ultimate source of light, it would have to be something purely negative, something non-existent, undefinable, meaningless, something that lay in absolute darkness. Although Plato's picture does not encompass anything so purely negative, the innermost wall of the cave itself comes close to such a condition. This is the point at the furthest remove from the sun. Here the light comes not from the rays of the sun but from its pale imitation, the fire. From the sun's point of view, the cave wall is what lies at the innermost, or deepest extreme. One meaning of the Greek word *hystera* is 'further back', or 'behind', a sense that might explain how it could become the term for uterus.

Irigaray picks up on this word, which Plato uses only once in the course of the cave myth, to illustrate the kind of distortions, inversions and mystifications that Plato employs in his text. She points out that Plato's image of the cave is constructed around various axes of symmetry, such as up-down, in front-behind, before-after, outer-inner, light-dark. All these are inverted in the course of the brief narrative. The orientation of these axes is always linear – which for Irigaray means phallic (*Speculum*, p. 244f.[6]). Plato uses the word *hystera* (*Republic* 516d) as a temporal adverb in the sense of 'later', or 'afterwards', from which it has obtained a normative meaning, namely, that which is derivative, that which is of lesser value since it is contrary to the original. The connection between the temporal and normative senses of the word becomes particularly clear in the context of Plato's thought. This kind of linguistic ambivalence also attaches to the word that expresses the contrary of *hystera*, namely *protera*, which can be translated as 'earlier', or 'former'; that which is earlier in time is also that which is ontologically and ethically of greatest value. For Plato, that which can most truthfully be said to exist, the True and the Good, is also what 'precedes', or goes before all else, that is, that which is the source of all other things, which themselves are consequently mere derivations and hence manifestations of a secondary type of existence. And like *hystera*, *protera* also has a spatial meaning, which is 'in front'. However, the spatial meanings of *hystera* and *protera* can be dissociated from the temporal and normative senses of the words, and Irigaray maintains that it is precisely this dissociative potential that Plato exploits in using these and similar words in his visual analogy.

In describing the cave at the beginning of the myth, Socrates emphasizes not so much the fact that the wall of the cave lies at the innermost extremity, but rather that the prisoners are placed with this wall directly *in front of* them, whereas the fire, daylight and the sun are all *behind* their backs and therefore out of sight. The words used to signify 'in front of' and 'behind' (*prosthen* and *opisthen*; *Republic* 514b) also have a temporal and normative sense, which may be said to correspond to the prisoners' grasp of reality. For them, what happens on the wall of the cave is reality itself, and of course it takes ontological priority over that which remains hidden behind them. Later we are also told that the shadow reality is of considerable importance to them (*Republic* 516c–d). But for anyone who has seen the genuine truth, things look very different indeed. The liberated prisoner who is shown genuine reality returns to the cave in the knowledge that what passes in front of him across the wall of the cave are no more than pale and ill-defined imitations of what can be seen outside, behind (*hystera*) him.

Although these reflections are only implicit in Irigaray's work, they under-lie her use of the confusing expression *hystera protera*; Irigaray introduces this term during the first few pages of her chapter on the cave myth, and uses it from time to time to spice up the ensuing argument. At face value the term seems to be self-contradictory ('later earlier', or 'behind in front'), but by using *hystera* in a merely spatial and *protera* in a temporal and normative sense, she contrives an expression for that which is located behind (*hystera*) but which in terms of time and status nevertheless takes priority over (*protera*) what is spatially in front. Irigaray uses the expression *hystera protera* to characterize what lies outside the cave, in particular, the sun. On the one hand, the sun is located behind the prisoners, meaning in effect behind *us*, since we all live in the world of sensory experience, while on the other, it is both of higher value in itself than our various mundane concerns, and also the source and prime cause of those preoccupations.

But on looking more closely at the expression *hystera protera*, we discover persuasive reasons to regard it as a fitting epithet for the uterus, such as we commonly conceive of it. The uterus (Greek: *hystera*) is that which lies deepest within the female body, yet it is at the same time the place where all human life begins, a place known to each and every one of us as *prior to* (*protera*) the commencement of life in the light of day. *Hystera protera* can therefore signify both the form of the Good (when taken in a Platonic sense) and the physical, female uterus (taken in an everyday sense). If we accept Irigaray's interpretation of the cave as a uterus, then Plato's representation of it flatly contradicts the sense that we associate with that organ in everyday experience: the innermost cave wall of the uterus is what the prisoners have in front of (*protera*) their eyes, and the things that play across this surface are derivations – reproductions – at several removes from their true origin, that is, they are posterior to (*hystera*) the forms from which they derive. In other words, if we turn the whole thing around and give *hystera* a temporal and normative meaning ('later', 'afterwards') and *protera* a spatial sense ('in front of'), then the uterus becomes a *hystera protera* also in the Platonic sense. Plato's image of the cave is therefore an inversion in at least two different ways. It constitutes both an inverted picture of the uterus as the source of life, and an inverted projection of the form of the Good.

As we begin to delve deeper into Irigaray's analysis, we should bear this basic insight in mind: by means of apparently innocuous metaphors, Plato turns a great many ideas upside-down, inside-out and back-to-front, in ways that can become more than a little confusing as we struggle to orientate ourselves in the landscape of his cave. Although Irigaray sometimes seems intent on maintaining a certain level of confusion, still I would claim that, by means of these inverted and doubly inverted images and concepts, she nevertheless discovers new and fruitful dimensions in Plato's thought.

THE UTERUS SEEN THROUGH A DISTORTING AND INVERTING MASCULINE MIRROR: A CAVE OF DEATH

Such as it emerges from Irigaray's analysis of Plato's cave myth, the uterus seems condemned from the very start to be an inferior site for reproduction, and this suggests that the genuine phenomenon of birth takes place elsewhere – such as out in the daylight. The cave wall is cold, dark and dead. It plays a totally passive role in Plato's allegory: as a background, a mere screen for the shadow images.

Irigaray remarks that, if the world outside the cave is the realm of light, then the cave itself is the realm of darkness. To the extent that the latter resembles the former, it does so in an inverted sense. Inside the cave, the light that gives meaning to the world outside is significant in terms of its own negation, in other words, as shadows. For this reason it would be quite mistaken to suppose we are dealing here with a cave of life. On the contrary, the uterus is represented as a cave of death (*Speculum*, p. 355). The shadows in this realm are born of lifeless imitations (the figures that are transported back and forth above the partition) of living creatures. The shadows cast on the cave wall put us in mind of Hades, the abode of dead souls, which are often represented in Greek mythology as lifeless shadows, or 'shades'. Plato himself suggests such a reading (*Republic* 516d).

The world outside the cave is pervaded by *Logos*, the highest form of reason, symbolized by the sun, and it is this that renders it perfect and meaningful. By contrast, the shadows on the cave wall offer nothing more than the suggestion of a meaningless puppet show being played out behind the prisoners' backs. This show is a thoroughly arbitrary spectacle resembling nothing whatsoever and is thus a reproduction without a model.

This absence of a model is an anomaly in Plato's otherwise so careful picture. We might regard it as a Freudian slip. Irigaray points out that, no sooner has Plato introduced the puppet theatre than he seems to forget it. Having freed the prisoner from his shackles and led him out of the cave, the 'teacher', or Platonic philosopher, does not demonstrate the workings of the figures that are the immediate source of the shadows on the cave wall: 'None of the scenographic, cinematographic apparatus is "unveiled" to him. Not the tricks of the director, not the architectonic of the cave, not the cunning of the magicians, not the mechanism of projections, not even the principle of the moving pictures, to say nothing of the principle of the echo' (*Speculum*, p. 271). In other words, the peculiar nature of the relationship between the shadows and the puppets remains obscure for the liberated prisoner. It is also noteworthy that, although Socrates comments systematically upon the other elements in his own interpretation of the cave myth (*Republic* 517b–518b), he does not say a word about the puppet theatre.[7] Irigaray herself characterizes the cave as an artificial and theatrical pregnancy: the cave wall is made pregnant by meaningless sound and light effects, and the progeny – the shadows – are no better than one would expect of such parents.

In the cave myth, the form of the Good serves as the unifying force of the cosmos, in other words, as that which creates a meaningful connection between things, which provides a degree of order and sense, and which hinders the world from falling apart and from ending in a state of chaos. However, the light from the form of the Good – the life- and sense-giving daylight – does not penetrate into the depths of the cave. It is only an artificial simulacrum of this light that gives the cave its quasi-unity, making it into a quasi-world with a quasi-sense. The cave wall propagates an illusion that cannot be discovered as such; the cave wall does not in fact reproduce anything. It merely feigns, or mimes, reproduction (*Speculum*, p. 255). Genuine reproduction takes place elsewhere.

Although the sunlight does not penetrate as far as the cave wall, Socrates nevertheless interprets the shadows that inhabit that space as owing their existence, ultimately, to that supreme source of light. But when one scrutinizes the myth as thoroughly as Irigaray does, one discovers that there is in fact no direct causal relation between the shadows on the wall and the sun. And since the shadow-play and the echoes of the puppeteers' voices are essentially arbitrary and meaningless, there are no clear criteria for how the prisoners should interpret what they see and hear; they are free to find their own meaning in the show. In other words, what arises in the cave is a man-made reality that has no precedent either in nature or in the realm of forms (cf. *Speculum*, p. 287). It is therefore difficult to see how the reality within the cave can be compared to that of the world outside, since the two are in certain respects quite independent. What this implies is that Plato's analogies and inversions are in fact faulty, although Plato himself fails to see any irony in the situation. But having escaped the attention of Platonic reason, this unintended irony offers a starting point for a non-Platonic reading of the cave myth.

From a Platonic point of view, however, the inner wall of the cave seems to constitute a direct negation of clear reason. The wall is also, according to Irigaray's interpretation, an image of the feminine in its purest possible form; it represents, in effect, female matter. The sole purpose of the wall in Plato's myth is – as with the female – *reproduction*, although the way it performs this job leaves much to be desired. The wall reproduces living creatures as lifeless, and things that have clear, conspicuous and recognizable features as murky, undefined silhouettes. Irigaray does not say so explicitly, but the point she seems to be making is that, due to its material properties, the wall is an unsuitable medium for the reproduction of pictures: a surface of rough stone will absorb most of the light that falls on it, rather than reflect it as a mirror image. What this means for Irigaray is that the cave wall is insufficiently virginal, or alternatively: it is not sufficiently frigid (*Speculum*, p. 302). It does not repulse and transmit the masculine rays of light that are thrown at it, but rather receives and absorbs them, so that no more than shadows remain. The light needs something more virginal than a cave wall for adequate reproduction to occur; it needs something smooth and impermeable, such as the shining surface of a mirror.[8]

VIRGINITY AS A MODEL FOR IDEAL REPRODUCTION

It is here, I believe, that we find some of the most original, exciting and valuable aspects of Irigaray's reading of Plato. What her analysis reveals is that Plato's light metaphors serve to justify an attitude that sees *virginity* as the ideal condition for reproduction and propagation. In this context 'virginity' refers to that which is impervious and permits no penetration (*Speculum*, p. 345). Insofar as the virgin gives birth at all, she does so not to her own offspring, but to that of the father; she produces his duplicate. The virgin does not contribute any features to her progeny, or leave her own mark on it. She throws back the best possible replica of the original, namely, of the father, of the One and of the Good. Irigaray's point is that the monist metaphysics of the cave myth also implies a notion of asexual, masculine – or 'virginal' – reproduction.

Of the five senses, sight enjoyed an elevated status not just in the work of Plato, but among a number Greek thinkers. In both the myth of the sun and the cave myth, Plato employs the analogy between the eye, or the sense of sight, on the one hand, and the soul, or reason, on the other. Just as the eye needs light in order to see, so the soul can only think where the light of reason shines, and the source of the latter illumination is the form of the Good. Irigaray herself makes use of these metaphors of sight and light in her own text. She asks her readers to visualize the cave not just as an inverted phallus, but also as an inverted eye; it is an analogy that functions on several levels, for among other things, it implies an eye that cannot see. The cave is like a dead, petrified eye, whose retina cannot conceive images but only shadows. Once again, we find ourselves in the cave of death. Of course, it is not just the analogy between the cave and the eye that Irigaray emphasizes, but also – and above all – that between the eye and the womb, that is, between sight and birth. Sight is capable of producing pictures, and for Irigaray this means it functions metaphorically. The pictures on the retina are more or less adequate copies ('offspring') of the things that the eye looks at and which therefore provide the model for the picture (cf. *Speculum*, p. 254f.).

Whereas the prisoners inside the cave are in a metaphorical sense blind, since all they see is illusions, the liberated prisoner who emerges into daylight is fully able to see, albeit after some painful acclimatization. He sees things as they really are, and for Plato this means he is able to see the forms. In other words, he can think rationally. The seeing eye can be regarded as a new image of the female, as that which gives birth and is creative. But like the cave and the petrified eye, also the seeing eye constitutes an analogy to the female which is in itself inverted, even if the inversion is in this case rather different. Whereas the cave is portrayed as a site of death, that is, as a negation of the cave where life has its origins, as a negation of the female principle of birth, the picture of the seeing eye can be read as a masculinization of the feminine, or alternatively, as a masculine subjection of the feminine. Outside in the light of day, the absorbent, female material, that is, that which is capable of being fertilized, is abandoned in favour of pure reason, which allows pure, virginal reproduction. Thus the seeing eye is not just far more fertile but also more virginal than the cave wall.

The notion of the virginal as something masculine is a fairly familiar feature of the Greek world view. Since a woman's female aspects are associated with her sexuality, the absence of her sexuality will in a sense entail the absence of femininity. And for Irigaray it is just such a pattern of thought that we find in the cave myth: the more virginal the activity of perception / reproduction, the more masculine it is. As the myth progresses steadily up towards the daylight, the female aspect becomes increasingly absorbed in the masculine, a process that gradually deprives the feminine of its physical embodiment. This requires further explanation.

One aspect of Irigaray's interpretation that is likely to be fairly uncontroversial is her claim that Plato envisaged thought to be an activity that produces pictures and metaphors. To think is therefore to create imitations of forms that are as similar to the original as possible. Perception also gives rise to pictures, but at a lower level. For Plato, reproduction and cognition are two aspects of the same thing, and we should therefore expect there to be some form of continuity between sense and thought. And indeed, it is this continuity that we find expressed in the gradual ascent from the dark interior of the cave to the daylight outside. As already mentioned, although the meaningless speculations of the prisoners inside the cave can be equated with physical, female parturition, Plato's text also implies an alternative picture of the feminine as something cleansed of all physicality. In this case, 'the feminine' carries a very limited and rather paradoxical meaning. It signifies the woman's reproductive function, that is, her ability to serve as a reflective background for masculine seed in one form or another. The paradox is that the perfection of 'the feminine' depends on the extent to which it repels light in a virginal way. By the time we emerge into the clear daylight of rationality, the feminine, light-absorbent material has been left far behind, and this explains why more truthful progeny can be born in the daylight than in the cave. The world outside is governed exclusively by masculine reason. The mirror-like surface of the spiritual, masculine eye throws back almost perfect reflections of the forms.

The ultimate aim of Plato's philosophy is to create the truest possible – meaning the most masculine and virginal – images of the form of the Good, or of the Father, as Irigaray calls it. A reflective female background is a necessity also on this spiritual, masculine level, otherwise there would exist only one thing, namely the form of the Good, or the One itself. Even so, thinking in terms of metaphors entails that the Other, in the sense of the Not-One, meaning all things other than the One, is controlled within the economy of the One. Or to put it another way: for Irigaray metaphorical thinking presupposes that the Father (the model) occupies a seemingly all-powerful position, while the mother remains seemingly superfluous. But the father's omnipotence and the mother's effacement are no more than appearance; the mother is there and must be there, even if invisible. The function of the female is always to be a passive, reflective surface for the father, for without this surface the latter would remain totally unreflected (cf. *Speculum*, pp. 301 and 306f.).

Irigaray characterizes the meeting between the philosopher's soul and the One (the Father) as a relationship that is both homoerotic and incestuous (*Speculum*, p. 344). It requires little ingenuity to demonstrate that Plato's rational soul is essentially masculine in character. This is a theme I have discussed elsewhere and which need not detain us here. I shall only mention the reference Julia Kristeva makes in her *Histoires d'amour* to Plato's *Phaedrus*, where Socrates describes how the soul in love – that is, the philosopher's soul – grows warm, swells up, and sprouts great wings; in due course it raises itself in its desire to fly towards its beautiful lover, and together with him towards Beauty itself (*Phaedrus* 251). The phallic connotation is clear, and Kristeva laconically remarks that, when we consider Plato's description of the soul's erection, it is not so difficult to understand why the Church Fathers hesitated in attributing souls to women.[9]

FROM THE PRISON OF ILLUSIONS TO THE PRISON OF TRUTH

Irigaray's analysis draws particular attention to the aspect of coercion to be found in the cave myth. When a prisoner turns about and ascends from the cave into daylight, he does so only because he is forced. The reorientation – or education – is forcefully brought about by someone who has experienced more than the prisoners. The emancipation and release – delivery and birth – from the darkness of the cave depends on the master's authoritarian violence. The liberated prisoner is shown how all the things that he formerly considered true were nothing more than illusions. Initially he refuses to acknowledge the painful, dazzling light; he is thoroughly confused and would rather return to his former companions, to the place where reality was something that *he* had created in cooperation with his fellow captives. Nonetheless, Plato's prisoner does not require much persuasion. In Irigaray's formulation, he soon becomes ensnared by something other than the chains of illusion; in due course it is the chains of rationality that constrain him. He no longer wants to live under the intoxication of magic, Irigaray writes, but rather under the intoxication of authority.

Inside the cave the prisoners were free to talk among themselves, and by means of their conversation they developed ideas about the shadows and how they were related. Outside the cave the prisoner is obliged to accept the master's claim that reason functions hierarchically and metaphorically, in other words, he has to take the master's word for it that the analogies are valid, and that things out in the daylight are truer and more authentic than the shadows inside the cave. Plato's text emphasizes that a master and his authority are essential for anyone who wishes to discover rational truth. This can be read as a statement about the Platonic dialogues themselves: since they are composed by a master, they are ultimately monological in form. If we peruse the cave myth in search of dialogue, the only place we will find it is down inside the cave, among the prisoners, and not outside.

Whereas Plato would say that force is needed to liberate someone from deceit to truth, Irigaray claims that this Platonic coercion merely creates a new type of prisoner, one in thrall to rationality (*Speculum*, p. 268ff.). The sun and the form of the Good govern the philosopher's field of vision in a way that is just as brutal as the fetters and braces that kept the prisoner staring straight ahead. In this way Irigaray situates Plato himself among the prisoners: he is so obsessed with the form of the Good that he fails to see the irony that governs his own text.[10]

Irigaray's point is that the prisoners in the cave enjoy a kind of freedom that the liberated prisoner no longer has. There are no clear originals for the shadows on the cave wall, and the meaning these shadows acquire has to be ascribed by the prisoners themselves. Reality within the cave is man-made and hence capable of change, whereas the ideal truth that reigns outside is singular and unambiguous and lacking in scope for human interpretation. The heterogeneous, ambiguous and unclear reality inside the cave stands in contrast to the homogeneity and clarity of the ideal reality. Evidently Irigaray prefers the cave to the light of day since it offers latitude for interpretation. Inside the cave, she writes, it is still possible to constitute oneself as something original (see for example *Speculum*, p. 292f.). As a child of the cave one can regard oneself as an individual with a personal – empirical – history; as children of the sun we are all the same, impersonal, and quite lacking in individual traits.

Irigaray thus develops a picture of reality within the cave that differs considerably from the one we are used to. Life in the cave is not just a pale imitation of truth; the cave turns out to be quite a different place, where the yoke of the One and of Truth is partly avoided. It is a place that can accommodate heterogeneous values. It is a place that has space for women, whom Irigaray believes cannot be measured by the same standards as men. Wherever there is only one norm, women will be excluded, for in such a place woman will be regarded as an imperfect man. Women are above all 'the sex that is not one',[11] the sex that is not embraced by the phallic, unambiguous, 'Platonic' discourse of the West. Through her analysis of the cave myth, Irigaray has shown that there are gaps in this discourse, and it is these gaps – or free spaces – that she wishes to focus upon: it is in the examination of these intervals that we might discover unforeseen meanings that tell us something about the Other; they constitute points that cannot themselves be unlocked with a Platonic key.

Does an apparently meaningless puppet show contain some Other meaning, as Irigaray suggests it does through her highly individual style of writing? Regardless of how that question is answered, her interpretation of the cave myth presents us with something entirely new – an alternative that ought to inspire even those Platonic scholars whose first impulse would be to dismiss her reading as absurd.

CHAPTER 7

From Pederasty to Philosophy
On Foucault's view of sexuality in antiquity

Michel Foucault's projected work on the history of sexuality was never completed. Following the publication of the first volume, *La volonté de savoir* (*The History of Sexuality*, vol. 1), which discusses sexuality from the seventeenth to the nineteenth century, he fell silent for eight years. When he at last published the next two volumes, shortly before his death in 1984, many people were surprised at the new direction of his work. Instead of continuing his study of the history of modern sexuality, he had turned his attentions to antiquity. In *L'usage des plaisirs* (*The Use of Pleasure*) Foucault writes about sexual morals in the fifth- and fourth-centuries BCE, while in *Le souci de soi* (*Care of the Self*) his interest is how people reflected on sexual morality in Greece during the Hellenistic period and in imperial Rome during the first few centuries CE.

Foucault must have devoted his eight years of silence to a diligent study both of classical languages (Greek and Latin) and of central philosophical, ethical and medical tracts. Some classical scholars would nevertheless say that he was not diligent enough. Among other things, Foucault is accused of dilettantism in his handling of these texts. In a review of the English translation of *L'usage des plaisirs* in the *New York Times Book Review* (10 November 1985), for example, Martha Nussbaum claims not only that Foucault 'lacks all the usual scholarly tools, including knowledge of Greek and Latin', but also that he is 'pretty well ignorant of Greek political and social history and of the problems of scholarship surrounding the texts he uses', and that he is therefore unable to situate what he has read in the contexts where they belong. Thus the entire result is awry. In addition complaints were made about Foucault's selection of texts. He focuses his attention exclusively on texts in which sexuality constitutes the explicit subject matter, such as medical texts (first and foremost Hippocrates) and texts of a more moral-philosophical hue (not least Xenophon, Plato and Aristotle). Foucault ignores for example the comedies of Aristophanes, which are packed with sexual remarks, and thus fails to give an opinion on texts that turn a more ironic or humorous gaze on the sexual practices of the Greek citizen.[1]

From the standpoint of the classical scholar it is indisputable that Foucault's books on the sexuality of antiquity have faults and deficiencies, and these will form a crucial aspect of my analysis of *The Use of Pleasure*. Even so, there is more to these books than their shortcomings. Foucault's incisive scrutiny and consistent analysis of antique culture has opened the eyes of many a philosopher, philologist or anthropologist who considered himself an expert on the very texts and issues that Foucault addresses. In the years following the publication of Foucault's works an intense debate arose on the subject of sexuality in antiquity, perhaps primarily in feminist and homosexual circles, although by no means exclusively.[2] It has to be said that feminist classical scholars have been far from unanimous in their enthusiasm for Foucault. Those writing in English have criticized him for having neglected earlier studies that in some cases anticipate his ideas,[3] and for turning a blind eye on the misogynous attitudes of classical authors.

It is true that Foucault's *The Use of Pleasure* does not explicitly address the overtly misogynous aspect of Greek reflections on sexuality. On the contrary, he seems to identify with the male Greek writers. But to my mind it is precisely this strategy of cultivating the masculine perspective that helps to bring out the misogynous attitudes so clearly. I for one am certainly indebted to Foucault's works for helping me to recognize the full extent of masculine narcissism in ancient Greece. The fact that Foucault did not intend to provide material for feminist studies, and the irony of the fact that this is just what his analyses did, is quite another – yet in itself interesting – matter. It is a theme I shall return to. But no matter what one thinks of Foucault's books, it has meanwhile become difficult, if not impossible, to say anything on the subject of antique sexuality without acknowledging those works in some way or other.

One of Foucault's main ideas is that what we now refer to as 'sexuality' is strictly speaking a modern construction that simply did not exist in antiquity. There were numerous sexual practices, yet these could not be associated with the individual's identity or inner self. Effectively, they lacked the concept of a sexual identity. For example, it was common for the male Greek citizen to have sexual relationships with young men, yet it would be an anachronism to call him homosexual since such sexual relationships belonged to accepted social practice. To the extent that one can talk about sexuality in antiquity, the term must be taken to refer to something one *did*, rather than to something that defines what one *was*.

What was it that motivated Foucault to return to an epoch and to texts with which he had hitherto been only poorly acquainted? Why did he not continue with his original project, namely to write the history of modern sexuality? He suggests an answer in an interview that was published shortly after his death: 'I have tried to investigate three substantial areas of difficulty: truth, power and individual behaviour. These three areas of experience can only be understood in relation to one another and not independently. It has bothered me that in my earlier books I dealt only with the first two types of experience without paying attention to the third' (*Les Nouvelles*, 28 June–5 July 1984, p. 38). What characterizes both *The Use of Pleasure* and *Care of the Self* is precisely this interplay between the three areas of difficulty mentioned in the interview: truth, power and individual behaviour, whereby the latter stands at the very focus of his analysis. Perhaps Foucault had to turn to what was for him a new epoch in order to distance himself from his earlier methods of analysis, in which the individual – or the subject, as he generally calls it – is all but absent.

In many ways it is therefore a new Foucault that we meet in these books. This is true not just of the questions he addresses and the historic period, but also of his style. The rather inaccessible, highly individual and dazzlingly intellectual style to which we are accustomed from his earlier works has been set aside. One French reviewer claimed that his writing had become so simple that even a child could read it. Even so, the earlier Foucault is visible in the way he approaches his theme: how did the ancient Greeks and Romans problematize sexuality, its desire and its enjoyment? Foucault's concern is not the prevailing sexual morals or practices of the era as such – it is not his intention to write empirical history. Instead he analyses moral-philosophical and medical texts that discuss sexuality as a problem. To what extent and in what ways, he asks, was it possible for the free man to indulge in the pleasures of sexuality while still retaining his self-control? Foucault sketches out what we could call an aesthetic of morals, or perhaps rather, an aesthetic morality – what he himself calls an 'aesthetics of existence'. The crucial moral problem is how one should form one's life to be as beautiful as possible. The moral subject, for example, is described as the craftsman who has to make his life into an artwork with a certain aesthetic value and which satisfies certain stylistic demands (p. 10f.[4]). Key terms in Foucault's analysis are 'art of existence' (*art de l'existence*), 'stylisation of existence' (*stylisation de l'existence*), 'technique of the self' (*technique de soi*) and 'technique of existence' (*technique de vie*).

THE GREEKS' SEXUAL-MORAL PROBLEM: HOW TO STYLIZE ONE'S LIFE?

The question that sets the direction for Foucault's analysis is this: 'how, why and in what forms was sexuality constituted as a moral domain?' (p. 10).

Foucault suggests an answer already in the introduction: it was not some basic sexual precepts that determined how the Greeks regarded sexuality, but rather the freedom they enjoyed in this area of experience. The Greek citizen had the right, the power, the authority and the freedom to engage in whatever sexual relationships he desired, both inside and outside the institution of marriage, and of course with both sexes. The fact that Greek writings on sexual morals nevertheless seem to reveal a consistent austerity (*austérité*) has to be understood, in Foucault's opinion, as an attempt to impose some form and style on an activity that constitutes one of the areas in which the citizen exercised his power and freedom.

In this regard Foucault seems to credit the Greeks with a peculiarly modern form of moral reflection: the free and enfranchised individual establishes rules for his own actions, even though these rules might not apply universally and need not be formulated as prohibitions, but rather as attempts to give shape to the individual's behaviour. The strict moral demands one tends to find among Greek authors are evidence not of actual moral rules, but should be understood rather as recommendations – almost like luxury extras – that might give a more beautiful form to the individual's sexual activities, thereby helping him to exercise greater control over himself. Foucault emphasizes time and again that it is an entirely masculine morality we find among the Greeks, a morality written by men for men ('une morale d'homme, faite par et pour les hommes'). Women are represented merely as objects that serve the man's sexuality, and the moral writings he studies therefore have nothing whatsoever to do with women.

Already in early antiquity, the stylization of sexual activity comes to expression in terms of four focal concerns – which Foucault refers to as a 'thematic quartet': care for one's own body, the relationship to one's wife, homosexual relationships, and the relation between sexuality and truth, that is, between the form and the place of sexuality in the life of the philosopher. In accordance with this structure, *The Use of Pleasure* is divided into four main sections (following a general introductory discussion of some length): *Dietetics*, which deals with the effects of sexuality on the body's health; *Economics*, which deals with the man's role as the head of the family; *Erotics*, where homosexuality is discussed; and *True Love*, where philosophy is constituted as *philo-sophia*, the love of wisdom. These chapter headings might at first sight seem rather off-putting, since they suggest that in this work Foucault intends to approach morality and sexuality from an angle very different from the one we are used to. It is an expectation he meets to the full.

Foucault's general view of what constitutes a moral action is by no means as original as his analysis of Greek morality, even though the former is presupposed in the latter. For an action to be described as moral, he writes, it is not enough for it to accord with a set of rules for how we should behave. A moral action presupposes that the agent adopts a particular stance towards himself; it presupposes that the agent constitutes himself as a *moral subject*. In this context, to adopt a stance towards oneself entails an attempt to understand, to control, to test, perfect and change oneself. A moral action implies an 'exercise', an 'ascesis' (Greek: *askēsis* = exercise) or a 'practice of the self' (Foucault's basic term is 'pratique de soi'). A morality will therefore have two aspects: the rules of action that it embraces, and various forms of subjectivisation or 'practices of the self', which will, among other things, determine the individual's attitude towards the rules for behaviour. Certain types of morality emphasize the first of these aspects (Foucault cites Christian morality as an example), while others emphasize the second, and the Greek morality is among the latter. It is obvious that Foucault himself lays his principal emphasis on the subjective nature of morality, and it is here, I believe, that we will find at least one of the reasons for what strikes me as Foucault's overtly positive attitude towards Greek writings on morality.

Taking the moral subject as his point of departure – the subject being someone who is aware of sexual desire and urges, and engages in sexual acts – Foucault endeavours to write the genealogy of subjectivity. But when put like this, Foucault's project seems somewhat problematic, since it proves rather difficult to discover in the realm of Greek thought any term corresponding to 'moral subject', or even one for 'subject'. As we would expect, Foucault is aware of this himself, and one of the places where he mentions the problem is in the above-mentioned interview in *Les Nouvelles* (p. 41): 'Since no Greek thinker ever developed a definition for the subject, nor even attempted one, I would say quite simply that there is no such thing as the subject' (that is, not for the Greek thinkers). Nevertheless, he uses the term 'subject' in a range of specific textual analyses without discussing the problems thereby raised. This is a point to which we will return.

A MASCULINE, VIRILE MORALITY: TO BE MASTER OF ONESELF AND OTHERS

Greek morality was masculine and 'virile'; in all circumstances the Greek citizen's first concern was to conduct himself like a man. Reasonably enough, manly behaviour stood in contrast to womanly behaviour. In Foucault's analysis, this opposition between the womanly and the manly corresponds to the opposition between passivity and activity, which can be taken as fundamental to Greek thinking in general, to its ethics in particular, and above all to its sexual morals. The distinction here is between the active agent and the one who is subjected to the action or who is, as it were, acted upon. It is masculine to be active, that is, to be someone who takes initiatives, is decisive and assumes leadership, whereas it is feminine to be passive, that is, to be subjected to the decisions and rule of another.

Thus the distinction between the masculine and the feminine does not correspond neatly to the distinction between men and women in classical Greece. Although the citizens of the city states were expected to conduct themselves like men, it was not only women, but also slaves and children, who were regarded as 'feminine', or who had to submit to the authority of the citizens in all matters. Or to put it another way, it was expected of this latter group that it should behave in ways that were passive, submissive and hence 'feminine'. The distinction between the masculine and the feminine was therefore not just a distinction between the sexes, but also one of a political nature.

One of Foucault's achievements is the clarity with which he exposes how these three analogous and fundamental distinctions crop up again and again in Greek writings on sexuality: activity and passivity, masculine and feminine, citizen and non-citizen. These oppositions govern Foucault's own analysis, even if not always explicitly.

This is true, for example, of Foucault's detailed discussion of one of the cardinal virtues of the Greeks, namely *sōphrosynē*, which is usually translated as 'moderation', 'soberness' or 'temperance'. He bases his discussion on Plato's definition of the word in the *Republic*: 'Soberness (*sōphrosynē*) is a kind of beautiful order (*kosmos*) and a mastery (*enkrateia*) of certain pleasures (*hēdonai*) and appetites (*epithymiai*)' (*Republic* 430e). Foucault undertakes a deeper analysis of one of the words used in this definition, namely *enkrateia*, or mastery. The root of this word is *kratos*, which can mean 'strength', 'victory' and 'power', and is generally used to designate the superior contender in combat. The person who displays *enkrateia* has therefore struggled against and overcome inner enemies in the form of his own urges and desires: 'He is not wise (*sōphrōn*),' writes the Sophist Antiphon, 'who has not tried the ugly and the bad; for then there is nothing he has conquered (*kratein*) and nothing that would enable him to assert that he is virtuous (*kosmios*)' (fragment 16; *The Use of Pleasure*, p. 66).

Sōphrosynē therefore implies a kind of conflict with oneself. The individual's enemies are a part of himself. This kind of morality demands the paradoxical feat of being 'master of oneself' (Plato, *Republic* 430e). For Plato this implies a distinction between the 'better' and 'worse' parts of the soul (*Republic* 431a), where, as we might expect, the 'worse' part consists of one's desires and urges. Thus Plato does not moralize over the presence of desires, but rather quite the opposite; if anything it is a necessity that we feel them, for what counts is our victory in the struggle to overcome them.

The moderate person is master of himself, and for Foucault this is a prerequisite for the ability to 'constitute oneself as a moral subject' (p. 82). What Foucault quite fails to mention is that, for Plato, the 'better' part of the soul is reason, and that it is reason that must control the sensual desires for the subject to be considered moderate. What Foucault calls 'subject' seems here to coincide with what Plato and Aristotle call *nous* or *epistēmē*, which can also be translated as 'reason'. These latter terms are far from straightforward, and this is hardly the place for a detailed clarification of their meanings. Even so, we should be in no doubt that, although *nous* and *epistēmē* occasionally bear certain resemblances to what we call 'subject' – as in the current Platonic case – the scope of these concepts is far from identical. The issues here are complex, and it is a conspicuous shortcoming of Foucault's work that he fails to discuss them at any point where the 'constitution of the moral subject' is the focus of his attention.

The *sōphrosynē* of ethical relevance to the individual is of the same structure as that which is relevant to family life. The head of the family – the family's 'better' part – is expected to govern his wife, his children and his slaves. And the same structure recurs in the city state as a whole. Free citizens have mastery over the less-deserving members of the community, a group that consists once again of women, children and slaves. Foucault thereby demonstrates that *sōphrosynē* is a purely masculine virtue; it presupposes freedom and mastery, both of which are the province of the free citizen. To be moderate implies to be a man, in relation both to oneself and to others. The masculine man has control over his desires, whereas the feminine one is swept along by them (p. 84f.). What underlies Foucault's discussion of *sōphrosynē* is therefore an implicit distinction between active and passive. The moderate person assumes an active, dominant stance towards his desires and urges, and this is taken to be a sign of masculinity; by contrast, the person who is 'unrestrained', who passively follows his desires, is characterized as feminine, regardless of whether it be a man or a woman.[5]

Thus a person's reason constitutes their masculine, active aspect, whereas their desires and urges constitute the feminine side of their nature. What Foucault calls 'the moral subject' ought therefore to be equated with the free citizen's rationality, at least to the extent that the citizen does exercise control, on the one hand, over his own desires, and on the other, over women, children and slaves. The fact that Foucault once again prefers to leave reason unmentioned strikes me as tantamount to obscuration. His peculiarly modern mode of thought seems to permit him an apparently unreflected approach to Greek texts, with the result that their uniqueness vanishes from view.

THE GREEK FOR SEXUALITY: APHRODISIA

Following these rather general remarks, let us turn to Foucault's explicit theme: sexuality. At first glance, the Greek writings on sexuality on which he focuses seem to lack the 'depth' we are accustomed to in other branches of Greek thought. I would suggest that this can be attributed to the very tangible nature of the theme, which in Greek is *ta aphrodisia*, that is, the 'things' that are owing to Aphrodite, the goddess of love, which include both the sexual act itself and the various desires most commonly associated with it. In other words, we are not dealing with sexuality in the modern sense, where its scope is far broader, or, as Foucault puts it, where 'it refers to a reality of another type' (p. 35).

We are used to thinking of sexuality as something that is *expressed* through numerous apparently non-sexual phenomena – we need only mention key Freudian terms such as sublimation and repression, concepts which Foucault tells us were unknown to the Greeks. He illustrates this point with a fine example: 'And when philosophers are laughed at for claiming to love only the beautiful souls of the boys, they are not suspected of harboring murky feelings of which they may not be conscious, but simply of waiting for the tête-à-tête in order to slip their hand under the tunic of their heart's desire' (p. 47f.). It is tempting simply to translate *aphrodisia* – at least as Foucault uses the term – with 'sex'. Foucault, however, prefers to use the Greek word.

According to Foucault, the foundation for the Greek conceptualization of *aphrodisia* is not the form of the sexual act but the manifestations of an activity. The theme is the 'dynamics' of *aphrodisia* rather than its 'morphology' (cf. p. 42). What Foucault means by 'the dynamic of the sexual act' is the movements that constitute the act, the pleasure (Greek: *hēdonē*) that accompanies it, and the desire (Greek: *epithymia*) associated with it (p. 42). Together, the act, the pleasure and the desire constitute an insoluble unity characteristic of the Greek attitude to *aphrodisia*.[6] These three components pursue one another in a circular fashion. Desire leads to the act, which results in pleasure, which once again stirs desire (p. 42f.).[7] For Foucault, it is this dynamic relation between the act, the pleasure and the desire that forms the core of Greek moral writings on the topic of *aphrodisia*. The ethical question concerns not so much the permissible desires, acts and pleasures, but rather the possibility of gaining control over this circular dynamic, such that one does not become a slave to one's own sexual desires and pleasures.

Here as well we see how the Greek notion of *aphrodisia* is founded in the distinction between active and passive. The verb *aphrodisiazein* expresses the so-called masculine role in the sexual act, the apparently 'active' function, which is defined as penetration, whereas the passive form of the verb expresses the so-called feminine sexual role, which involves the passive acceptance of penetration and of being reduced to the object of someone else's desire. The latter is also the role of the young boy in a homosexual relation. It seems then, that for the Greeks every sexual relationship encompassed an active and a passive pole, regardless of whether those poles were male or female.

Once again we should note that Foucault seems to identify the active figure with 'subject' and the passive, or 'sufferer', with 'object'. Through this use of the modern concepts of 'subject' and 'object' Foucault interposes a considerable distance between himself and the Greek way of thinking and experiencing. When in Greek a person is described as 'suffering' (*paschei*) it can mean one of two things, either that he is the victim of circumstances beyond his own control, or quite simply that he is experiencing a certain mental state. Both of these are very different from the situation of being objectivized by another subject.[8] I believe we would get closer to the realm of Greek experience by taking 'subject' and 'object' in their strictly grammatical senses. The woman can be regarded as the object of the sexual act in the sense that she does not do anything, but is rather the thing to which something is done.

For the free adult male the only morally acceptable thing to do is of course to assume the active, masculine role that conforms to his social and political status in the city state. The passive role, on the other hand, is suitable for women, slaves and children. It should be noted that this places women in a very particular position relative to the other two groups, one that doubly justifies her sexual inferiority. It is not just her social status that makes it appropriate for her to assume the passive role, but also her nature.

As far as the free man is concerned there are two forms of sexual immorality: one is to allow desire and pleasure to gain the upper hand, that is, to show no self-restraint in sexual matters, and the other is to assume a passive role in sexual relationships. We have meanwhile seen that anyone who leads a life of licentiousness and gets carried away by their desires is passive according to the Greek way of thinking, for such a person displays a lack of self-mastery. Ultimately, therefore, the two forms of sexual immorality can be reduced to one (although Foucault fails to make this point explicitly), namely passivity.

Now, the Greek citizen is of course subject to other desires than just the sexual, for he also craves food and drink. Admittedly, the sexual urge is particularly powerful and seems to function by some trick of nature, for it is this that persuades men and women to seek each other out, thereby enabling propagation and guaranteeing the continuation of the species. Foucault tells us that, in the texts of Plato, Aristotle and Xenophon, the morality of the table and the bed are equivalent, and they use the same terminology in discussing different types of physical excess: sexual abandon and immoderate drinking and eating. In this regard, all desires are seen as having the same objective, which is the maintenance of the species, the one by keeping the individual alive from day to day, the other compensating for the individual's mortality. For the Greeks, the desires and the activities they strive after – eating, drinking, the sexual act – are both natural and perfectly necessary, but still they threaten constantly to exceed the limits of necessity, to overcome reason, and to take control of the individual. This implies that there is nothing evil about *aphrodisia* itself, but that it is nevertheless associated with a potential evil, since it is capable of reducing the individual to a passive slave of his desires. It is this that Foucault identifies as the wellspring of the Greeks' moral reflections on *aphrodisia*.

Personally I believe this insight to be the wellspring of a certain ambiguity of which Foucault himself falls foul. When it comes to imposing specific limits on *aphrodisia*, what counts is not so much nature's 'need' for reproduction, but rather the free man's need to satisfy his urges and to rid himself of certain bodily fluids. Homosexuality, which from the point of view of the species' reproduction is about as useful as a candy stick, is no less effective than heterosexuality when it comes to satisfying the appetite and ridding the body of excess fluids. Much the same is true of masturbation, which the cynic Diogenes provocatively described as the simplest possible way of satisfying the requirements of sexuality. For Foucault, 'the scandalous gesture of Diogenes' (p. 54) is an extreme consequence of Socrates' ideal, which Xenophon tells us was only to give in to one's most pressing urges. By satisfying himself without the involvement of others, the free man is able to exercise complete mastery over his sexuality, although not without problems. For in isolation, the masculine activity will be practised without its passive counterpart, and will thereby lack, as it were, any material on which to work. In effect it would be a punch at the empty air. In this context, the basic dichotomy seems rather weak. It is a problem that Foucault fails to discuss, but I myself consider it to be of decisive significance and will therefore return to it in due course.

At this point, with this general discussion of *aphrodisia* in mind, I shall turn to the four 'grand thèmes d'austérité' on which Foucault concentrates for the remainder of his work: 'dietetics', 'economics', 'erotics' and 'true love'.

THE PRINCIPAL THEMES OF FOUCAULT'S ANALYSIS OF SEXUALITY: DIETETICS, ECONOMICS, EROTICS AND TRUE LOVE

DIETETICS

In his analysis of Greek dietetics, or health theory, Foucault discusses the relation between *aphrodisia*, health, life and death. It is probably this part of the book that causes the most surprise. We are not accustomed to reading, in a book on ethical writings, how often one ought to vomit or have sexual intercourse at different times of year in order to maintain the body's natural balance between moist and dry, hot and cold. Yet the main idea is clear: Foucault wants to show that here as well we are dealing with 'a whole manner of forming oneself as subject' (p. 108), namely as a subject that takes care of his body and who refuses to succumb to any form of excess either in the one direction or the other. Once again, it is a matter of control, or mastery. '*L'usage des plaisirs*', the use of pleasures, must therefore be governed by a strict rationality that strives to maintain an illusory balance between wet and dry, warm and cold. In this context, the man's ejaculation is equated with vomiting.

Foucault never tires of repeating that the Greek citizen did not regard sexuality as an evil in itself. The assertion is, however, always followed by a 'but'. Sexuality is a potential evil, partly because it can turn a man into the slave of his desires, and partly because it can have unfortunate physical consequences (such as bodily dehydration), and partly because it has negative metaphysical connotations. What is meant by 'sexuality' is first and foremost the sexual act, which the man sees as something frightening. The reason for this is that during sexual activity, one's entire attention becomes focused on the orgasm, an experience that Hippocrates characterized as 'a minor epilepsy', in other words, as an infirmity.

What is emphasized is the violent, almost compulsive aspect of sexuality. It is not only penetration that can be seen as violent, but also the orgasm. The unfortunate thing is that it seems impossible to gain mastery of this 'mécanique violente', and that the otherwise moderate man is for a brief moment reduced to a slave. Philosophers (the Pythagoreans, together with Plato and Aristotle) and physicians (Hippocrates, Diocles) all give the citizen more or less the same advice, which is to limit sexual activity to a minimum. Although not essentially evil, for the philosophers and the physicians it is at least potentially so, and certainly it is not a good in itself. We could perhaps say that sexuality is regarded as a necessary evil: necessary for the maintenance of the species and of one's own physical equilibrium, an evil not just because it obstructs the citizen in gaining full mastery of his life, but also because it is associated with death. Let us take a closer look at this ambiguous aspect of sexuality – the fact that it is linked with both life and death.

Sexuality, Foucault tells us, stands at the point where life and death intersect: it is inscribed in the individual's death and the species' immortality. By means of sexuality people can compensate for their own, individual mortality by helping the species as a whole to continue. It seems clear that sexuality stands at the service of life – or perhaps we should say, of immortality – and therefore has an indisputably positive function. But it is precisely because it contributes to the maintenance of life that sexuality is also associated with death. Semen is regarded as man's life-giving substance, and the loss of any amount of it therefore amounts to a step closer to death. This conception is mainly physical, but it also has metaphysical connotations. It is interesting to note, for example, that in the work of a later Greek author – the oneirocritic Artemidor of the second century CE – the word *ousia*, an important philosophical term which in this context means 'essence' or 'being', can also mean 'seed' (*Le souci de soi*, p. 40). For the man, ejaculation therefore represents a certain loss of existence, or of vital force. And this is precisely what it means for Aristotle, who credits semen with a metaphysical function. In his opinion it is the semen that transmits the father's form, or essence (*eidos*) to the offspring – albeit by mechanisms that are not entirely clear – and which therefore determines that father and child are of the same species.

Aristotle believes that semen is an element of the material that remains once the body has absorbed the nutrients from food. This residue can either be distributed through the body as a kind of 'growth substance', or it can give life and growth to a new individual in the form of semen. During childhood the entire residue is used as 'growth substance' – which explains why boys have to reach a certain age before they themselves can produce semen (cf. Aristotle, *De Generatione Animalium*, Bk. I, 724–725). In women this substance is converted into menstrual blood, which for Aristotle is a form of semen, albeit one that lacks life-giving force. This explains why sexuality and propagation are less problematic for women than for men. Since it is only the man that gives life, he is also the only one who can guard against the potentially threatening loss of life-giving substance. Rather typically, these latter reflections about the different meanings of sexuality for women and men are given no mention in Foucault's book. They fall outside the scope of his interests, which seem to coincide with those of the Greek authors; he concentrates instead on what he calls the Greeks' 'ejaculatory schema' (p. 129).

Foucault's use of the term 'ejaculatory schema' alludes to the conception that regards male penetration, culminating in the ejaculation of semen, as sexuality's sole concern. By accepting this view without discussion, that is, by adopting uncritically this thoroughly masculine attitude, Foucault blinds himself to highly significant aspects of the Greeks' speculations about sexuality and its relation to life and death. The consistent absence of women in the Greek texts about sexuality and reproduction is hardly accidental. To my mind this can only be understood as the attempt to deny individual mortality. Let me briefly explain what I mean.[9]

The relation between vegetative and sexual reproduction was evidently a matter of concern in antiquity: whereas sexual propagation leads to the birth of an entirely new individual, one that is different from and independent of its progenitors, the product of vegetative reproduction – in the form of either a sucker or a slip – is regarded as an identical replication of the original. Whereas vegetative propagation ensures the immortality of the source, the same cannot be said of sexual reproduction. Sexual reproduction and individual death can therefore be seen as indissolubly linked. Aristotle hints – albeit only hints – at such a view in the first book of *De Generatione Animalium*, as Foucault points out. We also suspect the same theme in another work that Foucault discusses, although in this case the context is rather different, namely Plato's *Symposium*. In reporting Diotima's discussion of the possibility of man's participation in immortality, Plato's aim seems to be to establish a vegetative theory for human propagation. In this part of the dialogue, propagation and birth are seen as extensions of the individual's growth and of the physical renewal that constitutes an ongoing aspect of life (*Symposium* 207c-208b). Thus, strictly speaking, the thing that is born is not a new individual, but rather an extension of its origin. This view opens the prospect of immortality, not just for the race as a whole, but for the individual himself. By taking vegetative propagation as the model for human reproduction, Plato avoids the problem of sexuality, or rather, he avoids the problem of sexual differentiation, or the painful fact that the division of humankind into males and females entails the inevitable death of the individual. Foucault also avoids this issue and fails to notice that it lurks behind what he refers to as the Greeks' 'sexual schema', which largely revolves around 'penetration and male domination' (p. 242).

ECONOMICS

Foucault discusses the relation of sexuality to propagation in the section entitled *Economics* (Greek: *oikonomia*), a term that could be glossed as 'the management of one's household'. The citizen's aim in maintaining an *oikos*, which can mean both family, house and home, is first and foremost the creation of legitimate heirs. Whereas Foucault's analysis of 'dietetics' focused on the citizen's relation to his own body, his analysis of economics addresses the issue of the citizen's relationship to his wife.

Foucault begins this analysis with a famous quote from a defence speech of Demosthenes: 'Mistresses we keep for the sake of pleasure (*hēdonēs heneka*), concubines for the daily care of our persons, but wives to bear us legitimate children and to be faithful guardians of our households' (*Against Neaera*, 122).[10] In other words the realm of pleasure seems clearly to lie outside marriage. The sexual status of the wife is also clear: her task is to bear legitimate children and thus to secure the survival of the family and the city state. And just as self-evident as her duty to remain faithful to her husband is the husband's right to engage in a range of extra-marital sexual relationships. In addition to enjoying full sexual rights over the household slaves, men as well as women, and to having both lovers (*hetairai*) and concubines (*pallaka*), the man can also indulge in homosexual relationships with young boys, a practice that was common and widely accepted. The total subjection of the woman to the man's control stands in blatant contrast to the man's utter freedom in sexual matters.

One reflection of this situation is found in attitudes towards rape. A rapist offended not against the woman but against her husband. Foucault informs us that in Athens the seduction of a married woman carried a higher penalty than rape; the man who rapes only uses the woman's body, whereas the seducer gains a degree of power over her soul and thereby threatens her husband's absolute authority. Accordingly, infidelity was an offence of married women alone. A man was not unfaithful, although he might cause another man's wife to be such (p. 146).

This asymmetry between the man and the woman is also apparent in the arrangements that led to marriage. The man would negotiate with the young woman's father concerning the conditions on which he would accept to marry her. The man set conditions on his own behalf, the father on behalf of his daughter. The woman was excluded not just from these marital negotiations, she also remained extraneous to the family to which she was linked via her husband: 'she is not "at home"' (p. 178), that is, she does not belong to her husband's household (*oikos*). Her status is therefore ambiguous. Although she does not belong to her new family, her function is still to perpetuate it by reproducing the man's line. Foucault emphasizes the woman's weak position: alien and homeless, she seeks refuge and protection at her husband's hearth, and is thus utterly dependent on his goodwill.

Despite the man's sexual freedom within the marriage institution, he was still expected to curb some of his sexual activities once married. Greek writers on sexual morality go further. They call on men to devote their sexual activities to their wives alone.[11] At this point, Foucault asks how the sexual relationship of the husband to his wife could come to be viewed as problematic, since her duties were strictly defined and his freedom was all but total. His answer depends on his analysis of what it means to be a husband. To be married means above all to be the head of one's family, to have authority and to exercise power within the home (p. 150f.). And the first imperative for the person who has power over others is to show that he has mastery of himself, that is, that he is able to control his own urges.

As already mentioned, for the Greeks, the structure of sexuality was the same as that of society – and also, for that matter, of the individual – in that it involved active and passive elements, masters and subordinates. (Foucault applies the notion of *isomorphism*, that is, these phenomena manifested analogous forms.) This structure is also apparent in the individual household, where the man is the master of the house, its natural leader and commander. The accounts that Foucault discusses, of the Greek man's relations to himself, his wife, his children and his slaves, draw on the model of monarchy (either historical or utopian),[12] or on one of aristocracy, such as described by Aristotle. The good monarch exercises righteous and moderate sovereignty over his subjects without abusing his power and his freedom. This is something he can do insofar as he is master of himself. And this is also how the free man should behave in relation to those things over which he has power, including his own desires.

This, in my opinion, puts the Greek democracy in perspective. The Greek citizens are a pole in need of a counterpole; the one cannot subsist without the other. Democracy consists of those men who are independent of their subjects, not just in practice, but on the purely structural level. Foucault's analysis makes this brilliantly clear, even though he does not explicitly address the theme. Due to his tacit identification with the Greek citizen as both a sexual and political focus, Foucault is unable to take in the periphery. The basis of his analysis is always the active-passive polarity. Foucault hardly spares a thought for the necessary but miserable existence of those who exemplified passivity in ancient Athens. He seems to get carried away by his enthusiasm for the enviable privileges of those who were active – both sexually and politically.

One of Foucault's main points is that the moral ideas about the man's position as the paterfamilias are best explained in terms not of moral prohibitions but rather of the Greek man's freedom: how can he manage his *oikos* in the best possible way, how can he be a good monarch in relation to the subjects of his family? Above all it is crucial for him to preserve his *enkrateia*, his mastery over himself. He who allows his desires to gain the upperhand will ruin his own body, his soul, and his home (p. 160). Also at stake is his position as a citizen. Those moral writings that deal with the man's relations to his wife seem largely concerned with 'the art of managing one's house', so that the subject here is effectively the same as in politics, namely the governing of other people. The form of rule most appropriate when dealing with women is described as 'soft'. The woman should be educated to become the man's colleague (*synergos*). Man and wife have a shared objective, which is to preserve, or preferably to increase, the family's wealth and to produce legitimate heirs. The relationship of a man to his wife is therefore shaped by the interests of his *oikos*.

Foucault is aware that the strict demands the Greek authors imposed on the sexual activity of married men must be kept in perspective. The aim was not mutual fidelity, and neither was it a matter of establishing with one's wife a relationship of trust and love. This is not to say that a husband and wife could not enjoy a close and loving relationship, but where they did so it was largely a result of chance and had nothing to do with their reciprocal roles as husband and wife. Foucault notes that the faithful husband was not necessarily the one who renounced all and every sexual partner other than his wife, but rather the one who respected her status as the first woman of the house, and who begrudged her none of the privileges that belonged to that position. The man's fidelity – regardless of what the word entails – is a kind of reward for 'the good wife', who in turn is defined as the one who serves her husband like a good colleague. The woman is obliged, the man merely recommended, to abstain from extra-marital sexual activity. For the woman fidelity means that she is subject to the man's control; for the man it was 'the most elegant way of exercising his control' (p. 151). Of greatest importance to the Greek citizen was the need to stylize an actual asymmetry.

If the exercise of power is beautiful enough, then it will also be morally defensible. Foucault does not himself draw this conclusion from his analysis, and he expresses neither approval nor disapproval for what he regards as the Greeks' 'existential aesthetic'. This is a pity, and indeed it is rather remarkable that Foucault does not present any reflections of his own on the aesthetics of power and freedom, which, as we shall see, eventually modulates into an aesthetic of truth. Although, as master of his *oikos*, the Greek citizen was dependant on his wife in order to exercise power and freedom, when it came to his truth-seeking activities, she was always condemned to total exclusion. The one who wanted to become a philosopher had to turn to his own sex.

EROTICS

It might seem surprising that a chapter devoted exclusively to homosexuality among the Greeks should be given the title 'Erotics'. But Foucault has chosen his title with care. For the subject is no longer pure *aphrodisia*, the carnal desire that provided the focus in the foregoing discussions. At this point Foucault introduces a new divinity. It is no longer Aphrodite who rules, the goddess who tempts the man to yield to his own feminine aspect, but the love-god Eros, who knows how to raise desire onto a higher, more masculine level, or who has known it at least since Socrates delivered his speech in praise of Eros in Plato's *Symposium*.[13]

Foucault objects to the term 'homosexuality' to describe the Greeks' sexual relationships with members of their own sex. He prefers to speak of 'bisexuality', since a desire for women was quite compatible with the desire for young men. Foucault clarifies the point by saying that – in contrast to modern sexual attitudes – the Greeks did not consider there to be two types of desire that were generally divided between two types of person, the heterosexual and the homosexual. Desire (*epithymia, orexis*) remained the same, although it might take either a woman or a boy as its object. What one preferred was 'a matter of taste' (p. 190).

While certainly true that the terms homosexuality and heterosexuality do not do justice to the Greek citizen's sexual relationships, Foucault fails to mention another important distinction. Desire assumed two essentially different forms: there was the desire for young boys, in other words, for the sons of citizens, and there was the desire for women and slaves. The significant distinction here is that the citizen's desire for a person who is free and active, and hence – potentially at least – his equal, is different from his desire for someone who is utterly subject to his control. The citizen's desire for a young boy is a desire for someone masculine, whereas his desire for a woman or a slave is a desire for a feminine person. In the one case he yearns for something similar to himself, in the other, something that is different. In this sense the terms 'homosexuality' and 'heterosexuality' clearly have a degree of relevance, although we should not forget that the senses suggested here differ significantly from the way the terms are used today.

Foucault, however, is not prepared to subdivide the citizen's desire in this way, even though his analysis – so it seems to me – suggests such a distinction. One of Foucault's main reasons for discussing Plato's *Symposium* is to demonstrate that the Greeks acknowledged only one form of desire (p. 188f.). As we saw in Chapter 5, Pausanias, one of the speakers at the symposium, distinguishes between the earthly and the heavenly Eros. The earthly Eros is oriented towards both women and boys and is merely interested in the 'act' (*Symposium* 181b), not in the person towards whom the desire is directed. The heavenly Eros is oriented towards that which 'by nature is stronger and more intelligent' (*Symposium* 181c), and as we might expect this is found only among boys. Foucault therefore thinks that the distinction is not simply between homosexuality and heterosexuality, but between a lower and a

higher form of desire. The nobler form of desire occurs only in the context of
a certain type of homosexuality, namely pederasty. We will shortly return to
this theme.

One of the speakers at the symposium whom Foucault rather surprisingly
fails to mention at this juncture, is Aristophanes, who has his own theory
about the origins of sexual desire.[14] Originally humans were roughly spherical in shape. They had two faces, one at the front and one at the back, two
pairs of legs and two pairs of arms, and two sets of genitalia etc.. Among this
species there were three sexes: male, female and hermaphrodite. It came
about that these creatures were divided in two, and it was then that desire
arose; henceforth, each half went in search of his or her missing counterpart,
or other half. Those who were originally one-sexed became homosexual,
whereas those who had formerly been hermaphrodite became heterosexual.
Aristophanes regards as homosexual (this word does not occur in Greek and
consequently not in Plato's text either, which uses instead the terms 'pederast' and 'philerast') only those men who love young boys. In other words, the
distinction that Aristophanes draws does not correspond to the one conveyed
by the modern words homosexuality and heterosexuality, but distinguishes
rather between heterosexuality and what we today would regard as a rather
special form of homosexuality. According to Aristophanes, the peculiar characteristic of the latter is that it entails that like seeks like (*to syngenēs*; *Symposium* 192b). Thus, here as well we find the distinction that was made above
between the desire for that which is similar in nature (the same) and the
desire for that which is different in nature (the other). And as we shall see, it
is here as well that we find the most crucial of all the moral problems that
arise for the Greeks in response to pederasty.

As in other contexts, Foucault's analysis of Greek pederasty ('l'amour des
garçons') begins with acknowledged freedoms. It was thoroughly permissible
for a citizen to have sexual relationships with other men, and under particular
conditions, such relationships were not only widely accepted, but also highly
respected. Even so, such relationships tended to be problematic. Relationships that complied with the respected form of homosexuality generally
involved a significant, if not always considerable, difference in age. One of
the pair, namely the lover (*erastēs*) was a grown man in possession of his full
rights as a citizen, while the other, the beloved (*erōmenos*) was a young and
sexually immature boy who stood on the threshold of manhood and of acces-
sion to his rights as a citizen.

Greek pederasty was more than just a widespread sexual activity; it was
effectively an institution, and one that played an important role in the process
of educating young boys to become men. In his analysis of Greek pederasty,
Foucault tends towards an interpretation that treats the practice like a kind of

initiation rite, a perspective that I consider rather promising. The boy was on the verge of becoming a man, and his conduct towards the men that courted him would reveal whether or not he was worthy of assuming his place as the lovers' equal in the city state. Moreover, the relationship between the man and the boy was in many ways ritualized. The lover was the one who took the initiative, who did the courting, who paid calls on the young boy, gave him presents, did him favours, provided social support, and in some cases training in a profession. The boy for his part was expected to be reserved, although without rejecting his lover entirely, provided the latter was respectable. The boy had the freedom to choose and rebuff suitors as he pleased. This freedom was something the lover had to accept, and we can imagine how the game between the older lover and the beautiful, highly-coveted boy could lead to the use of cunning, thus becoming more complex and infinitely more challenging than the relationship of the man to his wife, who was thoroughly subject to his will.

The young boy's body was valued in terms of its own aesthetic. What was appreciated was not its feminine character, so much as its developing aspects of manliness ('the signs and guarantees of a developing virility', p. 200), such as for example strength and endurance. A handsome boy embodied the promise of manhood but not yet the manhood itself. It was in this, Foucault believes, that the attraction lay, and boys had to exploit the quality while they had it, for it lasted only a short while.

Between the man and the boy a personal relationship would develop in which sexuality was an essential element. As we have already seen, any sexual relationship – as viewed by the Greeks – presupposed an active and a passive pole. And it was here that the pederast encountered the moral dilemma. The active position was relatively unproblematic since it was a role that the adult lover could assume quite naturally, whereas it was morally impossible for the young boy to identify with the passive position – provided, that is, that he wished to retain his honour.

Foucault calls this problem 'the antinomy of the boy' (p. 221). Whereas for the lover the young boy was an object of desire, it was impermissible for the youngster to see himself as such for as long as he was in the process of developing as a moral subject. Pederasty therefore constitutes a moral problem primarily from the viewpoint of the boy. Foucault claims that, from the perspective of the Greek citizen, there was nothing problematic in the idea of taking a boy as a lover. The problem lay entirely on the side of the beloved. As it stands this view seems unsatisfactory, as Foucault himself seems tacitly to admit in generalizing the problem thus: 'The young man – between the end of childhood and the age when he attained manly status – constituted a delicate and difficult factor for Greek ethics and Greek thought' (p. 213). Let

us take a closer look at what it means for the young man to constitute 'a delicate and difficult factor' for Greek ethics.

There is a certain ambivalence in Greek texts about whether pederasty
should be ascribed a positive or negative value. In some cases it is regarded
as something 'natural', in others as something 'unnatural'. It is natural to the
extent that it involves a desire for the beautiful. But the sexual act itself is
unnatural since it expects of the boy a feminine, passive role. This contradicts the dynamic that binds the elements of *aphrodisia* into a single unit; the
desire itself is accepted, but not its satisfaction. Another way of putting it is
to say, sexuality is hereby deprived of its passive aspect and is therefore
unable to function as it should. 'Between the man and the boy, there is not –
there cannot and should not be – a community of pleasure' (p. 223). The difficulty – or rather, the impossibility – lies in the attempt to regard the boy as
an object of desire.

In the case of the man's relationship to his wife, the objective was 'the stylization of an actual dissymmetry' (p. 151), but where his relationship to the
boy is concerned it is precisely such an asymmetry that is problematic and
'delicate'. This asymmetry is not enduring, as it is between the man and the
woman, but of a passing nature. The problem for 'erotics' is therefore not the
same as it was for 'economics'. The question is, how is one to acknowledge
the freedom and potential sameness of the other in the relationship? This
formulation captures the essence of the problem. It is the potential sameness
of the lover and the beloved that seems to form the basis for the peculiar type
of attraction between the man and the boy. Or rather, the crucial tension
seems to result from the temporary difference between the man and the boy,
a difference that can at any moment tip over into identity. The eagerly
coveted youngster ought by now 'already to conduct [him]self as the man
[he] has not yet become' (p. 200). In this context, Foucault is preoccupied
with the aspect of time. The boy's body is maturing rapidly, and the least
change threatens to destroy his charm. Pederasty is based on the experience
of 'a fleeting time that leads ineluctably to an end that is near' (p. 252). It
involves an experience of time that is full of expectation, excitement and
worry, and which therefore stands in stark contrast to the time dimension
that gives shape to marriage, namely that of the species, the continuity of
generations, and the maintenance of the hierarchy. The boy's 'not yet' pro-
mises future sameness. And it is here that the lover's social responsibility
comes into play. His duty is to educate the youngster to become a man, and
this means creating him in his own likeness. Referring to a text by Demosthenes (*Erōtikos*), Foucault remarks that the young boy's life is regarded as an
artwork, which the suitors of the beloved had a responsibility to shape to the
greatest possible perfection.

Was it his own mirror image that the Greek citizen loved above all else? Or was it rather that the highest object of his love was the model on which he himself was based, and that he strove to mould the boy into a still-more perfect copy of that model than he was himself? Whatever the answer, the Greek citizen seems to have loved sameness, if not indeed identity. Or perhaps it would be more correct to say, he loved the potential for sameness and identity, and that he dreamt of attaining a utopian embodiment of these qualities, a dream that young boys were able to nourish. It was a dream in which women had no place. Whether or not Foucault would have approved of these speculations, to my mind they are implicit in his text.

TRUE LOVE

The last of Foucault's four 'grands thèmes d'austérité' – following the relationship to one's own body, the relationship to the wife and the relationship to boys – is the relationship to truth. The notion that the 'use of pleasure' should have something to do with truth is by no means self-evident, but by altering the terminology to use the word 'love' rather than 'pleasure' the connection becomes clearer. For the meaning of the term 'philosophy' is love of wisdom, or alternatively, the love of truth. Among the Greek philosophers it was Plato in particular who treated philosophy as a form of love, and it is Plato whose voice we get to hear in the concluding chapter of Foucault's work. This is no coincidence. In the introduction to the book, Foucault announced that his project was to discuss sexuality in relation to truth. Prior to this point he has not done so. By taking Plato as his route to this theme in the final chapter, he effectively invests that philosopher with a certain authority. Foucault neither condemns nor concurs with Plato. As in other contexts, he remains irritatingly neutral, but even so it seems to me that he uses Plato to express the truth about the problems associated with Greek sexual morals. Foucault is saying something more. In his own way he hints at a truth about Plato's philosophy.

The starting point for Plato's discussion of Eros is pederasty. His two dialogues that take love as their theme – *Phaedrus* and *Symposium* – both open with speeches in praise of Eros, which Foucault regards as reiterations of a more traditional view of love than the one Plato wishes to convey. One of the moral questions posed is how the lover and the beloved should behave in relation to one another. This applies first and foremost to the beloved, that is the boy: whom should he choose as his lover, to whom should he yield, and under what conditions? As Foucault puts it, it is a 'question of conduct, grounded in a preexisting concept of love' (p. 236). When Socrates eventually takes the floor, he frames the question very differently. By relating a conversation he once had with the wise woman Diotima, he changes the subject to the true nature of love. Diotima criticises the view that equates Eros with love's passive aspect – embodied by the beloved (*to erōmenon*) – rather than with the active aspect embodied by the lover (*ho erōn*; *Symposium* 204c).

In Foucault's terminology, what Diotima does is take a step back from the object of love to its subject. Even so, Diotima does not ignore the question of love's object, but puts it rather in a new perspective; it is the analysis of what constitutes love itself that determines its object. In Foucault's interpretation of Plato, the object of love is truth (p. 237f.). And it is here we find the solution to the 'the antinomy of the boy': the beloved is swept along by the lover's love for truth, so that he too becomes a lover; 'it is right that he should actually become a subject in this love relation' (p. 240). At this point it seems as if the two lovers are on an equal footing, since the asymmetry has been transformed to a symmetry between two subjects. But the transformations do not stop there. The roles undergo a further change thanks to the introduction of a new figure, namely the master, 'le maître de vérité', who takes over in the position of the lover and, thanks to his absolute self-mastery, renounces all forms of *aphrodisia*. For the youngster who yearns for truth, love's object is this 'master of truth' (p. 241).

The love relationship has grown complex, and it is regrettable that Foucault takes his analysis no further. His account of Plato becomes terse, at the very point where we begin to glimpse the possibility of a foundation for Foucault's own perspective on Greek sexual morality. Foucault says nothing about his own understanding of Platonic truth, neither does he tell us why he prefers to take truth as the object of love rather than beauty, which Plato explicitly focuses on in the two dialogues that Foucault selects for study. Moreover, it is of course a highly problematic move to call Platonic truth an object, and even more so to use the term 'master of truth'. To be master over something implies that the subject in some sense constitutes, or at least controls, the object; the subject assumes priority over the object. For Plato, beauty (or truth) has to be assumed as a precondition for any desire for such a thing. Truth, or the form of Beauty, are absolute, whereas the desire for it is relative. The term 'maître de vérité' would simply be meaningless from the Platonic point of view. Since truth is absolute and beyond time and space – and in this sense divine – no human, at least not in the mortal realm, will ever 'master' a comprehensive view of it. Foucault fails to address problems of this nature.

But returning to the relationship between the lover (a role now assumed by the boy), the lover / master, and truth, which Foucault now sees as triangular, let us ask, who loves who? (Foucault does not put the question, and the answer will have to be my own.) The boy loves the master, not for what he is in himself, but because the master knows the truth. The master does not seem to love anyone. He is 'maître de vérité', which implies that he possesses truth and is consequently no longer motivated by any deficit, which, according to Socrates / Diotima, was a precondition for the ability to love. This scheme preserves the active-passive polarity, but now in quite a different form. The youngster has become the active participant, whereas the master has become passive, albeit not in the traditional sexual sense. The master is passive in the sense that he has now become more or less indifferent towards his enthusiastic lover. The master is only concerned with the truth, so that it hardly makes sense to speak of there being any kind of relationship between him and the boy. Such is the situation in the case where the philosopher becomes master, as he does in Foucault's interpretation, and in the case where the philosopher attains his goal by glimpsing the form of Beauty, a situation which, according to more plausible interpretations of Plato, would still fail to qualify him as master of either *logos* or truth (*Symposium* 210e–211b).

Foucault presents the apotheosis to master as the story's climax: the master of truth has power over the loving youth, a power he is qualified to exert insofar as he demonstrates full mastery over himself. In other words the relationship is characterized by the exercise of power. The boy is left alone with his feelings of love, and the chance of any relationship based in equality has vanished. One feature of the traditional concept of pederasty, as Foucault himself presented it, was that such relationships involve a certain tension and liberating potential on account of the 'delicate' ambiguity that attached to them: the ambiguity between the citizen's commanding position and the boy's freedom, between the ostensible asymmetry and a potential equality. Certainly, this ambiguity is overcome by what Foucault calls 'true love'. But personally I can only see that love has been replaced by power.

The two participants in Plato's love story – as dramatized by Foucault – are essentially the same: two men, both equipped with the same faculty of reason, even if it is still underdeveloped in the case of the boy. What the lover seeks in his beloved is not his lost other half – as he does in Aristophanes' account of sexual love – but rather the beauty of which the other's soul is a reflection (p. 243). The potential equality that exists between the lovers, which has, as it happens, been annulled and replaced by domination, crops up again in terms of what the two figures relate to, namely the beautiful, or truth: the beautiful 'subsists of itself and by itself in an eternal oneness' (*Symposium* 211b), in other words, it is eternally like itself. For Plato this is a vital and decisive consideration, for it constitutes the very basis of his theory of forms. It is, however, an idea that makes no appearance in

Foucault's text, and its absence is conspicuous. Why does Foucault, in an analysis of Plato's transformation of pederasty to philosophy, fail to mention that the all-important truth (the beautiful) is characterized by unity and sameness? In Plato, the homosexual – or pederastic – Eros, that which desires its equal, undergoes transformation to a philosophical eros, which desires absolute oneness, identity and equality. Foucault's analysis certainly prepares the ground for a view of Plato's philosophy as a kind of sublimation of Greek pederasty, but it stops short of actually expounding such a view at the conclusion.

Despite my fundamental objections to Foucault's interpretation of Plato, I believe that, ultimately, he exposes a truth about Plato's philosophy: philosophical eros is an extension of the pederastic eros. Plato's philosophy is essentially homoerotic. And for Plato himself this would hardly have been an objectionable evaluation. In the *Symposium*, for example, we read that true insight is attained by 'loving boys correctly' (*Symposium* 211b). This is a theme that deserves serious thought, not only in relation to Plato's own work, but also in relation to the philosophy that stands in his debt.

*

In the conclusion of his book on Greek sexual moral reflections, Foucault focuses on three concepts that have crystallized out of the study: *freedom*, *power* and *truth*. What the Greeks were attempting to do, he believes, was develop an existential aesthetic, such that they could give form to their freedom, and to their own power games. Foucault emphasizes that this morality would apply exclusively to free citizens, although he does not reflect on the fact that the Greek citizen needed the non-citizen in order to define himself. There is no master without a slave. Superiority presupposes inferiority. Foucault's silence on this theme is disturbing.

Although Foucault does not explicitly say so in his text, it seems reasonable to suppose that he considered the moral attitudes of the Greeks to offer a suitable foundation for our own – which is not to say that he wished to adopt them as such. In an interview in *Magazine Littéraire* shortly before his death he compares our moral situation with that of the Greeks. Numerous moral prohibitions, which for a long time were regarded as necessary for the smooth functioning of so-called capitalist society, have, he tells us, gradually fallen into disuse without having solved any problem of a political or moral nature whatsoever. If anything, he sees the opposite to be the case: it is freedom that creates the problems. He formulates our modern ethical problem in the same way as he formulated that of the Greeks: how are we to give form to our own actions? His genealogy of sexual moral reflections, and of the constitution of the moral subject, is therefore clearly written within a framework of contemporary relevance, as he himself asserts in the interview (*Magazine Littéraire*, May 1984, p. 21).

It is freedom – not prohibition – that leads to moral reflection. The starting point for Foucault's project is in itself rather astonishing since it contradicts the usual notion of what prompts us to reflect on morality. The Christian tradition, up to and including Freudian theory, identifies fundamental sexual prohibitions as the motivating force behind our morals. This tradition goes back to the Greeks, who were themselves highly preoccupied with the prohibition against incest. It is no accident that Sophocles' *King Oedipus* was of such immense importance for Freud, who speculates on our subconscious desires to break the prohibition against incest. By contrast, Foucault regards this kind of prohibition to be only marginally relevant for the way the Greeks reflected over sexual morals. Referring to a passage in Xenophon, he suggests his own idea of what incest meant to the Greeks. Xenophon tells us that it is unfitting for the wife to be much older than her husband, as she would be if a man married his mother. And the reason for this, we learn, is that such an age difference might lead, among other things, to sickly offspring. On this point, Foucault – and Xenophon with him – strikes me as unforgivably naive. The fact that he limits his material to philosophical and medical texts means that the problem itself gets defined too narrowly. Had he also included some of the Greek tragedies, which quite obviously contain what Foucault calls sexual moral reflections, he would, I believe, have been forced to reconsider several of his theories.

THE RECEPTION OF FOUCAULT'S AND IRIGARAY'S PLATONIC STUDIES: THE HISTORY OF WOMAN'S EXCLUSION IN REPEAT?

Foucault and Irigaray have both made contributions to the study of Plato, and in both cases their efforts find a focus in the same two themes: love and sexuality. Both are interested in Plato's philosophy to the extent that it can throw light on their own philosophical concerns, and from a traditional perspective, both their studies are idiosyncratic, each in its own way. Neither of them is a classical scholar in the strict sense. But when it comes to the reception of their work, the differences are considerable. Foucault's work has been read and criticized, but also embraced by many classicists, and above all it has stimulated an intense and fruitful debate on the issue of sexuality in antiquity. By contrast, Irigaray's Platonic study has hardly been commented on. This is true not only of her account of the cave myth in *Speculum*. For neither does her interpretation of Diotima's role in the *Symposium*[15] seem to have stirred much interest among Plato scholars. Why this enormous discrepancy in the reception of Irigaray's and Foucault's work?

A possible explanation is of course that Irigaray's Platonic analysis is so beside the point that it simply deserves to be ignored, whereas Foucault's work, on antique sexuality in general, and on Plato's philosophy in particular, is of quite another quality – even if it is controversial. I myself have tried to show that Irigaray's account of Plato's philosophy is by no means beside the point, and that it is perfectly possible to engage with it on a constructive level. Admittedly, Irigaray's texts demand patience, but this is hardly a quality that classicists lack. Considering the amount of writing that Plato's philosophy prompts, and how much of that writing becomes a subject for discussion in specialized journals, I see no academic reason why Irigaray's Platonic studies should be so neglected. One possible objection might be that she seems less interested in Plato's text than in her own thoughts. But this critique would apply to Foucault to an equal degree.

The biggest difference between Irigaray's and Foucault's readings of Plato lies in the different contexts in which they chose to place him. Whereas Irigaray aims to read the cave myth from a 'woman's perspective' – in the 'mirror of the other woman', as it says in the title of her book – Foucault's focus is on the man and his desires and urges. It is here, I believe, that we find the explanation for the immense difference in response to Irigaray's and Foucault's work. Irigaray's extreme 'woman's perspective' strikes us as far more off-putting than Foucault's extreme 'man's perspective'. For a feminist it is hard not to see the silence that surrounds Irigaray's interpretation of Plato as yet another episode in the history of the exclusion of all things female from our tradition of European philosophy.

Notes

Introduction

1. Cf. Vernant's phrase: 'This dream of a purely paternal heredity never ceased to haunt the Greek imagination' ('Hestia-Hermes: The Religious Expression of Space and Movement in Ancient Greece', in Jean-Pierre Vernant, *Myth and Thought among the Greeks*, p. 134). The phrase has been used in several feminist studies of Greek myths and literature before me. See for instance Marilyn B. Arthur, 'The Dream of a World without Women: Poetics and the Circles of Order in the *Theogony* Prooemium'; Froma I. Zeitlin, 'The Dynamics of Mysogony: Myth and Mythmaking in the *Oresteia*', p. 180, n. 21; Nicole Loraux, *The Children of Athena: Athenian Ideas About Citizenship and the Division Between the Sexes*, p. 64, n. 145 and p. 120.

Chapter 1

1. Translation Philip Vellacott.
2. Pierre Vidal-Naquet, *The Black Hunter*, p. 206.
3. Here I take up a thread suggested by Jean-Pierre Vernant, Nicole Loraux and Pierre Vidal-Naquet. The present chapter is greatly indebted to their work (see bibliography).
4. The significance of the Greek myths for philosophy has long been a subject for feminist philosophers, first and foremost Simone de Beauvoir, *The Second Sex*. Cf. also Robin Schott, *Cognition and Eros: A Critique of the Kantian Paradigm*.
5. Cf. Apollodorus 3.14.6.
6. Cf. Loraux, *The Children of Athena*, p. 38.
7. Translation Philip Vellacott.
8. Both this and the next section build on Vidal-Naquet, *The Black Hunter*, p. 216f.
9. In fairness we should note that Loraux refers to passages in Aristophanes which modify this claim: at *Lysistrata* 56 we find the expression *attikai gynaikes* ('women of Attica'; Loraux, *The Children of Athena*, p. 117, n.28) and in *Thesmophoriazusae* we find the word *astai* ('female citizens'; ibid. p. 119, n.38). But these are isolated occurrences.
10. Translation Philip Vellacott.
11. Concerning quotations from Hesiod's *Theogony* and *Works and Days*, see Translator's Note at the beginning of the book.

12. Plato's theory of principles is part of his so-called 'unwritten philosophy', which has been reconstructed by, among others, Hans-Joachim Krämer and Konrad Gaiser. See Krämer, *Arete bei Platon und Aristoteles*, and Gaiser, *Platons unges-chriebene Lehre*. In his interpretation of the dialogues, Egil A. Wyller identifies something similar to the theory of principles. See especially his doctorate thesis, *Platons* Parmenides *in seinem Zusammenhang mit* Symposion *und* Politeia, and, *Den sene Platon: en studie i Platons henologi*.

13. J.-P. Vernant, 'Hestia-Hermes: The Religious Expression of Space and Movement in Ancient Greece', in Vernant, *Myth and Thought*.

14. See R. Waterfield, *The First Philosophers: The Presocratics and the Sophists*, p. 111.

15. Xenophon, *Oikonomikos* 8.23. Cf. Vernant, *Myth and Thought*, p. 133.

16. Cf. Froma I. Zeitlin, 'Cultic Models of the Female: Rites of Dionysos and Demeter'.

17. Pseudo-Aristotle, *Oikonomikos* A4.1344 a.

18. It might be objected that women played an active role in the religious festivals that played such an important role in the public life of the city state. But insofar as these festivals seem to confirm and underline the masculine ideology of the *polis*, women's participation in them seems somewhat ambiguous. See e.g. Zeitlin, 'Cultic Models of the Female'.

19. In a number of articles, Vidal-Naquet has analysed both the parallels and the contradictions implied by the various fringe groups of the Athenian *polis*. See in particular 'The Black Hunter and the Origin of the Athenian *Ephebia*', 'Recipes for Greek Adolescence' and 'Slavery and the Rule of Women in Tradition, Myth, Utopia', all in *The Black Hunter*.

Chapter 2

1. Concerning translations of Parmenides, see Translator's Note at the beginning of the book.

2. The relation between Hesiod and Parmenides has been demonstrated in numerous studies. See e.g. Hans Schwabl, 'Hesiod und Parmenides: Zur Formung des parmenideischen Prooimiums', and Maja E. Pellikaan-Engel, *Hesiod and Parmenides: A New View on their Cosmologies and on Parmenides' Proem*.

3. See for instance P. Philippson, 'Genealogie als mythische Form. Studien zur *Theogonie* des Hesiod'.

4. The account of Parmenides' philosophy offered here differs significantly from prevailing interpretations on a number of points. Firstly, the research tradition has not been commonly concerned with the issue of gender and sexuality in relation to Parmenides. It is only in the course of the last ten years that such themes have received any attention whatsoever, and evidently they still belong on the fringe of Parmenidean research, to put it mildly. My interpretation of Parmenides' poem shares a number of features with Arlene W. Saxonhouse's analysis in *Fear of Diversity: The Birth of Political Science in Ancient Thought*. Saxonhouse stresses above all that there is room for neither generation nor sexual difference within Parmenidean Being, which is also a central point in my analysis. Adriana

Cavarero, in her essay 'Die thrakische Dienstmagd' (*Platon zum Trotz*), also touches on questions of gender. My interpretation of Parmenides, however, differs fundamentally from Cavarero's.

I also distance myself from some of the most widely accepted notions in Parmenidean research in regarding the concept of Being as a kind of *life*: Being as something immobile, absolutely inert. See, e.g. W. K. C. Guthrie, *A History of Greek Philosophy. Vol. 2: The Presocratic Tradition from Parmenides to Democritus*, p. 36: 'The complete immobility of the real, the impossibility of *kinesis* in any sense of the word, is for Parmenides the climax of his message.' There are, however, some exceptions, in particular analyses influenced by Heidegger's work on Parmenides. See, e.g. J. Schlüter, *Heidegger and Parmenides*, p. 248ff. The present work also draws inspiration from Heidegger, not least from M. Heidegger *Vorträge und Aufsätze* and *Was heisst Denken?*

5. The authenticity of verses 118 and 119 has been disputed. See Hesiod, *Theogony*, ed. M.L. West, p. 193ff.

6. Cf. Giulia Sissa, *Le corps virginal*.

7. Cf. Annie Bonnafé, *Eros et Eris: mariages divins et mythe de succession chez Hésiode*.

8. In his article 'Politische Gemeinschaft auf dunklem Grund: Das Negativ und seine Transformationen in Hesiods *Theogonie*', Thomas Oser shows convincingly how the three genealogical principles are mutually dependent on one another throughout the poem.

9. Translation Kirk, Raven and Schofield, *The Presocratic Philosophers*.

10. Anaximander, who according to Simplicius was the first of the philosophers to use the term *archē*, seems to have applied it in the sense intended here. One of Aristotle's definitions of *archē* runs as follows: 'It is common, then, to all beginnings (*archē*) to be the first point from which a thing either is or comes to be or is known' (*Metaphysics* 1013a 17–19; translation W. D. Ross).

It is common to claim that, at this point in the poem, Hesiod is coming closer to what would later be called philosophy. Cf. for example, Hermann Fränkel, who believes that what we are looking at here is '(p)rofunde ontologische Spekulationen' (*Dichtung und Philosophie des frühen Griechentums*, p. 117).

11. In etymological terms, the Greek word for 'threshold' – *oudos* – is clearly related to *hedos*, the term for 'foundation', or 'groundwork', used at the opening of the poem to describe Earth (Hesiod, *Theogony* 117, cf. O. Becker, *Das Bild des Weges*, p. 15). The fact that terms with similar meanings are used at *Theogony* 117 and 812 – 'secure' at the former to describe Earth, and 'unshakeable' at the latter to describe the threshold – suggests that the threshold offers the same kind of security as was formerly provided by Earth.

12. See Ch. 5, 'Sexuality and philosophy in Plato's *Symposium*'.

13. Cf. Vernant, *L'individu, la mort, l'Amour*, p. 18f.

14. Cf. Hesiod, *Works and Days*, 90–92. These evils (*kaka*) are brought into circulation with the opening of Pandora's box (*Works and Days*, 94ff.).

15. Cf. Hesiod, *Theogony* 573–84; the quotes are from Hesiod, *Works and Days* 66, 67 and 78.

16. It is worth noting that the sense of wonder (*thauma*), which is the source of the man's desire for the woman, is later characterized as the source of philosophy:

'Philosophy has no other origin (*archē*)' (Plato, *Theaetetus* 155d; cf. Aristotle, *Metaphysics* I, 982b12ff.). Plato seems to regard wonder as a kind of philosophical desire (*eros*) for the thing that arouses wonder: that which can never be fully grasped, the supreme One, the divine. Without going into details, I merely wish to point out a possible connection between Hesiod's notion of woman as the source of man's insatiable desire for immortality on the one hand, and philosophical desire (*eros*) on the other.

17. One of these verse lines is most probably an interpolation, yet it is difficult to know which. Cf. Hesiod, *Theogony*, M.L. West, ed. p. 329f.

18. Cf. Hesiod, *Works and Days* 92 (see also 113–116).

19. Cf. Arthur, 'The Dream of a World without Women', p. 102ff.

20. This is a translation of the Greek word *hēmeros*, which was a common designation for 'human being'.

21. Cf. Sissa, *Le corps virginal*. In a number of contexts, Sissa discusses the word *chasma* ('fissure', p. 32; 'cavité', p. 166) as an allusion to the female body. She points out that Hesiod's description of the *chasma* in the passage on Tartarus is reminiscent of an inverted vase (p. 166). Pandora is also associated with a vase (*pithos*) full of misfortunes, and her body, which is made of clay, also implies a reference to the same *pithos*. Tartarus, *chasma*, woman, misfortune – each element refers to the other.

22. References to the Parmenides fragments, and, unless otherwise stated, to the fragments of other Presocratic philosophers, are given according to the numbering established by Diels and Kranz in *Die Fragmente der Vorsokratiker*. References are prefixed with either an A to indicate a testimonium, or a B to indicate an authentic fragment. Concerning the English translations, see the Translator's Note at the beginning of this book.

23. Regrettably, historians of philosophy and Parmenides scholars have rarely shown much interest in Parmenides' prologue, which is usually dismissed as mere lyrical embellishment. See, for example, Jonathan Barnes, *The Presocratic Philosophers*, p. 156: 'The poem began with a long allegorical prologue, the interpretation of which is for the most part of little philosophical importance.' A few commentators, however, have seen significance in the proem, e.g. Uvo Hölscher, in his work *Parmenides*.

24. Heraclitus, fragment 94. Translation Kirk, Raven and Schofield, *The Presocratic Philosophers*.

25. Cf. J. Sihvola, 'Decay, Progress, the Good Life? Hesiod and Protagoras on the Development of Culture', p. 49 ff.

26. Cf. Hans Schwabl, who has pointed out the clear parallel between the many uses of *entha* in Hesiod's depiction of Tartarus, and Parmenides' *entha* in the prologue ('Hesiod und Parmenides: Zur Formung des parmenideischen Prooimiums'). I have also studied these parallels more closely in my doctoral thesis, *Zwiefältige Wahrheit und zeitliches Sein. Eine Interpretation des parmenideischen Gedichts*, pp. 29–33.

27. For Xenophanes, who is supposed to have been Parmenides' teacher, the notion of god is clearly corporeal: 'All of him sees, all thinks, and all hears' (Xenophanes B 24). Man, on the other hand, has a deficit of both rationality and perception. In other words we find a fundamental distinction here as well between unity and

multiplicity, although this does not necessarily imply a distinction between body and soul/rationality.

28. It should be noted that the translation of this fragment is much disputed.

29. See Jesper Svenbro's interesting discussion of this word in his book *Phrasikleia*, p. 18ff.

30. The translation and intepretation of this line are widely disputed. See Jürgen Wiesner, 'Überlegungen zu Parmenides, fr. VIII, 34'.

31. Cf. Heidegger, *Was heisst Denken?*

32. Cf. fragment 8.29: 'Abiding as the same in the same (place) it rests by itself'.

33. I shall develop this 'political' interpretation of Parmenidean Being in the next chapter.

34. We might also mention *Themis* (B 8.32) and *Pistis* ('persuasion', B 8.28), but these two are not so clearly personified in the poem as the other three goddesses.

35. Cf. H. Schreckenberg, 'ANANKE', pp. 20 and 31.

36. This discussion draws on my book *Zwiefältige Wahrheit und zeitliches Sein*, p. 71f.

37. Cf. David Ross, *Aristotle*, p. 82.

38. Cf. Günther Bien's article 'Praxis, praktisch' in *Historisches Wörterbuch der Philosophie*.

39. Loraux, ('Das Band der Teilung', p. 41) 'Le lien de la division', p. 108.

40. Cf. Sissa, *Le corps virginal*. The term *parthenos*, translated here as 'virgin', is perhaps closer to the English 'maiden'. It meant 'young unmarried woman' without necessarily implying that she was what we understand by 'virgin'. Sissa points out that there were both genuine and ungenuine virgins: a virgin who gives birth is 'une fausse vierge' (p. 113).

41. Cf. Hippocrates' Aphorism V.51: 'As soon as conception takes place, the mouth of the uterus is closed.'

42. Cf. Paula Schmitt, 'Athéna Apatouria et la ceinture', p. 1063f.

43. One word occasionally used for the woman's belt is *desmos*, which Parmenides uses as a term for the bands that hold Being. Cf. Schmitt, 'Athéna Apatouria', p. 1063.

44. Cf. Euripides, *Helena* 61, where we find the expression *asylos gamōn*: to be protected against marriage.

45. I will return to this theme in Chapter 5.

Chapter 3

1. Here I have in mind Hippodamus of Miletus. Cf. Vernant, *Myth and Thought*, p. 185f.

2. Cf. Vernant's essay, 'Geometrical Structure and Political Ideas in the Cosmology of Anaximander' (in his *Myth and Thought*).

3. See Moses I. Finley, 'Was Greek Civilization Based on Slave Labour?' in M.I. Finley (ed.) *Slavery in Classical Antiquity*.

4. Quoted from Finley, ibid., p. 70.

5. In addition to Vernant's book *Les origines de la pensée grecque* I shall refer first and foremost to the following articles of his, all of which are published in *Myth and Thought*: 'Geometry and Spherical Astronomy in the First Greek

Cosmology', 'Geometrical Structure and Political Ideas in the Cosmology of Anaximander', 'Space and Political Organisation in Ancient Greece'. I shall also draw upon Lévêque and Vidal-Naquet's book *Clisthène l'Athénien.*

6. Herodotus, 6.130. The word 'democracy' seems not to have existed in Cleisthenes' time. There is no record of its use prior to Herodotus. *Isonomia* ('equality before the law') was the term most commonly used. Cf. Herodotus, 3.80.6, where he speaks of democracy as the system of government that has 'the most beautiful of all names: *isonomia*'. Concerning the relation between 'democracy' and 'isonomia', see Lévêque and Vidal-Naquet, *Clisthène l'Athénien*, Ch. 2, 'Isonomie et démocratie'; G. Vlastos, 'ISONOMIA POLITIKE'; C. Meier, 'Demokratie. Einleitung: Antike Grundlagen' and *Die Entstehung des Politischen bei den Griechen.*

7. Lévêque and Vidal-Naquet, *Clisthène l'Athénien*, p. 15f.

8. Lévêque and Vidal-Naquet, *Clisthène l'Athénien*, p. 21: 'Le découpage politique doit aboutir non à dissoudre l'unité du *demos*, mais à lui assurer plus de cohésion. Aussi l'espace politique de l'Agora, centre géométrique de la *polis*, se voit-il nettement délimité et circonscrit.'

9. For a more thorough account of *hestia*'s symbolism and political significance, see L. Gernet, 'Sur le symbolisme politique en Grèce ancienne: le foyer commun' and Vernant, *Myth and Thought.*

10. This corresponds to Socrates' line of thought when he suggests, in Plato's dialogue *Apology*, that rather than be condemned to death he ought to be maintained for the remainder of his life in the Prytaneum and at the state's expense. In his opinion, his philosophical activity does not represent a crime against the *polis*, but rather a service: his philosophical cross-questioning of the Athenians did not endanger the state, as his opponents claimed, but rather reinforced its unity. Cf. *Apology*, 36b–e.

11. Vernant refers for instance to Herodotus' account of the tyrant Maiandros of Samos, who came to power after Polycrates around 510 BCE. Following the death of Polycrates, Maiandros erected an altar to Zeus Eleutherios, the liberator. He called together the citizens and told them that 'the sceptre and the power' were now in his hands, but that he had no wish to rule over his equals: 'I therefore place the power in the middle (*es meson*) and proclaim *isonomia* for you (i.e. that you have equal political rights)' (Herodotus, 3.142; quoted in *Myth and Thought*, p. 191). To 'place power in the middle' clearly means transferring power to the community, i.e. the introduction of democracy.

12. Cf. Lévêque and Vidal-Naquet, *Clisthène l'Athénien*, p. 17.

13. Vernant, *Myth and Thought*, p. 190.

14. Cf. Charles H. Kahn, *Anaximander and the Origins of Greek Cosmology*, p. 233.

15. Cf. Aristotle's rather convoluted discussion of the comparative contributions of the male and female in reproduction in *De Generatione Animalium* 1. See e.g. 729b13ff.

16. See my article 'Materia, genere e morte in Aristotele', in Michele Marsonet, *Donne e Filosofia*, pp. 10–20.

17. Cf. Krämer, 'Die Grundlegung des Freiheitsbegriff in der Antike', p. 259: 'Im Begriff der Autarkie liegt . . . das Moment der Selbsterhaltung, das Vermögen, sich selbst aus sich heraus im Sein zu halten.'

18. I have discussed such strategies in Chapter 1.
19. In *L'écriture d'Orphée*, Detienne sketches similar connections between the central fire (*hestia koinē*) and the city state's ideal of autonomy and autarchy. For a thorough investigation of the *hestia* symbolism and its political significance, see also Gernet, 'Sur le symbolisme politique en Grèce ancienne', and Vernant's essay 'Hestia-Hermes' in *Myth and Thought*.
20. Translation Kirk, Raven and Schofield, *The Presocratic Philosophers*.
21. Lévêque and Vidal-Naquet, *Clisthène l'Athénien*, p. 66.
22. See Sissa, *Le corps virginal*, p. 166.
23. Diogenes Laertius, 1.35. The reference is from Vernant, *Myth and Thought*, p. 197.
24. This might seem to contradict the claim made above that Thales suggested founding the state on principles of a democratic nature. Yet it should not surprise us that one or two of these early thinkers advocated ideas that were in some respects 'old' and in other respects 'new'. We can regard Thales as a thinker with one foot in the 'mythical', 'monarchic' world of thought, and the other in the realm of new and 'democratic' concepts.
25. Cf. e.g. Anaximenes, B 2: '. . . the whole universe is surrounded by wind and air'.
26. Cf. Anaximenes, fragment B 3.
27. Vernant (*Myth and Thought*, p. 199ff.) discusses in detail whether or not we can accept Hippolytus' text as an accurate rendition of Anaximander's words. This is of greatest significance in the case of the expression *ou kratoumenon* ('not governed'). He concludes that the expression must be considered authentic. I follow Vernant on this point.
28. Cf. Vernant, *Myth and Thought*, p. 191.
29. Aristotle, *Physics* 187a20 = A 16 (Diels and Kranz). However, *apeiron* is not mentioned explicitly at this juncture, but is rather called 'the One' (*to hen*).
30. Cf. Vlastos, 'Equality and Justice in Early Greek Cosmology', p. 156f.; Lévêque and Vidal-Naquet, *Clisthène l'Athénien*. p. 30.
31. Vlastos, 'Equality and Justice', p. 168.
32. There is no general consensus for the view that opposites return to *apeiron*. Most Anaximander commentators of the past 40–50 years have concluded that the elements repay their debts to one another by being transformed into their opposites. Accordingly, stability (*dikē*) consists in a process of constant change between contraries. In her article 'Cosmic Justice in Anaximander', Joyce Engmann argues convincingly against such an interpretation. In this regard Engmann agrees with Heidegger's 'Der Spruch des Anaximanders' (in *Holzwege*), to which there is however no reference in her article. I myself am indebted to Heidegger's Anaximander analysis.
33. Cf. Vernant, *Myth and Thought*, p. 204f.
34. C. Kahn, *Anaximander and the Origins of Greek Cosmology*.
35. Cf. e.g. Mansfeld, *Die Vorsokratiker I*, p. 24. See also Vernant, *Myth and Thought*, p. 223: 'With Parmenides philosophy becomes independent. Each type of discipline, at grips with its own problems, has to develop its own ways of thinking and its own terminology and elaborate its own logic.'
36. Vlastos ('ISONOMIA POLITIKE', p. 163). As far as I know, few people other than Vlastos have pointed out the relevance of the political discourse in

Parmenides' poem. G. Jameson ('"Well-rounded truth" and circular thought in Parmenides', p. 26) speaks of 'a military metaphor which, though never precisely formulated, runs through the Way of Truth', a number of aspects of which he also examines (pp. 26–9). He does not, however, discuss the meaning and relevance of this metaphor, due to the rather different aim of his own inquiry, which is to show that it is Being and not thought (or truth) which Parmenides regards as spherical. Even so, I acknowledge that my own reading of Parmenides is indebted to his analysis. In addition, W. Detel 'Zeichen bei Parmenides' has shown that Parmenides' concept of a sign (*sēma*, fr. 8,2) is of military origin (cf. Detel, 'Zeichen bei Parmenides', pp. 221–39).

37. Cf. Euripides, *The Suppliant Women*, 312.
38. Cf. Vlastos, 'Equality and Justice', p. 157 and footnote 13.
39. In his 'Parmenidesstudien', Fränkel translates *isopales* as 'das ausgeglichene Kräftespiel' (*Wege und Formen frühgriechischen Denkens*, p. 196). Herodotus, a contemporary of Parmenides, uses the word to describe two armies that are exactly equal in strength (1.82.4; cf. 5.49.8).
40. Plato discusses this ontological problem in depth in the *Sophist*, which deals explicitly with Parmenides' unifying principle. Even so, Plato finds no solution to the problem, and one of Aristotle's main objections to Plato's political philosophy is that it lays so much emphasis on the unity of the state that the state itself threatens to break down as a political community of separate individuals: 'Is it not obvious that a state may at length attain such a degree of unity as to be no longer a state? – since the nature of a state is to be a plurality, and in tending to greater unity, from being a state, it becomes a family, and from being a family, an individual' (Aristotle, *Politics II*, 1261a. Translation W. D. Ross).
41. This principle can also be found in medical treatises, which occasionally dealt with the effects of the climate on health. The heat of summer is overcome by the cold of winter, which interacts in turn with the body's own cold and warmth. In time, the interplay of the fluctuating forces of the body and of nature leads to a state of equilibrium (*isonomia*). Cf. Vlastos (1947) p. 158, where he speaks of 'the idea of rotation in office'.
42. Cf. Jameson, '"Well-rounded truth",' p. 28: '*ētor* is here placed in the normal context of self-defence against attacks'.
43. See Jameson, ibid., p. 28.
44. See p. 51.
45. Cf. e.g. Euripides, *Medea* 728 and 387 respectively.
46. Cf. J. Bollack, whose study 'La cosmologie parménidéenne de Parménide' lays particular stress on the principle of stability. To the best of my knowledge, Bollack is the first to have given a consistent interpretation of this part of the poem, both on its own terms and relative to the rest of the poem; the concept of stability is fundamental for both *alētheia* and *doxa*.
47. Bollack has persuasively emphasized the strict symmetry that holds between the male and the female in Parmenides: 'Dans la première évocation du mélange, les qualités de mâle et de femelle représentent les forces opposées. La symétrie des mouvements, le femelle allant vers le mâle, et le mâle vers le femelle, illustre jusque dans l'union qu'ils amorcent leur stricte équivalence.' To my knowledge, no other scholar has made this point.

48. I have adopted the term 'one-sex model' from Thomas Laqueur's book *Making Sex. Body and Gender from the Greeks to Freud*. In contrast to Laqueur, I myself believe that the one-sex model still survives today.

Chapter 4

1. Cf. Aristotle, *De Generatione Animalium* I, 730.
2. Cf. Toril Moi, *Simone de Beauvoir: The Making of an Intellectual Woman*.
3. See Chs 1 and 5. The idea of woman as the negation of man is the target of most of what I say about Plato in this book. It will be the main theme of Chapter 6.
4. Cf. Martha C. Nussbaum, *The Fragility of Goodness: Luck and Ethics in Greek Tragedy and Philosophy*, p. 25. My inspiration for setting 'tragic conflict' up against 'Platonic harmony' is the distinction Nussbaum draws between what she calls human fragility and divine perfection. According to Nussbaum, one of the characteristics of the Greek tragedies and of Aristotle's view of human life and ethics is their belief in people's fundamental fragility. By contrast, Plato adopts divine perfection as a standard also for human life. I therefore differ from Nussbaum in treating Aristotle as a representative of the Platonic tradition. Neither does Nussbaum address the possibility that gender difference might constitute an aspect of human 'fragility'. It is my aim to make good that omission in this chapter.
5. There are many opinions about which gods the various elements correspond to. One person to have considered this question in detail is Peter Kingsley in his *Ancient Philosophy, Mystery, and Magic*. Kingsley claims that Empedocles identified, or at least associated, Hera with earth, Zeus with air, Hades with fire and Nestis with water (see Part I, 'Philosophy').
6. For a more detailed study of Empedocles' views on love, conflict and sexual difference, see my book *Tanker om opprinnelsen* (Ch. 10, 'Empedokles. Kjærlighet og hat').
7. Translation Lane Cooper, in *The Collected Dialogues of Plato*, ed. Hamilton and Cairns.
8. Cf. e.g. Karl Popper, *The Open Society and its Enemies*. Vol. 1: *The Spell of Plato*.
9. Translation Paul Shorey, in *The Collected Dialogues of Plato* ed. Hamilton and Cairns.
10. Cf. Nussbaum's depiction of Socrates (*The Fragility of Goodness*, p. 183f.).
11. Cf. Saxonhouse's interpretation of Plato's philosophy, in *Fear of Diversity*, where she demonstrates the decisive role that the dialectic between the ideal of self-sufficiency and human dependence on others plays in Plato's reflections on *eros*, sexual difference, life and death.
12. Translation Michael Joyce, in *The Collected Dialogues of Plato*, ed. Hamilton and Cairns.

Chapter 5

1. In this chapter, unless otherwise specified, the numbers in parentheses refer to the *Symposium*. Quotations from the *Symposium* are taken from the translations by Joyce and Nehamas & Woodruff (see bibliography).

2. This picture of the philosopher – as one who fertilizes, becomes pregnant and gives birth – focuses on slightly different aspects of philosophical activity than those intended by the Socratic image of the philosopher as midwife (cf. especially Plato, *Theaetetus*, 149ff.). The image of the philosopher as midwife suggests first and foremost the dialogical aspect of philosophical activity: it is Socrates' task to deliver his interlocutors of their spiritual offspring, i.e. he must help them think true thoughts, or achieve true insight. The midwife metaphor is in itself neutral with regard to sexual difference, whereas the metaphors I am concerned with in this analysis provide an opportunity to reflect on the role that sexual difference plays in Plato's philosophy.

3. For another and somewhat deeper discussion of the view that Plato was looking for the most masculine women as instruments of government, see Julia Annas, 'Plato's *Republic* and Feminism'. See also *An Introduction to Plato's* Republic, by the same author, and A.W. Saxonhouse, *Fear of Diversity*, p. 148 ff. Saxonhouse calls the equality of women and men in the *Republic* 'the figurative murder of the female' (ibid. p.148).

4. For further references to Plato's disparaging view of women, see Dorothea Wender, 'Plato: Misogynist, Paedophile, and Feminist'.

5. Many readers are likely to object: but what about Diotima, the woman who lectures Socrates and the other participants in the *Symposium* on the topic of love? I shall address this question later in the chapter.

6. B. Freeman, '(Re)writing Patriarchal Texts: *The Symposium*', p. 168.

7. Cf. Hesiod, *Theogony* 120ff.; Parmenides, fragment 13; Aristophanes, *The Clouds* 973ff. (1084ff.) and *The Birds* 704ff. On the basis of Parmenides' fragment 13, it cannot be said for sure that the function of Eros in Parmenides' cosmology is to unify the male and the female elements, but this is still the most likely interpretation, and to the best of my knowledge, quite uncontroversial.

8. Cf. Sophocles, *Antigone* 781ff., and Euripides, *Hippolytus* 1268ff.

9. This point requires some qualification: it can be claimed that Plato is following a thread suggested by Sappho, who depicts Eros as a god of love between women. My thanks to Gro Rørstadbotten for this reminder.

10. Of course, the fact that there was no god for the love between men does not mean that there were no appropriate role models in Greek mythology. Zeus' love for the young Ganymede could be described as a prototype. See e.g. B. Sergent, *L'homosexualité dans la mythologie grecque*.

11. For a thorough study of Greek pederasty, see above all Kenneth J. Dover, *Greek Homosexuality*, and H. Patzer, *Die griechische Knabenliebe*.

12. This is the dilemma that Foucault refers to as 'the antinomy of the boy' ('l'Antinomie du garçon'). I shall discuss this in greater detail in Chapter 7.

13. See Dover, *Greek Homosexuality*.

14. The best available discussion of this theme is in my opinion David Halperin's 'Why is Diotima a Woman?' in Halperin, *One Hundred Years of Homosexuality and Other Essays on Greek Love*. This work also contains a comprehensive bibliography. Cf. also Martina Reuter, 'Feministiska synpunkter på Platons dualismer', and her unpublished thesis *Kunskap, kropp och kvinnor: Några synpunkter på den feministiska kritiken av Platons og Descartes dualismer*, in which she makes a detailed examination of Diotima's role in the *Symposium*.

15. L. Irigaray, 'l'Amour sorcier. Lecture de Platon. Le banquet, "Discours de Diotime"' (in Irigaray, *Éthique de la différence sexuelle*). In her article 'Diotima of Mantinea' (in Waithe, *A History of Women Philosophers. Volume 1*) Mary Ellen Waithe also claims to discover a particularly female view of love in the *Symposium*. I myself have discussed Irigaray's reading of the *Symposium* in the article 'Luce Irigaray rakkaudesta ja ihmetyksestä' ('Luce Irigaray on love and wonder').

16. See note 14.

17. Cf. Saxonhouse, whose interpretation of Socrates'/Diotima's speech contradicts my own in most respects; she says for example about this point: 'Plato via Socrates via Diotima brings the female fully into the process of generation' (*Fear of Diversity*, p. 175).

18. Cf. J.S. Morrison, 'Four notes on Plato's *Symposium*', p. 53f. Morrison refers to *Timaeus* 91cf., where Plato's description of human procreation can be interpreted in this way.

19. See e.g. John Brenkman, 'The Other and the One: Psychoanalysis, Reading, *The Symposium*'.

20. Aeschylus, *Eumenides* 658ff.

21. In this I follow Morrison, 'Four notes on Plato's *Symposium*', p. 53. Halperin argues that on the few other occasions in the literature where such expressions are used of men, they serve as metaphors for death. Halperin also regards it as innovatory that Plato uses the notion of birth as a metaphor for the man's creative agency (Halperin, *One Hundred Years of Homosexuality*, p. 138).

22. I accept Creuzer's conjecture here that the Greek text reads *adynaton* ('impossible' i.e. 'no other way') rather than *athanaton* ('immortal').

23. I acknowledge here the inspiration of Egil A. Wyller's account of the role played by the phenomenon of suddenness – *exaiphnēs* – in Plato's philosophy. Of particular relevance in this regard is Wyller's doctoral thesis *Platons* Parmenides *in seinem Zusammenhang mit* Symposion *und* Politeia.

Chapter 6

1. The English translation *Speculum of the Other Woman* was published in 1985.

2. Toril Moi, 'Patriarchal reflection: Luce Irigaray's looking-glass', in *Sexual/Textual Politics*.

3. Cf. for instance the following quotation from Galen: 'Think first, please, of the man's (external genitalia) turned in and extending inward between the rectum and the bladder. If this should happen, the scrotum would necessarily take the place of the uterus with the testis lying outside, next to it on either side' (quoted in Laqueur, *Making Sex*, p. 25). Laqueur argues that, although we do not find such explicit evocations of the woman as an inverted man in the texts of Plato's time, it was nevertheless the 'one-sex model' that dominated.

4. Margaret Whitford, *Luce Irigaray. Philosophy in the Feminine*, p. 106.

5. Some readers might find this section rather technical. It can be skipped without serious consequences for the general argument.

6. Page references are to the English translation, *Speculum of the Other Woman*.

7. Irigaray comments extensively on the significance of the wall from behind which

the puppet theatre is performed. She seems to regard it as an inexplicable aspect of the myth: how have the prisoners entered the cave when it is blocked by such an unpassable barrier?

And how do the liberated prisoners manage to pass through or over this wall? I myself am not convinced that this problem is significant, since the text does not specify that the barrier blocks the passage through the cave by extending from one wall to the other. It is quite possible that Plato imagined the prisoner passing around the end of the wall. Irigaray seeks to interpret the wall as a metaphor for the virginal hymen and thus to raise the question of the role of fertilization within this picture, for it seems that fertilization simply does not occur, i.e. there is no 'mingling' of the masculine and the feminine. Moreover, she ascribes quite another crucial function to the wall. It divides the cave into two, creating a further distinction between inside and outside, and this in turn allows, or implies, a doubling and inversion of other inside/outside distinctions.

8. Although Irigaray characterizes the cave wall as 'virginal' (*Speculum*, p. 328), the text nevertheless implies that the virginity of the cave wall is not of a pure nature.

9. Julia Kristeva, *Histoires d'amour*, p. 84.

10. For several of the points mentioned in this and the foregoing sections, I am indebted to Gro Rørstadbotten and Kristin Sampson.

11. Cf. the title of Irigaray's book *Ce sexe qui n'en est pas un*.

Chapter 7

1. This is one of the complaints that Simon Goldhill levels against Foucault in his book *Foucault's Virginity*. Foucault is criticized in particular for ignoring the ironically humourous texts of late antiquity and the Hellenistic period.

2. Among the influential studies that have emerged in response to Foucault's work, the following deserve particular mention: Jesper Svenbro, *Phrasikleia. Anthropologie de la lecture en Grèce ancienne*; John J. Winkler, *The Constraints of Desire*; D.M. Halperin, *One Hundred Years of Homosexuality and Other Essays on Greek Love*; Larmour, David H., Paul Allen Miller and Charles Platter (eds), *Rethinking Sexuality: Foucault and Classical Antiquity*; D.M. Halperin, J.J. Winkler and Froma I. Zeitlin (eds), *Before Sexuality: The Construction of Erotic Experience in the Ancient Greek World*. The latter work reveals the extent of Foucault's influence on the study of gender and sexuality in antiquity, mythology, philology, literature, art and anthropology.

3. This applies in particular to a number of studies of Roman sexuality, such as Marilyn Skinner, 'Parasites and Strange Bedfellows', and Amy Richlin, *The Garden of Priapus*. For a severe critique of Foucault and his adherents for having overlooked feminist studies, see A. Richlin, 'Zeus and Metis: Foucault, Feminism, Classics'.

4. Unless otherwise indicated, references are to Foucault, *The Use of Pleasure*.

5. It should be noted that Foucault's analysis of *sōphrosynē* as a masculine virtue differs from Plato's account in the *Republic*, where *sōphrosynē* constitutes the *aretē* of the state as a whole and is therefore both active and passive in character. Those who govern show moderation when exercising their rightful power over their

subjects, whereas the subjects themselves show moderation in allowing their masters to control them. In the *Laws* Plato regards *sōphrosynē* as a feminine virtue (*Laws* 803). In Aristotle the type of ambiguity that is here an aspect of *sōphrosynē* seems to attach to all the virtues. Aristotle gives the virtues complementary meanings depending on whether they are applied to a man or a woman (or a slave or a child). For men, the virtues relate to the ability to govern, whereas for women, the virtues relate to the ability to *be* governed (cf. *Politics* I, 1260a20ff.).

6. Foucault claims that it is the dissolution of this unity that characterizes Christian morality (p. 42).

7. Foucault refers to a number of passages in Plato, Aristotle and Xenophon, where pleasure and desire occur repeatedly as a conceptual pair in relation to *aphrodisia*. The hypothesis of three-part circularity is his own, but to me it seems a reasonable interpretation of the Greek notion of *aphrodisia*.

8. This can be illustrated by a simple example from Plato's *Symposium*: 'That, he said, caused him to find himself in a very embarrassing situation'. For Aristotle a 'non-sufferer' (*mē paschōn*) is a man who is immune to the influence of feelings (*Magna Moralia* 1203b21; reference from Liddel, Scott and Jones, *Greek-English Lexicon*).

9. Whether directly or indirectly addressed, this theme is central to most of the chapters of this book, but especially Chs 1, 2 and 5.

10. Translation A.T. Murray, Loeb Classical Library.

11. Foucault analyses texts by Xenophon (*Oeconomicus*), Plato (*Laws*), a so-called pseudo-Aristotle, probably a pupil of Aristotle (*Economics*), and by the rhetorician Isocrates (*Nicocles*). Plato not only encourages fidelity within marriage, but makes it obligatory under the rule of law that he envisages.

12. Xenophon bases his model on the rule of the Persian king Cyrus (*The Use of Pleasure*, p. 153f.). Isocrates also uses an (imagined) monarch as his model for the ideal paterfamilias (*The Use of Pleasure*, p. 170ff.).

13. Foucault takes it for granted that Eros stands on a 'higher' plain than Aphrodite without explaining the different functions of these divinities. It is doubtful whether the distinction between the corporeal Aphrodite and the more spiritual Eros was clearly established in the fourth century BCE. In Plato's *Symposium*, for instance, two versions of Eros are described to correspond to two Aphrodites, in each case there is both a heavenly and an earthly embodiment. The earthly Eros is more representative of love's physical aspect, whereas the heavenly Eros is more spiritual and is the preferred symbol for the love of the free citizen for a young boy (*Symposium*, 180dff.). See also Ch. 5.

14. For a more detailed discussion of this myth, see Ch. 5.

15. This is presented in the essay 'Sourcerer love: A reading of Plato's *Symposium*, Diotima's speech', in *An Ethics of Sexual Difference*. I myself have analysed this text in 'Luce Irigaray rakkaudesta ja ihmetyksestä'.

Bibliography

Classical texts

Texts by Greek authors referred to in this work are available in numerous editions and translations, such as the dual-language (Greek–English) versions published in the *Loeb Classical Library*. The major exception of the *Loeb* edition is the Presocratics. The surviving fragments of the latter are, however, collected and published in various other scholarly editions. In the current work these fragments are referred to according to the system established in Hermann Diels and Walther Kranz, *Die Fragmente der Vorsokratiker*, Berlin: Weidmann, 1951 (Greek and German text). English translations referred to in the current work include: G. S. Kirk, J. E. Raven, and M. Schofield, *The Presocratic Philosophers: A Classical History with a Selection of Texts*, Cambridge University Press, 1983, and Robin Waterfield, *The First Philosophers: The Presocratics and the Sophists*, Oxford University Press, 2000.

The following editions and translations have been consulted, are referred to, or are otherwise recommended (see also Translator's Note at the beginning of the book):

Aeschylus. *Eumenides*. Translated by Philip Vellacott. London: Penguin, 1956.

Apollodorus. *The Library of Greek Mythology*. Oxford University Press, 1997.

Aristotle. *The Works of Aristotle*. Ed. W. D. Ross. Oxford: Clarendon Press, 1997.

Euripides. *Medea*. Translated by Philip Vellacott. London: Penguin, 1963.

Hesiod. *Theogony. Works and Days*. Translated with an introduction and notes by M. L. West. Oxford University Press, 1988.

Hesiod. *Theogony*. Edition with commentary by M. L. West. Oxford: Clarendon Press, 1966.

Hesiod. *Theogony. Works and Days* (published together with Theognis. *Elegies*). Translated and with introductions by Dorothea Wender. Harmondsworth: Penguin, 1973.

Hippocrates. *The Aphorisms of Hippocrates*. New York: The Classics of Medicine Library, 1982.

Homer. *The Iliad*. Translated with an introduction by E. V. Rieu. Harmondsworth: Penguin 1950.

Homer. *The Odyssey*. Translated with an introduction by E. V. Rieu. Harmondsworth: Penguin 1946.

Parmenides. *Parmenides. A Text with Translation, Commentary and Critical Essays*. By Leonardo Tarán. Princeton University Press, 1965.

Plato. *Symposium*. Translated by Alexander Nehamas and Paul Woodruff, in *Plato. Complete Works*, John M. Cooper ed. Indianapolis and Cambridge: Hackett Publishing Company, 1997.

Plato. *The Collected Dialogues of Plato*, Edith Hamilton and Huntington Cairns ed. Princeton University Press, 1961.

Plato. *Platonis opera*, John Burnet ed. Scriptorum classicorum bibliotheca Oxoniensis: Oxford: Clarendon Press, 1900–07.

Other literature

Annas, Julia. 'Plato's *Republic* and Feminism'. *Philosophy*, 51 (1976), pp. 307–21.

Annas, Julia. *An Introduction to Plato's* Republic. Oxford: Clarendon Press, 1989 (1st ed. 1981).

Arthur, Marilyn B. 'The Dream of a World without Women: Poetics and the Circles of Order in the *Theogony* Prooemium'. *Arethusa*, 16 (1983), pp. 97–116.

Barnes, Jonathan. *The Presocratic Philosophers*. London and New York: Routledge & Kegan Paul, 1982 (1st ed. 1979).

Beauvoir, Simone de. *Le deuxième sexe*. Paris: Éditions Gallimard, 1949. English translation: *The Second Sex*. London: Jonathan Cape, 1953.

Becker, Otfrid. *Das Bild des Weges und verwandte Vorstellungen im frühgriechischen Denken*. Berlin: Weidmann, 1937. Hermes. Einzelschriften 4.

Bien, Günther. 'Praxis, praktisch'. *Historisches Wörterbuch der Philosophie*, vol. 7. Darmstadt: Wissenschaftliches Buchgesellschaft, 1989, pp. 1277–87.

Bollack, Jean. 'La cosmologie parménidéenne de Parménide', in R. Brague and J.-F. Courtine (eds), *Herméneutique et ontology: mélanges en hommage à Pierre Aubenque*. Paris: Presse Universitaire de France, 1990.

Bonnafé, Annie. *Eros et Eris: mariages divins et mythe de succession chez Hésiode*. Lyon: Presse Universitaire de Lyon, 1985.

Brenkman, John. 'The Other and the One: Psychoanalysis, Reading, *The Symposium*', in S. Felman (ed.), *Literature and Psychoanalysis*. Baltimore and London: Johns Hopkins University Press, 1982.

Cavarero, Adriana. *Platon zum Trotz*. Berlin: Rotbuch Verlag, 1992. From the Italian: *Nonostante Platone*. Roma: Editori Riuniti, 1990. English translation: *In Spite of Plato*. New York: Routledge, 1995.

Detel, W. 'Zeichen bei Parmenides', *Zeitschrift für Semiotik*, 4 (1982), pp. 221–39.

Detienne, Marcel. *L'écriture d'Orphée*. Paris: Éditions Gallimard, 1989. English translation, *The Writing of Orpheus: Greek Myth in Cultural Context*. Baltimore: Johns Hopkins University Press, 2002.

Dover, Kenneth J. *Greek Homosexuality*. Cambridge, MA: Harvard University Press, 1978.

Engmann, Joyce. 'Cosmic Justice in Anaximander'. *Phronesis*, 36 (1991), pp. 1–25.

Finley, Moses I. 'Was Greek Civilization Based on Slave Labour?', in M.I. Finley (ed.), *Slavery in Classical Antiquity*. Cambridge: Heffer, 1960.

Foucault, Michel. *La volonté de savoir*. Paris: Éditions Gallimard, 1976. Histoire de la sexualité, 1. English translation, *The History of Sexuality. Vol. 1: An Introduction*. New York: Vintage, 1980.

Foucault, Michel. *L'usage des plaisirs*. Paris: Éditions Gallimard, 1984. Histoire de la sexualité, 2. English translation, *The History of Sexuality. Vol. 2: The Use of Pleasure*. New York: Vintage, 1988.

Foucault, Michel. *Le souci de soi*. Paris: Éditions Gallimard, 1984. Histoire de la sexualité, 3. English translation, *The History of Sexuality. Vol. 3: The Care of the Self.* New York: Pantheon, 1986.

Fränkel, Hermann. *Dichtung und Philosophie des frühen Griechentums.* Munich: Verlag C. H. Beck, 1950. English translation, *Early Greek Poetry and Philosophy: A History of Greek Epic, Lyric, and Prose to the Middle of the Fifth Century.* New York: Harcourt Brace Jovanovich, 1973.

Fränkel, Hermann. *Wege und Formen frühgriechischen Denkens.* Munich: Verlag C. H. Beck, 1955.

Freeman, Barbara. '(Re)writing Patriarchal Texts: *The Symposium*', in H. J. Silverman and D. Welton, *Postmodernism and Continental Philosophy.* Albany: State University of New York Press, 1988, pp. 165–77.

Gaiser, Konrad. *Platons ungeschriebene Lehre.* Stuttgart: Ernst Klett Verlag, 1963.

Gernet, Louis. 'Sur le symbolisme politique en Grèce ancienne: le foyer commun'. *Cahier internationaux de sociologie,* 11 (1951).

Goldhill, Simon. *Foucault's Virginity: Ancient Erotic Fiction and the History of Sexuality.* Cambridge University Press, 1995.

Guthrie, W. K. C. *A History of Greek Philosophy. Vol. 2: The Presocratic Tradition from Parmenides to Democritus.* Cambridge University Press, 1978 (1st ed. 1965).

Halperin, D. M. *One Hundred Years of Homosexuality and Other Essays on Greek Love.* New York and London: Routledge, 1990.

Halperin, D. M., John J. Winkler and Froma I. Zeitlin (eds): *Before Sexuality: The Construction of Erotic Experience in the Ancient Greek World.* Princeton University Press, 1990.

Heidegger, Martin. *Holzwege.* Frankfurt am Main: Vittorio Klostermann, 1950. English translation, *Off the Beaten Track.* New York: Cambridge University Press, 2002.

Heidegger, Martin. *Vorträge und Aufsätze 3.* Pfullingen: Neske, 1954.

Heidegger, Martin. *Was heisst Denken?* Tübingen: Max Niemeyer, 1954. English translation, *What is called thinking?* New York: Harper & Row, 1968.

Hirzel, Rudolf. *Themis, Dike und Verwandtes: Ein Beitrag zur Geschichte der Rechtsidee bei den Griechen.* Leipzig: S. Hirzel Verlag, 1907.

Hölscher, Uvo. *Parmenides: Vom Wesen des Seienden.* Frankfurt am Main: Suhrkamp, 1969.

Irigaray, Luce. *Speculum de l'Autre femme.* Paris: Minuit, 1974. English translation, *Speculum of the Other Woman.* Ithaca: Cornell University Press, 1985.

Irigaray, Luce. *Ce sexe qui n'en est pas un.* Paris: Minuit, 1977. English translation, *This Sex which Is Not One.* Ithaca: Cornell University Press, 1985.

Irigaray, Luce. *Éthique de la différence sexuelle.* Paris: Minuit, 1984. English translation: *An Ethics of Sexual Difference.* Ithaca: Cornell University Press, 1993.

Jameson, G. '"Well-rounded truth" and circular thought in Parmenides'. *Phronesis,* 3 (1958), pp. 15–30.

Kahn, Charles H. *Anaximander and the Origins of Greek Cosmology.* New York: Columbia University Press and London: Oxford University Press, 1969.

Kingsley, Peter. *Ancient Philosophy, Mystery, and Magic: Empedocles and Pythagorean Tradition.* Oxford: Clarendon Press, 1995.

Krämer, Hans-Joachim. *Arete bei Platon und Aristoteles.* Heidelberg: Carl Winter Verlag, 1959.

Krämer, Hans-Joachim. 'Die Grundlegung des Freiheitsbegriffs in der Antike', in J.

Simon (ed.), *Freiheit: Theoretische und praktische Aspekte des Problems*. Freiburg and Munich: Verlag Karl Alber, 1977, pp. 239–70.

Kristeva, Julia. *Histoires d'amour*. Paris: Denoël, 1983. English translation, *Tales of love*. New York: Columbia University Press, 1987.

Laqueur, Thomas. *Making Sex. Body and Gender from the Greeks to Freud*. Cambridge, MA and London: Harvard University Press, 1990.

Larmour, David H., Paul Allen Miller and Charles Platter (eds). *Rethinking Sexuality: Foucault and Classical Antiquity*. Princeton University Press, 1998.

Lévêque, Pierre and Pierre Vidal-Naquet. *Clisthène l'Athénien: Èssai sur la représentation de l'espace et du temps dans la pensée politique grecque de la fin du VIe siècle à la mort du Platon*. Paris: Éditions Macula, 1964.

Liddell, Henry George, Robert Scott and Henry Stuart Jones. *A Greek–English Lexicon*. 9th ed. Oxford: Clarendon Press, 1996.

Loraux, Nicole. *Les enfants d'Athena: ìdées athéniennes sur la citoyenneté et la division des sexes*. Paris: Maspero, 1981. English translation *The Children of Athena: Athenian Ideas About Citizenship and the Division Between the Sexes*. Princeton University Press, 1993.

Loraux, Nicole. *Les expériences de Tirésias: le féminin et l'homme grec*. Paris: Maspero, 1989. English translation, *The Experiences of Tiresias*. Princeton University Press, 1995.

Loraux, Nicole. 'Das Band der Teilung', in J. Vogl (ed.), Gemeinschaften. Positionen zu einer Philosophie des Politischen. Frankfurt am Main: Suhrkamp, 1994. From the French: 'Le lien de la division', Le cahier du collège international de philosophie 4 (1987), pp. 101–24.

Mansfeld, Jaap (ed.). *Die Vorsokratiker I*. Stuttgart: Reclam, 1983.

Marsonet, Michele, ed. *Donne e Filosofia*. Geneva: Erga, 2001.

Meier, Christian. 'Demokratie. Einleitung: Antike Grundlagen', in O. Brunner, W. Conze and R. Koselleck (eds), *Geschichtliche Grundbegriffe: Historisches Lexikon zur politisch-sozialen Sprache in Deutschland*. Stuttgart: Klett-Cotta, 1972, pp. 821–35.

Meier, Christian. *Die Entstehung des Politischen bei den Griechen*. Frankfurt am Main: Suhrkamp, 1983.

Moi, Toril. *Sexual/Textual Politics*. London and New York: Methuen, 1985.

Moi, Toril. *Simone de Beauvoir: The Making of an Intellectual Woman*. Oxford and Cambridge MA: Blackwell, 1994.

Morrison, J. S. 'Four notes on Plato's *Symposium*'. *Classical Quarterly*, 14 (1964), pp. 42–55.

Nussbaum, Martha C. *The Fragility of Goodness: Luck and Ethics in Greek Tragedy and Philosophy*. Cambridge: Cambridge University Press, 1986.

Oser, Thomas. 'Politische Gemeinschaft auf dunklem Grund: Das Negativ und seine Transformationen in Hesiods *Theogonie*', in M. Hattstein et al. (eds), *Erfahrungen der Negativität: Festschrift für Michael Theunissen zum 60. Geburtstag*. Hildesheim, Zürich and New York: Georg Olms Verlag, 1992, pp. 29–53.

Patzer, Harald. *Die griechische Knabenliebe*. Wiesbaden: Sitzungsbericht der wissenschaftlichen Gesellschaft an der Johann Wolfgang Goethe-Universität Frankfurt am Main, 19.1 (1982).

Pellikaan-Engel, Maja E. *Hesiod and Parmenides: A New View on their Cosmologies and on Parmenides' Proem*. Amsterdam: Adolf M. Hakkert, 1974.

Philippson, P. 'Genealogie als mythische Form: Studien zur *Theogonie* des Hesiod', in E. Heitsch (ed.), *Hesiod. Wege der Forschung*. Darmstadt: Wissenschaftliche Buchgesellschaft, 1966.

Popper, Karl. *The Open Society and its Enemies*. Vol. I: *The Spell of Plato*. London: Routledge & Kegan Paul, 1966.

Reuter, Martina. 'Feministiska synpunkter på Platons dualismer', *Kvinnoforskning / Naistutkimus*, 7: 3 (1994), pp. 15–35.

Reuter, Martina. *Kunskap, kropp och kvinnor: Några synpunkter på den feministiska kritiken av Platons og Descartes dualismer*. Unpublished thesis. Helsingfors University, 1996.

Richlin, Amy. *The Garden of Priapus: Sexuality and Aggression in Roman Humor*. New York: Yale University Press, 1983.

Richlin, Amy. 'Zeus and Metis: Foucault, Feminism, Classics'. *Helios*, 18 (1991), pp. 160–80.

Richlin, Amy (ed.). *Pornography and Representation in Greece and Rome*. New York and Oxford: Oxford University Press, 1992.

Ross, David. *Aristotle*. London: Methuen, 1949.

Saxonhouse, Arlene W. *Fear of Diversity: The Birth of Political Science in Ancient Thought*. Chicago and London: University of Chicago Press, 1995 (1st ed. 1992).

Schlüter, Jochen. *Heidegger and Parmenides*. Bonn: Bouvier Verlag Herbert Grundermann, 1979.

Schmitt, Pauline. 'Athéna Apatouria et la ceinture: les aspects féminins des Apatouries à Athènes', *Annales. Économies, Sociétés, Civilisations* (1977), pp. 1059–73.

Schott, Robin May. *Cognition and Eros: A Critique of the Kantian Paradigm*. Boston: Beacon Press, 1988.

Schreckenberg, H. 'ANANKE: Untersuchungen zur Geschichte des Wortgebrauches'. *Zetemata*, 36 (1964).

Schwabl, Hans. 'Hesiod und Parmenides: Zur Formung des parmenideischen Prooimiums'. *Rheinisches Museum*, 106 (1963), pp. 134–42.

Sergent, Bernard. *L'homosexualité dans la mythologie grecque*. Paris: Payot, 1984.

Sihvola, Juha. 'Decay, Progress, the Good Life? Hesiod and Protagoras on the Development of Culture', Helsinki: Societas Scientiarum Fennica, 1989.

Sissa, Giulia. *Le corps virginal*. Paris: Librarie philosophique J. Vrin, 1987. English translation, *Greek Virginity*. Cambridge, MA: Harvard University Press, 1990.

Skinner, Marilyn. 'Parasites and Strange Bedfellows: A Study in Catullus' Political Imagery'. *Ramus*, 8 (1979), pp. 137–52.

Songe-Møller, Vigdis. *Zwiefältige Wahrheit und zeitliches Sein: Eine Interpretation des parmenideischen Gedichts*. Würzburg: Königshausen and Neumann, 1980.

Songe-Møller, Vigdis. 'Luce Irigaray rakkaudesta ja ihmetyksestä' ('Luce Irigaray on love and wonder'), in S. Heinämaa, M. Reuter and K. Saarikangas (eds), *Ruumiin kuvia: Subjektin ja sukupuolen muunnilmia*. Tampere: Gaudeamus 1997, pp. 23–36.

Songe-Møller, Vigdis. *Tanker om opprinnelsen. Tidlig gresk filosofia fra Hesiod til Demokrit*. Oslo: Cappelen Akademisk Forlag, 1999.

Songe-Møller, Vigdis. 'Materia, genere e morte in Aristotele', in Michele Marsonet, *Donne e filosofia*, Genoa: Erga Edizioni 2001.

Svenbro, Jesper. *Phrasikleia: Anthropologie de la lecture en Grèce ancienne*. Paris: Éditions la Découverte, 1988. English translation: *Phrasikleia: An Anthropology of Reading in Ancient Greece*. Ithaca, NY: Cornell University Press, 1993.

Vernant, Jean-Pierre. *Les origines de la pensée grecque*. Paris: Presse Universitaire de France, 1962. English translation, *The Origins of Greek Thought*. London: Methuen, 1982.

Vernant, Jean-Pierre. *Mythe et pensée chez les Grecs*, vol. 1. Paris: Maspero, 1971. English translation: *Myth and Thought among the Greeks*. London, Boston and Melbourne: Routledge & Kegan Paul, 1983.

Vernant, Jean-Pierre and Pierre Vidal-Naquet. *Mythe et tragédie en Grèce ancienne*. Paris: Maspero, 1974. English translation, *Tragedy and Myth in Ancient Greece*. Brighton: Harvester Press, 1979.

Vernant, Jean-Pierre. *L'individu, la mort, l'Amour: soi-même et l'Autre en Grèce ancienne*. Paris: Éditions. Gallimard, 1989.

Vidal-Naquet, Pierre. *Le chasseur noir: formes de pensée et formes de société dans le monde grec*. Paris: Maspero, 1983. English translation, *The Black Hunter*. Baltimore: Johns Hopkins University Press, 1986.

Vlastos, Gregory. 'Equality and Justice in Early Greek Cosmology'. *Classical Philology*, 42 (1947), pp. 156–78.

Vlastos, Gregory. 'ISONOMIA POLITIKE', in J. Mau and E.G. Schmidt (ed.), *Isonomia: Studien zur Gleichheitsvorstellungen im Griechischen Denken*. Berlin: Akademie Verlag, 1964, pp. 1–35.

Waithe, Mary Ellen (ed.). *A History of Women Philosophers. Vol. 1: Ancient Women Philosophers 600 B.C.–500 A.D.* Dordrecht, Boston and Lancaster: Marinus Nijhoff, 1987.

Waterfield, Robin. *The First Philosophers: The Presocratics and the Sophists*. Translated with Commentary by Robin Waterfield. Oxford University Press, 2000.

Wender, Dorothea. 'Plato: Misogynist, Paedophile, and Feminist'. *Arethusa*, 6 (1973), pp. 75–90.

Whitford, Margaret. *Luce Irigaray: Philosophy in the Feminine*. London and New York: Routledge, 1991.

Wiesner, Jürgen. 'Überlegungen zu Parmenides, fr. VIII, 34', in P. Aubenque, *Étude sur Parménide. Tome 2: Problème d'interprétation*. Paris: Vrin, 1987, pp. 170–92.

Winkler, John J. *The Constraints of Desire: The Anthropology of Sex and Gender in Ancient Greece*. London and New York: Routledge, 1990.

Wyller, Egil A. *Platons* Parmenides *in seinem Zusammenhang mit* Symposion *und* Politeia: *Interpretationen zur platonischen Henologie*. Oslo: H. Aschehoug, 1960. Skrifter utgitt av Det norske videnskaps-akademi i Oslo, 1959, no. 1.

Wyller, Egil A. *Der späte Platon*. Hamburg: F. Meiner, 1970.

Wyller, Egil A. *Platon I: Grunnvisjonen og det Skjønne*. Henologisk skriftserie, 4. Oslo: Spartacus Forlag, 1995.

Zeitlin, Froma I. 'Cultic Models of the Female: Rites of Dionysos and Demeter'. *Arethusa*, 15 (1982).

Zeitlin, Froma I. 'The Dynamics of Mysogony: Myth and Mythmaking in the *Oresteia*'. *Arethusa*, 11 (1978).

Index